GROWING
A BETTER
AMERICA

SMART | STRONG | SUSTAINABLE

CHUCK LEAVELL

with J. MARSHALL CRAIG

EVERGREEN ARTS | 2011

Published 2011
Printed in the United States of America

EVERGREEN ARTS, LLC
665 Charlane Dr.
Dry Branch, Ga. 31020
www.evergreenarts.com

ISBN 978-0-615-43458-2

All photos, unless otherwise credited, are from Chuck Leavell archives
or the source of the photo is unknown; credits will be amended
in future editions once brought to the publisher's attention.

Book design by Burt&Burt

www.mnn.com

Acknowledgements

My sincere thanks and gratitude go to the following ...

To my wife, Rose Lane White Leavell, who has been my partner in everything, and who guided my early steps to develop a love of the land and forestry after we inherited her grandparent's Middle Georgia plantation. She encourages my every step. To our daughters, Amy and Ashley, who have inspired me in so many ways and who have always been so good to their Dad; Amy's husband and our son-in-law, Steve Bransford, whom we are so proud to have in our family and who has shown sincere interest in land and environmental issues and who has helped to document the history and progress of Charlane in film and photographs; Miles and Rocco Bransford, Amy and Steve's two sons—our grandsons—whom I hope will help shape Charlane into an even better example of stewardship of the land in the years to come; to all our family, past, present, and future.

To my friends Skoots Lyndon, Scotty Simpson, Clay Huffman, Linda McDuffie, Herman and Dorsey Robertson, Evelyn Basley, Lois Height and the many other fine folks that have worked with us as staff at Charlane. These good people have helped to keep Charlane in top shape, whether Rose Lane and I are at home on the plantation or on the road for long stretches in my "other" life as a professional musician. All of them have made my life better through their friendship. My very special thanks to my friend and partner Joel Babbitt, CEO and co-founder with me of the Mother Nature Network (mnn.com), who changed my life by giving me the opportunity to expand my interest and involvement in environmental issues into the world of the Internet and in doing so, hopefully helping people to better understand our environmental challenges and giving them the information and tools to treat our planet better.

J. Marshall Craig

Chuck and I are not scientists—me in any sense of the word and Chuck not in the formal sense—but in our years of friendship I've learned a lot about forestry, land use, and the natural world from Chuck; I've absorbed an enormous amount of knowledge about being a good custodian of the land, and I've learned a lot by osmosis by simply spending time on his family's incredible Charlane Plantation in rural Georgia. I have learned, truly, about how the land can take good care of us if we take good care of the land.

Chuck has a long list of awards, recognitions, and accolades, and a substantial number of professionally recognized achievements and accomplishments that clearly make me the layman in our journey here of trying to tell you, as simply and hopefully as entertainingly as possible, where we are as communities, states, regions, a nation, and as a planet. And where, according to accredited experts, we need to go. With his family, Chuck is owner of a large working forest plantation in central Georgia. He has the desire and personal investment to keep families on the land and the land in families. Chuck spends a lot of his time on environmental matters and has served as a board member of the American

Forest Foundation, the US Endowment for Forestry and Communities, the Georgia Land Conservation Council, the Georgia Conservancy, and other non-profits. He is also co-founder and Director of Environmental Affairs for the world's premiere environmental website, the Mother Nature Network (mnn.com), which illustrates his deep love of our planet and his interest in what kind of environmental legacy he has within his power and his actions to leave his grandchildren, great-grandchildren and generations beyond.

During the years I've known Chuck and his wife, Rose Lane, they have been constantly exploring ways of lowering their carbon—their "human"—footprint on lands for which they're not just custodians, but those they touch in their travels. They are continually evaluating the environmental and economic implications of all they do at Charlane, in their main residence and in all the structures on the plantation. They are both acutely interested and involved in historic preservation, and have lovingly restored their own home as well as a historically significant home on the property known as the Bullard House, both built in the mid-1800s and both of which are now on the National Register of Historic Places. For the most part, restorative projects and new structures on Charlane were done using wood from their own land. Most of this wood was from trees that died from lighting strikes, insect infestation, or perhaps just from old age, and that would otherwise have gone to waste. This was a lightbulb that went on over my head more than a decade ago—long before Chuck and I discussed writing a book on these topics, of the wise use of resources and a clear illustration of sustainability in action.

The Leavells open up Charlane to a variety of guests on a commercial basis: Hunters can stay at Charlane in the quest for deer, wild turkey, wild boar, and, especially, quail. In fact, an active hunting plantation is part of Chuck and Rose Lane's vision of sustainability, just as their selective tree harvests are done to strict, sustainable, forestry standards. Outside the hunting season, they occasionally hold retreats that focus on everything from art (Rose Lane is an accomplished artist) to birding to outdoor appreciation of all sorts—and sometimes even just for relaxing or holding special meetings.

Entrance to Chuck and Rose Lane Leavell's Charlane Plantation in Middle Georgia.

I know they are constantly assessing "green" energy possibilities for the plantation's requirements and make positive changes when practical. As a tree farmer, Chuck is at the forefront of knowledge on practical forestry and is downright excited about the possibilities for the future—including biomass fuels, carbon sequestration, and other new uses of the forest resource.

Growing a Better America is not, and was never intended to be, an academic text; indeed, we've tried to keep it a simple, yet accurate, read that addresses the realities of the growth we have had and are going to have in the future, with suggestions as to how we might best handle that growth. From an accuracy standpoint, this has been somewhat of a challenge, with the vast, ever-changing, and mind-boggling amount of statistics and information out there.

Our world is changing so fast, Chuck and I quip, that the everlasting rewriting and updating has taken longer than it took to write the book in the first place. So, that said, it's a snapshot of a moment in time: mid-2010. Some things may get better; others, if disasters such as the BP oil spill of 2010 off the Gulf Coast continue to occur, will get much worse. If we don't support and invest in workable, alternative fuels and clean, renewable energy sources, arrest climate change, find better ways to build our buildings, plan our communities, solve transportation problems, and address all the other challenges connected to population expansion, things will get worse and we're going to leave our grandchildren and great-grandchildren a tainted legacy indeed.

Chuck and I are going to tell you some things that should frighten you. At least we hope they're going to frighten you! And we're also going to, through Chuck's own experience and deep interest in these subjects, provide a little illumination, a little knowledge on how even a few of us can make better choices and, I hope, make you go "wow, that's cool!" once in a while.

I've tried to help Chuck's work be as accurate as possible and cite sources of explicit figures, with the added intent of seeking the most current statistics. But I have not included a comprehensive footnote list (it would be as long as the book itself, frankly, and defeat Chuck's underlying intent), so any inaccuracies or unsourced statements the reader may find questionable are my fault alone. It has been my intention to help Chuck take you on a journey. If there are a few bumps along the road, blame me.

At the end of the day, we both have a deep and sincere desire to find ways to experience the inevitable growth we are going to have with realism, intelligence, grace, and innovation—and maybe with some good old-fashioned common sense thrown in.

Chuck Leavell

As a young fellow growing up in Alabama, I can recall some wonderful family times visiting our father's brothers and sisters. The Leavell brothers and sisters were fun people, always loud and proud, always giving big slaps on the back from the uncles and hugs and kisses from the aunts when we walked in the door.

We made road trips to see them, and I remember my older sister Judy and I being piled into the car, and sometimes our brother Billy as well, although Billy was quite a lot older than we were, and was off in college during some of these trips.

Our dad, Billy, Sr., had two brothers and three sisters. Emory was the eldest, the first-born. His family lived down in Orlando, Florida, and we enjoyed going to see him and to soak up some Florida sunshine. Emory played the banjo, which was, to me, a fun odyssey. On the way to see Emory, we would sometimes stop in to see our Aunt Gussie in the tiny community of LaPine, Alabama. Gussie was a very big woman, a countrywoman. She was not terribly attractive and was a little louder than her brothers and sisters, but she was very sweet. I can remember getting to her house, walking up to the door and knocking, and when the door opened she would have that big smile on her face. What was coming next was basically being smothered in her huge breasts and arms, and squeezed until my breath was gone. After recovering, the next thing was being offered food that was always a huge layout of country cookin'—and that included multiple desserts such as cakes, pies, cookies, puddings, cobblers, and of course a large glass of milk. We always left there with an extra three or four pounds on us.

Our Uncle Jay lived in Montgomery. Jay and Dad were very close, and we visited him more often than the others. Plus, two of Jay's kids were more our age, and we enjoyed playing with them. Our cousins Windy (short for Winston) and Candy were always fun, and Jay had an old carriage house behind his main house that we used to play in. It was great because we were on our own, away from the adults, and it gave us a special feeling of adventure. They had two other younger children, Tracy and Wiley, who were good kids, but as Windy and Candy were more our age, Judy and I played with them mostly. Jay was in the advertising business, and both he and his wife, Jo, were very good artists. Jay was also a good musician, a clarinetist. He had lived in New Orleans for a time when he was younger. It was after World War II, in which he served. I remember our Dad telling me that he went there to decompress, to recover from his experiences. He went to hear Pete Fountain, Al Hurt, and other jazz musicians there, learning some hot licks.

Sometimes, Emory and his family would come up to Jay's and they would have some fun jam sessions, with Emory banging out songs on his tenor banjo, Jay blowing high and hard on the clarinet, our dad playing spoons, and everyone else singing along and clapping hands.

Dad's other sister was named Frankie. She lived in North Carolina and I don't remember her as much as I remember the others, simply because we only saw her rarely, but I remember liking Frankie. She was a little quieter than her brothers and sisters, always very nice when we did see her.

But I especially remember our trips to the big city of Atlanta to visit our Aunt Lou. Atlanta was a landmark southern city, and, of course, it still is. Our own family had tried out three Alabama cities—Birmingham, Montgomery, and Tuscaloosa. Alabama's big city was the city of my birth, Birmingham. We lived there for about four years after I was born, moving to the country outside of Montgomery in 1956 for about three years, then back to Birmingham some time in 1959 before finally moving to Tuscaloosa in 1961. I was nine years old when we settled there. While I have fond memories of our times in Birmingham and Montgomery, it is T-Town where most of my childhood memories are.

It was a wonderful place to grow up—a nice, medium-sized southern town where the University of Alabama was established in 1841, one of the most prominent higher institutions of the South. My musical career began in Tuscaloosa, where my first band, The Misfitz, played every Friday night at the YMCA. Later on, we even had our own television show on Saturday mornings, modeled on Dick Clark's national show *American Bandstand* and very cleverly and creatively called *Tuscaloosa Bandstand*. As time went on, I played in other bands that found good-paying gigs in town—mostly fraternity parties at the University of Alabama—and we eventually branched out to play the "chitlin' circuit" of universities throughout the south, places like Oxford, Mississippi; Jackson, Mississippi; Auburn, Alabama; and the like. These were all small towns, but growing and doing pretty well due to the student populations. We also sometimes played up in Birmingham, which is, of course, Alabama's largest city. Two years before my birth, the 1950 census reported a population of 326,000 in Birmingham. Information from that same census tells us that Montgomery had 188,000 and Tuscaloosa had 94,000. But it was Atlanta that was truly the Big City of the South, and it was a very big deal for us when we would go there.

The drive up to Atlanta was quite pleasant, lots of beautiful countryside once you got outside of Birmingham. Beautiful little farms dotted the landscape, and there were thousands upon thousands of acres of forests. But when you rolled over the last hill and saw the Atlanta skyline, you knew you were in a metropolis.

Aunt Lou was a wonderful woman, a little loud (but not nearly as loud as Gussie!), always a big smile on her face and she was so much fun to be with, as she would take time to talk and play with my sister Judy, brother Billy, and me.

The year I was born, 1952, two years after the 1950 census, the city of Atlanta had grown from 326,000 to about 335,000 people, and the metro-Atlanta area had just topped the 1 million mark, the first southern city to do so. I have some vague memories of our family talking about how incredible it was to have that many people in a city in the south.

There is a famous sign that still exists on Peachtree Street in Atlanta that for decades has displayed the population in lights. And every year when we went to see Aunt Lou, that number got higher and higher. Aunt Lou was the secretary to the Secretary of State under Governor Carl Sanders, whose administration was from 1963 to 1967. Aunt Lou used to read the bills that were introduced on the Senate floor. In 1964, because of her position, Aunt Lou was able to get Judy and me positions as pages in the Senate. I was twelve at the time, and the population of metro Atlanta had hit 1.5 million. I remember how incredible that seemed, a million-and-a-half people was hard for us to fathom.

Today, in 2010, metro Atlanta boasts more than 5.5 million people. In my lifetime the city has grown more than five fold and is growing still at a rapid pace. The farms and forests that we used to watch go by the window of our 1962 Mercury Monterey have dwindled dramatically. Interstate highways I-20, I-75, I-85, and the I-285 loop and I-675 by-pass that all surround Atlanta, have spawned more and more exits, which have spawned more and more growth, more strip malls and convenience stores, fast-food and chain-type restaurants, gas stations, motels, and the like. Many of these have come and gone, been abandoned, some torn down to make way for more of the same, and some left to be derelict. Many of us have seen this occur all across America, in every state, in almost all our cities. More population, more growth and development, fewer natural lands.

We've seen many of our cities literally grow together, with strip mall after strip mall, residential section after residential section, trailer park after trailer park built until they connect one city to the next. While estimates vary, it's clear that metro Atlanta now loses somewhere between thirty and sixty acres of land a day to impervious surfaces and loses somewhere between fifty and a hundred acres a day of forests and natural lands.

Many other cities are seeing similar numbers. The South as a whole, from Virginia all the way to East Texas loses about a million acres a year of natural lands to growth and development. This is our reality. America's population topped 300 million in 2006 and at present in 2010 has reached 310 million. Predictions say that by around 2040 the US will have 400 million living on our shores. The world population passed 6 billion in 1999, is about 6.5 billion now, and estimates say we will grow to 8 billion by 2025 and 9 billion around 2047 or so.

The city of Atlanta has, for decades, been one of the fastest-growing urban centers in North America, and continues to grow at a remarkable rate. *Photo by Steve Bransford*

In my career as a musician, I have been privileged to travel a goodly portion of the globe, and have had many memorable experiences in those travels. My wife, Rose Lane, and I have seen the world grow, change, and expand in the thirty-eight years that we have been married. Some of the places we first visited on my early tours are hardly recognizable now, having doubled, tripled, or better in size and scope. A lot of land has been converted from natural states into concrete and asphalt. And when that happens, it is very difficult—almost impossible—to go back.

Now understand, I am not anti-growth. We are going to have growth whether we like it or not. It is an inevitable truth. Our population in the South, in the US and beyond is going to grow, period. These are the facts. But at this point, as we're talking about the population we already have and where we expect it to go from here, I believe we have to ask the question: is the growth that we are going to experience from here on out going to be rampant, rapid, and reckless? Or can it be smart, strong and sustainable? I certainly hope it is the latter, and that we can find ways to shape the growth we are going to experience in a way that will make sure we still have the lands we need for growing our food, the forests we love and depend on for things like materials to build our homes, schools, and churches; materials for books, magazines, and newspapers; and forests to help clean our air and our water and to provide home and shelter to all manner of wildlife—forests and natural lands that we like to walk in and renew our appreciation for and love of nature. Don't we all want to try to grow in ways that will have the lowest possible impact on all our precious natural lands?

In this book, we will explore ways we can achieve this. We will expose positive models of development being done by some really smart and talented people, like Steve Nygren's Serenbe Community in Georgia, Vic Mills's Poplar Grove in South Carolina, and others. We'll have a look at individual homes that are built in smart and energy-efficient ways, like Rutherford and Laura Turner Seydel's EcoManor. We will explore ideas like Janine Benyus's wonderful concept of biomimicry, the art of studying nature to find ways we can better do things ourselves.

We'll look into our options for energy use, transportation, home building, renovation, and other ways we can help grow smarter. We'll also discuss some older, tried-and-true ideas, like the English-village model of community living and architectural concepts that have withstood the test of time. We'll see what some big companies are doing to improve their situations and reduce their environmental impact, as well as individuals who are paving the way to a better world.

If we open our eyes and our minds to these concepts and possibilities, no doubt we can help each other to find a better future. Our children, grandchildren, and future generations—indeed, our planet—depend on it.

Chuck Leavell
Charlane Plantation, 2010

America

From Settlement to the Present,
and the Price We Have Paid

*"It's an America with strange mythic depths. I see it as a
distorting mirror; a book of danger and secrets, of romance
and magic. It's about the soul of America, really. What
people brought to America; what found them when they
came; and the things that lie sleeping beneath it all."*

Neil Gaiman

It wasn't easy to settle America. The Norse tried several times in the eleventh century with outposts in Greenland and a short-lived settlement on the very northern tip of Newfoundland thought to have been founded by Leif Erikson, who possibly even attempted colonies as far south as the St. Lawrence River and New Brunswick. But none survived.

By 1492, as history says, Christopher Columbus reached the Americas, but it's unlikely, according to most researchers, that he ever set foot on "American" soil or even, in fact, knew of the continent. But he sure "put the place on the map," as they say, by inspiring further exploration of the West. In the expedition led by Columbus was a fellow named Juan Ponce de León y Figueroa … one of what history books describe as "200 gentleman volunteers."

Ponce de León led his own expedition in 1508 with the permission of Ferdinand II of Aragon to what is now Puerto Rico. This led to his eventual expedition in February 1513 that landed him in what he named "La Florida," in recognition of the verdant landscape and because it was the season that the Spaniards called "Pascua Florida," or the Festival of Flowers. Most say that the landing occurred at St. Augustine, which calls itself "The Nation's Oldest City," although some historians cite areas south of there. In any case, this famous expedition is connected with the legend for the search for the "Fountain of Youth." Ponce de León is widely credited with the discovery of Florida, and he did indeed give it its name, but some say he was not the first European to reach the peninsula. There is some evidence that some Spanish slave ships made it to the shores around 1494.

What is documented is that Ponce de León explored the territory and eventually returned to Puerto Rico to find a party of Caribs from a neighboring island had raided the settlement of Caparra, killing several Spaniards and burning down the camp. He made a decision to return to Spain to give a report of his expedition. Upon his return, Ferdinand knighted him for his efforts, and he was regarded a hero. He made another trip to Florida in 1521 with about two hundred men, bringing farmers, artisans, and priests, as well as fifty horses and some other domestic animals. During this adventure, he was attacked by Calusa Indians and was injured with a poisoned arrow. He soon retreated to Havana, Cuba, dying there of his wound.

In 1526, Spaniard Lucas Vázquez de Ayllón began his attempts to colonize America, landing near what's now Georgetown, South Carolina, before moving south to build the short-lived colony of San Miguel de Gualdape near, or at, what's now Georgia's Sapelo Island. But they were ill-supplied, ill-prepared, and succumbed to hunger, disease, an uprising from the African slaves they'd brought with them (the first Africans in America), and conflicts with Native Americans. The whole experience lasted about three months and claimed hundreds of lives, including de Ayllón's.

The next known European settlement was a group of French, who built a colony at what is now Jacksonville, Florida, in 1564.

They lasted a little longer, only to be killed by Spanish troops the following year.

The next "permanent" European settlement, in 1587, also failed to survive. More than a hundred English men and women landed on Roanoke Island on North Carolina's coast. They knew little about living in the "new" world, arriving too late to even plant crops. Within three years, when English authorities again visited, the settlement—and the first European born in America, Virginia Dare—had vanished, although they hadn't been killed by the Spanish. Now called the "Lost Colony," it's a fascinating and tragic story, with no definitive proof, even today, of what happened to all of the settlers. Some scholars believe that at least some of the survivors were assimilated into the Croatoan tribe, the only people who understood and honored the nature of this land, and who knew how to survive here.

Spanish explorers began settling in New Mexico around 1598, and soon after, in 1607, the London Company established Jamestown in Virginia; it would, despite its tragedies, be the first colony to survive. Within roughly thirty years there would be a

Archaeologist Mary Anna Richardson and a team search an excavation site of a church built in 1608 at James Fort, part of the Jamestown settlement of 1607, which was the first European settlement to survive in America. The brick rubble layer belonging to an 18th-century church can be seen above her excavation layer.
Photo Courtesy Preservation Virginia

documented 26,600 Europeans or those of European descent living in America. One hundred years after that there were nearly a million and, by the early 1800s, the population was beyond 4 million, and European settlers had explored to the Pacific Ocean and back.

Aside from the American Revolution, one of the most significant events in American history has been, of course, the Louisiana Purchase in 1803. For all of the political, military, even constitutional implications, the purchase nearly doubled the size of the country, making America one of the largest in the world. With the completion of the Lewis and Clark expedition in 1806, the West was soon "open."

Then came what might be called a "perfect storm," the components of which (most notably the Industrial Revolution) made America what it became. Positive or negative, the course of events of the next century brought the true colonization of the country. This is unique: Even America's neighbor to the north, Canada, did not evolve, expand, and experience settlement the same way America did.

The discovery of gold; war with Mexico that ended in the annexation of the southwest, Texas, and California; war with Indian tribes, ending with the Indian Appropriations Act; practical events that made the settlement of the Midwest and the West easier and more enticing, such as the openings of the Champlain Canal connecting Lake Champlain and western Vermont to the Hudson River, and then the Erie Canal connecting New York with the Great Lakes; the transcontinental telegraph; the Homestead Act, encouraging settlement of "unoccupied" territories; the Mineral Act granting title to millions of acres of land to mining companies; and, especially, the completion of the Transcontinental railroad is uniquely American.

In addition to this, not insignificantly, was the Civil War, which had other unique effects on how America's urban and rural developments occurred. Obviously, despite the warring Union and Confederacy, America as a whole kept right on growing by an average of 434,000 a year, according to census records. While New York experienced a boom of immigrants to help with the war effort, Chicago entered into its status as one of the most important and influential cities in the country, taking over most industries, such as grain distribution and meatpacking, which had relied on the Mississippi River for a transportation route. It also developed heavy industries to support the Union effort. After the war, more than a million African Americans migrated from southern states to California and the northeast, while an influx of Scandinavian, Finnish, Italian, Slavic, and Jewish immigrants—the "New Immigration"—flooded various parts of the country.

In 1891, the US government created the Immigration and Naturalization Service and one year later opened the screening center at Ellis Island.

At the time of the Louisiana Purchase in 1803, the US population was more than 5 million. By the time that the one-year-old Immigration and Naturalization Service had opened the Ellis Island screening center in 1892, the population had boomed to more than 70 million and had spread across the country.

When the twentieth century dawned, America was gaining roughly nine hundred thousand people a year.

A lot was lost along the way, as usually happens when mankind thinks there's nothing standing in his way to an endless bounty. Most tragic was the treatment of Native Americans and the loss of their sovereignty and their lands, which wasn't seriously acknowledged until 1881 when Helen Hunt Jackson published *Century of Dishonor*, criticizing the US government's treatment of Indians. In 1804, when the first buffalo was killed by the Lewis and Clark expedition, it is estimated that there were more than twenty million of the animals roaming the American plains—the most numerous species of large wild mammal on Earth. By 1893, by most accounts, there were fewer than two thousand remaining.

By mid-2007, America's population topped 300 million, and between cities and towns, farms, ranges and managed lands such as working forests like my own family's, humans have now either developed or managed about 73 percent of all the land in America, according to compiled statistics from the US Census Bureau, the American Farmland Trust, and studies within the US Department of Agriculture.

Let's consider only land covered in impervious surfaces. According to a report on NPR, Dr. Christopher Elvidge of the

National Oceanic and Atmospheric Administration cites a three-year study using satellite photography that concluded about 9 percent of the country has been "developed." That means we have paved over an area the size of Ohio. That land is lost to nature and will forever have a negative impact on local ecosystems.

An EPA report on the environment states, "While the amount of developed land is a small fraction of the total, its ecological impact can be disproportionately high relative to other land use types. Paving and the creation of other impervious surfaces can change local hydrology, climate, and carbon cycling, leading to increased surface runoff, pollution, and degradation of wetlands and riparian zones (ecosystems located along the banks of rivers, streams, creeks, or any other water networks)."

I was happy to learn that re-forestation is occurring at a slightly higher rate than development on forestland.

Prior to European settlement in the US, "forests covered nearly one billion acres of what is now America. Since the mid-1600s, about 300 million acres of forest have been cleared, primarily for agriculture during the nineteenth century. Today, about one-third of the nation is forested, currently about 747 million acres. The total forest area has been relatively stable for the past one hundred years, but there have been significant regional shifts in the area and composition of the nation's forests," according to the Land Use Report.

Much of the marginal farmland in the east has been taken out of agricultural production and, to some degree, has been re-forested. Large-scale planting in the South has also taken place. Our own Charlane plantation was once mostly cattle pasture and agricultural land but is now almost entirely forested. While wildfires are still a threat, fire suppression all over our country has also contributed to increases in forest area. Factors contributing to loss of forests have been urbanization, conversion to agriculture, reservoir construction, and natural disasters. Of these, urbaniza- tion seems to be the leading cause of forest loss.

"Eastern forests cover about 384 million acres and are predominantly broadleaf (74 percent), with the exception of extensive coniferous forests and plantations in the southern coastal region. These are largely in private ownership (83 percent).

Western forests are quite the opposite, with about 363 million acres of predominantly coniferous (78 percent) and in public ownership (57 percent). America is somewhat unique in forest ownership, with some ten million private individuals owning about 422 million acres of forest and other wooded land. Most public forest land is held by four Federal agencies: The US Forest Service, Bureau of Land Management, National Park Service, and the Fish and Wildlife Service. Numerous state, county, and municipal government organizations round out the remainder.

Current major uses of American forests include timber production, naval stores products, recreation, hunting, fishing, watershed and fisheries protection, wildlife habitat and bio-diversity protection, and gathering non-timber products such as berries, mushrooms, and medicinal plants."

In 1982, the nation had 402.4 million acres of working forests (forests that are used for some type of production); that number steadily grew through to the most recent 2003 census of 405.6 million acres.

The numbers are opposite for cropland (419.9 million acres in 1982; 367.9 million acres in 2003), pastureland (131.1 million acres in 1982; 117.0 million acres in 2003), and rangeland (415.5 million acres in 1982; 405.1 million acres in 2003). While some percentage of this reduction is due to change in land use, such as pastureland becoming cropland or forested land, or the other way around, there is an ever-increasing amount of all but forestlands ending up under asphalt and concrete.

According to researchers Sugie Lee and Steven P. French in a 2009 *Journal of Environmental Planning and Management* article, metro Atlanta is expected to have about 1,639 square miles of impervious surface by the year 2030, when the population is expected to be just under 8 million people. This represents a 45 percent increase in land loss since the year 2000. From 2000 to 2008, the Atlanta area added 1.13 million people, and the city's population is now well past 5 million. The area's population growth was second only to Dallas, Texas, which added nearly a million and a half people.

Researchers have documented the impact of impervious surface on water resources: storm water runoff, ground water pollution, and reduced infiltration for underground water storage. More recent research shows that the increase of impervious surfaces is also closely correlated the urban heat island effect—the tendency of urbanized areas to become warmer than surrounding, undeveloped areas during the day and to retain this heat overnight—and associated air pollution problems. Lee and French suggest that future planners use light-colored pavement rather than dark pavement to help mitigate the increase in the UHI effect over the next decades.

According to another study by the Georgia Forestry Commission Atlanta loses 54 acres of natural lands per day to growth and development. That's 374 acres a week, or about 1,600 acres a month—more than 19,000 acres a year. Other estimates are even higher. Any way you look at it, these numbers certainly give us all something to think about, and that's just one metropolitan area of our country. These are staggering numbers, and should serve as a reality check and a wake-up call for America. In the face of this incredible expansion in the metro-Atlanta area, one bright spot is the ongoing efforts to keep a healthy urban forest. Since 1985, a wonderful organization called Trees Atlanta has planted and distributed more than sixty-eight thousand trees, and the group runs volunteer planting projects every Saturday.

And there is other good news. In some areas, farmland is being returned to wild pasture, as increased efficiency in food production requires less acreage than in decades past. (This has some downsides in the high use of fertilizers and massive chicken, hog, and cattle "factories" that increase pollution to groundwater and lakes and rivers from runoff, which I'll get to in a later chapter.) In other areas, farmland is being returned to forestland.

On our own property in Middle Georgia, we have a total of about 2,500 acres of land. Of this, forest cover now takes up approximately 80 percent of the total area, or some two thousand acres. However, when my wife's grandparents purchased some of this land back in the 1930s it was largely agricultural land.

While we don't have any hard data on the figures, we estimate that back then it was probably almost the reverse, with 75 percent row crops and cattle grazing and 25 percent forests. Rose Lane's grandparents began converting some of the land into forests in

Loblolly Pines planted by Chuck and Rose Lane Leavell in 1984 in what was former pastureland at Charlane Plantation.

1947 and continued to do so on a small scale until 1952. When the land was passed on to us in 1981, we converted even more into forests, bringing us to the current mix of forested and open land.

With all these changes in the American landscape through the last three centuries or so, when it comes to growth in this country, clearly, once we got started we haven't looked back.

The following photos depict three different areas of Charlane Plantation. Each photo shows the progression from agriculture to forests on the same tract from 1927 to 2010.

Tract 1

Tract 2

Tract 3   *Courtesy Chuck Leavell Archives*

* * *

You know the jokes about someone getting tricked into "buying swampland in Florida" or someone being such a good salesman as to pull off such a coup? The reference is, of course, to swampland being worth nothing, and that's how Europeans have thought for more than a thousand years. When they came to America, they brought the same philosophy with them. Native Americans always knew the importance of wetlands and used them and worked with them and learned from them.

The European descendants who settled America, however, saw them as blight to get rid of—especially after the late 1800s, when scientists learned that malaria and yellow fever was carried by mosquitoes, which breed in swamps and warm, standing water.

In 1850, Congress passed the Swamp Land Act, which granted millions of acres of federal wetlands to individual states, with the plan that they be sold off to private individuals to promote drainage and, eventually, farming.

By the end of the Second World War, demand for land for housing, farmland, and roads was so great that massive areas of wetlands were drained and destroyed, helped along by specific government subsidies. According to the US Fish and Wildlife Service, the country destroyed 54 percent of its wetlands, although, thankfully, the Everglades were protected by legislation in 1947.

A suggestion to drain the Everglades was first made in 1848; however, a real attempt was not made until 1882. A series of canals were constructed during the first half of the twentieth century and spurred the south Florida economy, prompting land development. But problems with some of the canals and floods caused by hurricanes forced engineers to go back to the drawing board and rethink their drainage plans. In 1947, Congress formed the Central and Southern Florida Flood Control Project, which built some 1,400 miles of canals, levees, and water control devices. This resulted in the south Florida metropolitan area growing substantially at this time, and water from the Everglades was diverted to cities. Some portions of the Everglades were transformed into farmland, where the primary crop put into place was sugarcane. Today, about 50 percent of the original Everglades has been turned into agricultural or urban areas. When the construction of a large airport was proposed six miles north of Everglades National Park, an environmental study predicted it would destroy the south Florida ecosystem. Restoring the Everglades then became a priority.

National and international attention turned to the environment in the 1970s, and UNESCO and the Ramsar Convention designated the Everglades as one of only three wetland areas of global importance. Restoration began in the 1980s with the removal of a canal that straightened the Kissimmee River. The water quality of Lake Okeechobee, a water source for south Florida, became a significant concern. The deterioration of the environment was also linked to the diminishing quality of life in south Florida's urban areas. In 2000, a plan to restore the Everglades was approved by Congress; to date, it is the most expensive and comprehensive environmental repair attempt in history, designed to redirect ocean-bound freshwater to areas that need it most. The Comprehensive Everglades Restoration Plan was signed into law, but the same divisive politics that had affected the region for the previous fifty years have compromised the plan that

A significant amount of America's wetlands have disappeared over the centuries—lost to development, railroads and agriculture all along the Louisiana, California and eastern seaboard coasts. Here, hundreds of acres of wetlands are being preserved as part of the environmentally sensitive Poplar Grove residential development near Charleston, South Carolina. *Photo courtesy Poplar Grove*

includes more than 60 elements, will take more than 30 years to construct, and was originally estimated to cost $7.8 billion.

Further legislation—such as the 2008 Farm Bill, which I was honored to be involved with shaping—and growing concern for the protection of wetlands has had a beneficial effect, but, by some estimates, the country is still losing about 1 percent of its wetlands every year.

Being biologically diverse and working as nurseries to fish and other creatures, wetlands have been accurately described as "kidneys" of the landscape. They filter water that would otherwise flow directly into oceans, rivers, and lakes. With the enormous increase in pollution from cities, roads, and farming especially, this lack of filtration has had a cataclysmic result. It has, in effect, destroyed a Connecticut-sized area of ocean into which the Mississippi flows. The pollution and fertilizer that flows into the river for hundreds and hundreds of miles upstream effectively chokes off the ability for the production of oxygen in the water—which supports all life that lives in it.

The loss of wetlands has also upset the natural balance of breeding and food chains, which sport hunters have noticed as bird populations have either declined rapidly or disappeared.

A more direct effect this drainage has had on mankind is that wetlands are there for an obvious reason: they act as sponges in times of flood, and never before has flooding caused so much damage to the very properties that wetlands were sometimes sacrificed for.

This is particularly noted in Louisiana, where flood-absorbing wetlands have been drained for more than two centuries, and low-level coastal development has soared—at the loss of 80 percent of the state's wetlands, according to census figures. And nowhere else has suffered such losses in times of flood and hurricanes as the coast of the Gulf of Mexico.

In one interesting and comprehensive report, the US Geological Survey said:

> "The Civil War focused attention on developing routes around, through, and over water bodies and wetlands that stood as logistical barriers to the movement of men and heavy equipment. Because accurate maps were critical to war efforts, an early glimpse of some of the nation's wetlands was finally gained. After the war, attention was focused on westward expansion and settlement. Railroads became an enemy of wetland habitat through both developing and draining these lands and as direct consumers of wetland forest products needed for railroad ties and fuel. Agricultural demands for large tracts of land caused increasing drainage of the abundant wetlands in the mid-continent, including prairie potholes in the North Central US, bottomlands of the lower Mississippi River's alluvial plains, and the Gulf plains of Texas. The Central Valley of California was also targeted during this time. California has lost as much as 91 percent of its original wetlands, primarily because of conversion to agriculture."

Another great area of swampland in America exists in my own state of Georgia: The Okefenokee. An attempt to drain this huge and beautiful wetland was made back in 1891 after the Georgia General Assembly authorized the Governor to sell the land to the highest bidder. That turned out to be a group of former Confederate officers who formed The Suwanee Canal Company in 1890. They paid a little over $83,000 for some 238,000 acres of the swamp. The intention was to drain it in order to log the vast stands of cypress and then to convert the acreage to crops. They did manage to cut some canals and to float about seven million feet of lumber to be sawn in a mill in Folkston, Ga., but for several reasons the attempt eventually failed miserably and the company went bankrupt. They abandoned further draining efforts in 1894 and went into receivership in 1897.

In 1901, the Hebard family of Philadelphia purchased the land and built a railroad on top of the swamp in order to log it. This was a successful endeavor, and they logged most all of the cypress from 1909 through 1927. Logging continued through 1942 by other companies and eventually ceased. Today the cypress stands are making a slow comeback, and the swamp is, thankfully, under sound management practices, with some 438,000 acres being restored to their original glory. Of this, 403,000 acres of the land makes up the Okefenokee National Wildlife Refuge, a true treasure of American lands.

A great place to visit, but in many cases we shouldn't be living there: The coasts.

According to the National Oceanic and Atmospheric Administration (part of the Department of Commerce) in the thirty years between 1970 and 2000, the number of people living in US coastal watershed counties increased to more than 34 million—the total population of California. In the fourteen years between 1982 and 1997, seven million acres of natural land in these same coastal watershed counties were converted to development.

Almost one-half of the nation's new construction occurs in coastal areas, and over the next fifteen years, coastal populations are expected to increase by approximately 27 million people. To illustrate how risky this is to the environment, when Hurricane Fran struck North Carolina in 1996, 120 million gallons of raw sewage ended up in rivers and streams, according to the NOAA (The National Oceanic and Atmospheric Administration). Almost half of the nation's gross domestic product—$4.5 trillion—is generated in those counties and in adjacent ocean waters.

Nearly one half of the nation's development takes place along coastal areas—which poses a challenge and even danger with rising ocean levels and proven vulnerability with oceanic storms and hurricanes. *Photo by US Government's National Oceanic and Atmospheric Administration*

A 2008 assessment by the Wharton School's Risk Center showed fast-rising economic losses worldwide along coastal areas from hurricanes. In the 1950s, losses were slightly above $50 billion. By the 1990s, losses were nearly $800 billion. In 2008, hurricanes Gustav and Ike mounted losses of $40 billion alone.

The Wharton School is one of several organizations that formed a coalition of insurers, public officials, risk experts, conservation groups, and builders to create a blueprint of policy-change suggestions and actions to stem losses from rising sea levels. The Resilient Coasts Blueprint, released in April 2009, calls on the Obama Administration and all levels of government and the private sector to implement recommendations: "The National Institute of Building Sciences showed that every dollar spent on mitigation saves society about four dollars on recovery costs. Despite this evidence, nearly all US coastal cities and towns lack adequate land use requirements and building code standards to realize these savings. The need to adapt is also an opportunity to restore our coastal ecosystems, which are a critical complement to defensive infrastructure. Wetlands provide an estimated $23.2

billion each year of storm surge and flood protection along our coastlines, according to a study by the University of Vermont. Yet the combined pressures of climate change and development—over half our population ... some 53 percent, live along the coasts—have led to the systematic depletion of protective wetlands. Clearly, the resiliency of our coastal populations and our ecosystems go hand in hand."

The Resilient Coasts Blueprint has so far been endorsed by the Travelers Institute, the Nature Conservancy, the National Oceanic and Atmospheric Administration, and the Wharton School. So why aren't we listening to these warnings—and even more importantly, why aren't we doing something about them? If we are to grow smartly, protect our citizens and our coastline ecologies, we should take heed and make changes.

Coastal areas are so ecologically sensitive to pollutants and increased erosion that marine and bird populations have been severely damaged, according to the National Resources Defense Council. Proof alone can be found in the collapse of the shellfish industry off the southern coast and the increased frequency at which beaches must be closed to swimmers every year because of dangerously high bacterial levels.

With global warming causing ocean levels to rise as well as heightening the frequency and severity of ocean storms, further coastal development seems foolhardy.

The historic city of Charleston, South Carolina, like most coastal cities, would be unable to handle a one-foot rise in sea level—such a rise would inundate some of the state's shoreline areas up to a half-mile inland, according to the Southern Alliance for Clean Energy. Charleston mayor Joe Riley, who has personally endorsed the Blueprint, says, "The pressures on our coast will continue unabated, making regional planning essential to shape growth and to protect our social, economic and natural well being. Charleston is one of our nation's treasures, and without serious action today to confront these risks it—and many other American cities—faces an uncertain future."

Thankfully, numerous groups all over the world are lobbying for shoreline regulation and management—for instance, the Sierra Club, the California Coastal Protection Network, America's

Wetland Foundation, American Shore & Beach Preservation Association, American Coastal Coalition, and others, are lobbying for shoreline regulation and management. Sadly, government isn't listening. In March 2010, the White House's Office of Management and Budget pulled the plug on coastal protection funding, declaring: "using Federal funds for periodic beach nourishment is contrary to Administration budget policy."

Federal resources have since been allocated to specifically assist with the BP Deepwater Horizon Oil Spill, but that is a special and crucial situation, according to the White House.

Global warming is also, scientists say, increasing the frequency, intensity, and duration of wildfires. With ever-increasing development and density in less urban, more natural areas, this puts more property and people at risk. The western United States in particular has been hard hit by this change. Since 1970, there has been a six-fold increase in acreage of forest burned, the wildfire season has increased by two months or more in some areas, and from week-long blazes, crews sometimes now spend more than a month containing fires, according to the University of Arizona and the Scripps Institution of Oceanography in San Diego. According to the US Geological Survey, wildfires are an increasing threat in most areas around the country. Some of this is due to poor or lack of proper forest management. The Native Americans knew the value of what we today call "prescribed" or "controlled" burns. This practice, along with careful and thoughtful thinning of our forests, can help reduce the occurrence of wildfires. These carefully planned and executed fires—and some naturally occurring fires—can have a beneficial component to the natural world, but devastating wildfires can lead to erosion, landslides (another hazard in California) and drops in water quality.

Particularly vulnerable to rising world ocean temperatures is coral, which for more than twenty-five years scientists have been calling the indicator of the health of the oceans—an early warning sign, much like the canary was for the coal miners.

According to the Global Coral Reef Monitoring Network, "reefs support at least a million described species of animals and plants, and another eight million coral reef species are estimated to be as yet undiscovered." But an estimated 25 percent of the world's reefs

For the past 50 years, the US government's Geological Survey department has been studying the decline and eventual death of coral in reefs such as the Carysfort Reef in the Key Largo Coral Reef Marine Sanctuary in Florida. *Photo by Eugene Shinn, USGS*

are dead or dying and another third are degraded or threatened. Beyond the climate crisis, coral is being killed by unsustainable fishing practices, and downright destructive fishing practices such as the use of explosives and cyanide. (In Komodo National Park in Indonesia, about half of the reefs have already been destroyed through the use of explosives, forming beds of coral rubble that can extend several football fields in length.)

According to the monitoring network: "In northern Jamaica, it is estimated that almost all of the reefs are dead or severely degraded from overfishing and coastal runoff. Fish stocks have declined to a point where local fishers are now straining fish larvae out of the sea for fish soup. In the Philippines, degraded reefs and fish populations have led to an 18 percent decrease in the amount of protein in the average diet. Human impacts are also occurring on US reefs, oftentimes for use as luxury items. For example, in Hawaii at Honaunau, the top 10 aquarium fish species have decreased by 59 percent over the last 20 years, and at Kona the most popular aquarium fish show declines in abundance from 38 percent to 57 percent."

Dr. Phil Dustan of the University of Charleston's Department of Biology claims that since 1975, more than 90 percent of the reefs in the Florida Keys have lost their living coral cover.

The primary threats to all reefs is coral bleaching—the coral loses its color due to warmer water and the changing pH of the oceans as a result of increased carbon dioxide in the atmosphere being absorbed into the water. While reefs also play a major role in protecting coastlines from erosion and storm damage, they also are a source of food, medicine, and income for tens of thousands of people, primarily those on Pacific Ocean coasts.

Despite it being federally protected, Australia's Great Barrier Reef, the largest in the world, has been severely threatened by pollution and rising ocean temperatures, according to the country's Marine Park Authority. Farm run-off is polluted as a result of overgrazing and excessive fertilizer and pesticide use. Water quality has also been declining due to sediment and loss of coastal wetlands, which act as a natural filter.

Thankfully, the Australian government is making steps toward making tourism ecologically sustainable at the reef. But worldwide, according to the Global Coral Reef Monitoring Network, in 2002 there was destruction or grave threat to at least 59 percent of the world's reefs. That rose sharply to 70 percent in 2008. Regionally, about 65 percent of the Persian Gulf's reefs have been destroyed, followed by South and Southeast Asia, where 45 percent and 38 percent, respectively, have been destroyed.

While it was the train that greatly accelerated the settlement of the west, it was the automobile that changed the landscape of how America developed.

At first a luxury only the rich could afford, the automobile nearly overnight changed people's lives once Henry Ford started producing the Model T. Simple and relatively inexpensive, more than fifteen million of the cars were sold during its nineteen-year production run, a quantity unchallenged until the Volkswagen Beatle surpassed it, according to Ford Motor Company. (And, for trivia's sake, Ford says, it didn't only come in black, as the urban legend goes … it came in blue, red, green and grey.)

With the freedom to go where and when they wanted people naturally took advantage of this development. They began to travel for pleasure and adventure rather than to a destination. With the evolution of old horse and buggy trails into a national network of roads and highways—perhaps the most famous being the cross-continental Route 66—came a whole new economic world of gas stations, garages, motels, and diners. Soon there was an alternative transportation method for goods as well, which led to the blossoming of villages and towns not on central rail lines making it more economical for some businesses to locate away from the new urban centers where real estate was escalating in price. It made it easier and made sense for new towns to start popping up deeper and deeper into the countryside.

Then came another invention that changed the way some people live: camping trailers. These, in turn, led to mobile homes and mobile home parks, which from their start were an alternative to apartments for those who couldn't afford homes and didn't necessarily wish to live in more urban areas. Soon, the mobile homes grew into "double-wides," that were not actually that mobile, yet changed the way some Americans lived, making them more vulnerable to severe weather, as most mobile homes are not as sturdy as permanent structures and are often located out of sheltered urban areas in more open, rural spaces. After Hurricane Andrew struck Florida with devastating results in 1992, new standards for mobile homes were adopted and their appeal has never been stronger, with an estimated thirty-five thousand mobile home parks in the country, according to one online database.

The American landscape began to change again in 1956 with the passage of the Dwight D. Eisenhower National System of Interstate and Defense Highways (the interstates). The president called for the creation of a network of limited-access highways not only to handle the burgeoning traffic load but also to make troop and military equipment transportation more efficient.

The spider web of highways was restructured over time, and some towns paid a heavy cost as they lost businesses, and residents, as they were bypassed. But the ribbon of multi-lane freeways, one of the largest public works projects in the world, again changed what the map of America looks like.

* * *

Amidst the unbridled expansion and establishment of settlements all over the country in the nineteenth century came the spark of the most important legacies Congress has ever done for the environment: The National Park Service.

While not fully enacted until a stroke of President Woodrow Wilson's pen in 1916, the park system had its start in the 1830s when artist George Catlin proclaimed of the beauty he saw on his travels that it should be protected "by some great protecting policy of government, in a magnificent park, a nation's park, containing man and beast, in all the wild and freshness of their nature's beauty!"

It took until 1872, but that's when President Ulysses S. Grant made Yellowstone the country's first national park. President William Henry Harrison created the first national forest preserve in 1891 when he signed on to the Yellowstone Timberland Preserve, and in 1903 President Theodore Roosevelt made Florida's Pelican Island the nation's first National Wildlife Refuge. Since then, according to the reserve, the system has grown to more than 150 million acres, 552 national wildlife refuges and other units of the refuge system, plus 37 wetland management districts. As a point of interest, there is a movement from some of the retired and existing officers of NWRS, as well as others, to take the system out from under the administration of the Fish and Wildlife Service where it is now administered and make it a stand-alone agency. This group, called the Blue Goose Alliance, believes that FWS is overwhelmed with what it takes to run their own lands as well as NWFS lands and that it would be better to set up a separate and autonomous agency. For more information on this, see: www.bluegoosealliance.org.

Today, according to the park service, there are 391 areas under its jurisdiction, which includes parks, lakeshores, seashores, rivers and trails, forests, and wildlife preserves. Historical parks and sites, monuments, and the White House are NPS designates as well.

And this is all good, the more than 130 years of such federally mandated protection. What's not so good is that in some years the national parks are a bit too successful when it comes to public appreciation. In fact, they are sometimes imperiled.

Park statistics indicate that visitation into the early 1990s had been rising about 10 percent a year, particularly at marquee spots such as Yellowstone and Yosemite. Use was becoming, some contend, overuse.

Many people, including environmental teachers and authors Donald G. Kaufman and Cecilia M. Franz from the University of Miami, argued that this increase in park visitors was destroying trails, damaging habitat, and that the litter and water pollution that inevitably trails people and their cars was having a markedly detrimental impact on the environment, which an under-funded park service was unable to successfully combat.

After a debate over federal funding and possible quotas, entrance fees were raised; attendance has fallen at most parks and remained steady at a lower level.

It wasn't just overuse that has, or may, threaten parks: As Kaufman and Franz point out, mining, oil drilling, and other unsound practices on adjoining lands can also impact parks. Pollution and soil erosion can both lead to broad negative effects on water quality for many miles, which in turn affects flora and fauna alike.

Don't get me wrong, as Wallace Stegner, the Western writer said, our national parks are our "best idea," and being our best idea, we need to be careful how we treat them and all of our precious American lands.

And so America was settled and grew, and grew, and grew—in some ways well, and in many ways rampantly and recklessly. As the population increased and Americans became more restless and adventurous, our landscape morphed and changed. Trains, planes, and automobiles gave us the means of moving people and things from here to there and beyond. The Industrial Revolution led us to build factories and create more and more jobs. New inventions did the same, and we built more cities and expanded the existing ones. We put a man on the moon and came into the computer and information age. We've come a mighty long ways since the pioneering days. Along the way we've left our mark. We expanded, explored, invented, built, and built, and built. As time went on, new concepts for planned communities came into play, such as William Levitt's Levittown on Long Island, New York, that was built between 1947 and 1951. Eventually we sprawled from our city and town borders and started building shopping centers, malls, and the like. Some of these ideas and concepts worked well, but many failed in the long term. We paved more roads, put down more impervious surfaces and didn't give much thought to the consequences. We put in more airports and highways, built bridges and tunnels, built in places we would have been better off leaving alone. We tore down and re-built and expanded some more; sometimes we learned from our mistakes, and sometimes we just made more mistakes. And now, here we are. We are no doubt at a crossroads, and it's time to take a good look at where we've been, where we are, and where we are going. We have to make some tough choices and some intelligent decisions going forward.

Settling America hasn't been easy. Nor is it going to be easy to find ways to deal with our continued growth. We all have to have places to live, to work, and to play. Can we do all of this in a way that will be smart, strong, and sustainable? Let's hope so.

A New World Is Born

The Awakening of the 'Sleeping Giant'

*"America was not made the industrial giant of the world
by the robber barons alone, … It was made the industrial
giant of the world by competition, by encouraging new
developments, by encouraging young entrepreneurs to break
into the market. It's the best system I've seen so far."*

Janet Reno

Something strange happened on the way to the twenty-first
century. Industry began to embrace environmentalists and
conservationists. Traditionally at odds—environmentalists
being seen as anti-business—the two sides are beginning to
meet because sustainable enterprises make good sense:
unsustainable models are slowly been seen as undesirable, if
not downright uneconomical, and with the shift in awareness
to protecting the environment, being considered a progressive
or even "green" company has enormous public relations
benefits which, in turn, enhance profitability. There's even
talk within industry of having an environmental ethic
standard of some kind.

If it can be said there's a leader in this movement, it would
be a man by the name of Ray Anderson, the chairman and
CEO of the Atlanta-based Interface, Inc.—the world's largest
producer of commercial, modular floor coverings. Anderson

Innovative industrialist and author Ray Anderson. *Photo courtesy Interface, Inc.*

wrote *Mid-Course Correction* and published it in 1998. In it, Anderson explains an epiphany he had when he learned that his companies, in 1995 alone, consumed 1,224 billion pounds of raw material—non-renewable resources—to produce carpets and other goods.

"It made me want to throw up," he writes.

Of that, 800 million pounds was petroleum based —two-thirds, burned up for energy, leaving pollution and product behind.

"When Earth runs out of finite, exhaustible resources and ecosystems collapse, our descendants will be left holding the empty bag. Someday, people like me may be put in jail."

Anderson pledged to make his multi-billion-dollar company the first industrial business in the world to be environmentally sustainable—and then restorative, putting back more than it takes.

He's made some remarkable progress, especially considering the underlying nature of the resources needed to make carpets, for instance. "It means creating and adopting the technologies of the future—kinder, gentler technologies that emulate nature."

Anderson contends that in the future, he won't have to make any new carpeting: it's already been made. His ingenious model is to take carpet that's already been manufactured and recycle it, endlessly, into new carpet. Inspired, in one case, by the patchwork patterns of a forest floor, Interface developed eighteen-inch patches, randomly colored, which come together to make a full carpet floor surface. When individual patches are damaged or worn, they alone can be replaced, then the core material recycled and turned into new patches.

His goal is for the company to become, by 2020, "closed loop," that is, feeding his factories entirely with recycled material.

As of 2009, the company diverted more than half the waste it used to send to landfills—roughly 100 million pounds. Seven of its plants operate with alternative energy such as solar. Interface uses 75 percent less water than it did in 1996, and has reduced its energy requirements by 45 percent. Anderson's company also plants three trees for every one calculated to offset the carbon cost of business air travel by employees.

"If we get it right during the next industrial revolution, we will never have to take another drop of oil from the Earth for our products or industrial processes," Anderson writes.

I highly recommend his book, as well as Anderson's more recent book, *Confessions of a Radical Industrialist*, in which he expounds even more on his journey. In that wonderful read, he talks about the "seven faces of Mt. Sustainability" and how to reach the summit. Both of these fine, sincere, and personal works show his visionary approach and reveal one man's bold desire to have a positive impact on our precious Earth. The model established by Interface is being adopted by other businesses, and Anderson himself is revolutionary beyond just his strong passion for sustainable industry—his views on turning the tax system upside down (tax the bad things—pollution, non-renewable resources—not good things, like income and property) are remarkable.

Interface is a long-existing business taking a different path, but with what many call the "next industrial revolution" comes an entirely new kind of business: green technology.

In his excellent and enlightening book, *The Plot to Save the Planet*, my friend and a fine business journalist Brian Dumaine, makes a case that the next, greatest industry in America will be that of "green" technologies.

He quotes maverick venture capitalist John Doerr as saying: "Green tech is bigger than the Internet. It could be the biggest economic opportunity of the 21st century."

And what drives this new economy should be carbon-free, or close, create wealth and jobs, and save the planet. UN Secretary-General Ban Ki-moon made the environment a centerpiece of his yearlong leadership and has gone so far as to say that the world doesn't have a choice but to embrace "the age of green economics."

"With the right financial incentives and a global framework, we can steer economic growth in a low-carbon direction," Ban said to a Chicago business group. Ban said global investment in green energy is projected to hit $1.9 trillion by 2020, an indication of an economic shift that will rival the industrial revolution and the technology revolution of the past two centuries.

For America, this green revolution may be the savior of the economy, a lasting savior, because many of the jobs can't be outsourced to other countries. For instance, (and I'll get into the details on this later) the Empire State Building is undergoing a $20-million retrofit; that can't be outsourced to China. Building and installing vast fields of solar panels on the roofs of existing buildings, building new high-speed mass-transit systems, and upgrading subways are other examples of a new-job economy that can't be outsourced.

At the forefront of green technology is the development of alternative fuels and ways to store energy, which, again, I'll address fully in a later chapter. Green technologies are being applied to how buildings are built and insulated, using markedly less energy and water, how non-toxic chemicals are developed, and to the burgeoning science of nanotechnology. Nanotechnology is manipulating material at the atomic level, on the scale of a nanometer—one-billionth of a meter. It is a controversial subject, and scientists basically don't know the limits to the technology but do know it could be used to make lifesaving medical robots or supercomputers one millimeter square in size that cost a penny or less and don't have the negative environmental impact of silicon-chip manufacturing.

Green nanotechnology may be able to help the environment in terms of pollutant filters and water filters that can clean water from any source other than radioactive.

Like most of our technologies, nanotechnology can also be put to evil use—perhaps by developing untraceable weapons of mass destruction or bio-weapons for which there is no treatment, so it's unlikely to remain uncontroversial and could become highly regulated.

In so many ways, we are at a standing point. Our environment is threatened and our economies coming into the second decade of the twenty-first century are in the deepest recession since the 1930s Depression. We have a chance to turn things right side up. In part, what I mean by that is that things have been upside down. Just look at the challenges even individuals face: Buying environmentally friendly, organic food is often more expensive than buying food made from farming practices that pollute the environment, erode soil, and demand excessive use of fossil fuels for production, processing, and transportation. Companies that have a desire to use raw materials such as wood that is "certified," or grown in a sustainable manner, often have to pay more for it. In my opinion, these things should cost less.

In his great book, *The Ecology of Commerce*, Paul Hawken states, "Without a doubt, the single most damaging aspect of the present economic system is that the expense of destroying the earth is largely absent from the prices set in the marketplace. A vital and key piece of information is therefore missing in all levels of the economy.... Markets are superb at setting prices, but incapable of recognizing costs."

I've yet to read a better or more concise explanation of this concept than Hawken's:

"Gasoline is cheap in the United States because its price does not reflect the cost of smog, acid rain, and their subsequent effects on health and the environment. Likewise, American food is the cheapest in the world, but the price does not reflect the fact that we have depleted the soil, reducing average topsoil from a depth of 21 to six inches over the past hundred years, contaminated our groundwater (farmers do not drink from wells in parts of Iowa), and poisoned wildlife through the use of pesticides.

When prices drop, effectively raising real income, people don't need to think about waste, frugality, product life cycles, or product substitution. When prices rise, people have to reconsider usage patterns. This may be painful at first, but it generally results in innovation and creativity."

It's been the traditional standoff between environmentalists and regulators and industry: The cost of sequestering toxins and carbon impairs business efficiency, it is claimed, and would result in loss of money, loss of jobs, and affect the economy—it is with these arguments that industries have, for decades, been able to often forestall regulation and prevent punitive taxes for polluting. We are, basically, as Hawken says, "stealing from the future in order to finance present overconsumption."

I'll get deeply into our energy options in a later chapter, but this concept so clearly applies to our conventional, fossil-fuel sources. Would nuclear, coal, and gas-fired energy plants really be considered cheaper than embracing wind, solar, tide, biomass or other alternate sources if the enormous cost of destroyed land from mining, compromised health of workers and residents, poisoned waterways and contaminated soil—and the millions of pounds of carbon dioxide (alone) dumped into the atmosphere—were added to the balance sheet? When one really thinks about it, shouldn't our current major non-renewable energy generators, by all rights, be the most expensive ways to harness energy given their enormous toll on the environment?

All it takes is being more in tune with nature. By this I mean taking lessons from nature, which is starting to happen in individual circumstances being now described as "industrial symbiosis." It's basically the belief that industry could behave like the natural ecosystem where everything is recycled, and by sharing information, services, and by-products, value is added, costs are reduced, and the environment is less affected.

As Hawken writes, "growth does not necessarily mean more waste, prosperity does not have to be described by kilowatts used, autos produced, hamburgers flipped and consumed."

The most often-cited example of this is in Kalundborg, Denmark.

In their 1997 article, "Industrial Ecology in Practice," authors John Ehrenfeld and Nicholas Gertler describe the Kalundborg complex as having at its center: "A 1500MW coal-fired power plant, which has material and energy links with the community and several other companies. This interesting web of energy distribution emanates from the Asnes Power Station. Surplus heat from this power plant is used to heat 3,500 local homes in addition to a nearby fish farm, whose sludge is then sold as a fertilizer. Steam from the power plant is sold to Novo Nordisk, a pharmaceutical and enzyme manufacturer, in addition to the Statoil plant, a crude oil refinery. This reuse of heat reduces the amount of thermal pollution discharged to a nearby fjord. Additionally, a by-product from the power plant's sulfur dioxide scrubber contains gypsum, which is sold to Gyproc, a wallboard manufacturer. Almost all of the manufacturer's gypsum needs are met this way, which reduces the amount of open-pit mining needed. Furthermore, fly ash and clinker from the power plant is used for road building and cement production."

This amazing network was not a planned effort; it just evolved as a collection of deals made between these entities that made

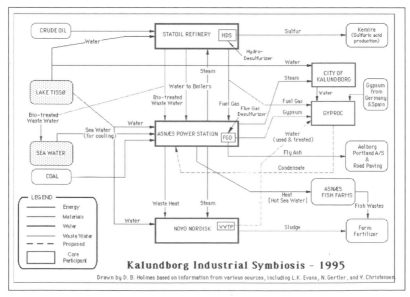

Kalundborg Industrial Symbiosis - 1995

Drawn by D. B. Holmes based on information from various sources, including L.K. Evans, N. Gertler, and Y. Christensen.

The remarkable "industrial symbiosis" of the massive complex at Kalundborg, Denmark. *Image © Douglas B. Holmes* economic sense for the participants. It all started when Gyproc located its facility in Kalundborg to take advantage of the gas fuel available from Statoil. Gyproc is still the only company to have located there to take advantage of an existing available supply.

Significantly, one of the best things about this "symbiosis" is that it occurred outside of government regulation; it happened because it made the most business sense and the most sense for the environment. The goal is to encourage companies to look beyond their traditional physical and sector boundaries in the pursuit of creating an environmentally sustainable economy.

England currently has the world's only national symbiosis program, which is inspiring the development of programs in China, Brazil, and in Illinois, USA. Since 2005, the British model (known as NISP: National Industrial Symbiosis Programme), has, according to its model: "diverted more than 5.2 million metric tons of industrial waste from landfill across the UK; generated £151 million in new sales for its members; reduced carbon emissions by more than 5.2 million metric tons; saved its members more than £131 million; eliminated 357,000 metric tons of hazardous waste; created and safeguarded 2,216 jobs; saved 7.9 million metric tons of virgin material being used in the UK; attracted more than £116 million in private investment in reprocessing and recycling; and saved more than 9.4 million metric tons of industrial water."

Considered a great success, the British organization is making efforts to export its model to other countries, including the United States. According to its head, Peter Laybourn: "Chicago is home to the US's first 'UK style' IS (Industrial Symbiosis) program, "Waste to Profit." Run in conjunction with the city of Chicago, the United States Business Council for Sustainable Development (USBCSD), and the Chicago Manufacturing Center with support from NISP, it is now in its third year. The Chicago Waste to Profit Network aims to continue to grow and promote economic development for the whole State of Illinois.

IS regional schemes have also been established in China, Mexico, and Brazil. Lessons learned in the UK helped shape a "circular economy" initiative in the Yunnan Province of South West China."

It's heartening to hear that this kind of progressive industrial planning is coming to America and is being embraced in its infancy, because it is a radical shift in corporate mentality, on the level of Ray Anderson's Interface efforts.

Another shift was the creation, by segments of the building community, of the Leadership in Energy and Environmental Design (LEED) Green Building Rating System, developed by the US Green Building Council. Building green has historically been more expensive and less profitable for developers, but having standards of design and development for new construction, existing buildings, commercial buildings, homes, and whole neighborhoods can be an incentive to more economical and sustainable materials.

LEED certification is based on a 100-point award system gauged to emphasize state-of-the-art strategies for sustainable site development, water conservation, energy efficiency, materials selection, and indoor environmental quality. There's a six-point bonus award for innovation in design, leading up to standings of Certified, Silver, Gold, and Platinum designations. Since its creation in 1998, LEED has grown to encompass more than fourteen thousand projects around the country and the world.

LEED-certified buildings are, of course, more environmentally friendly both during and after construction, and there are immediate, tangible benefits with water-and-electric-efficient appliances. But the programs architects suggest that a business with happier, healthier employees will incur added profitability from heightened productivity.

Ashley Katz at the US Green Building Council, which was instrumental in the creation of the LEED standard, said, "The LEED rating system is evolving to include regionally weighted credits, so that, for example, using solar panels in Arizona will be worth more than using solar panels in upstate New York. LEED-certified buildings are able to recoup the costs within the first one to two years of the lifecycle of the building and after that, you are saving money."

She suggested that what would normally cost $500,000 to construct, would cost $540,000 to meet the criteria for a LEEDS Platinum certification. I think having LEED and other similar standards is a wonderful idea and can truly help us build better, more efficient, and longer-lasting buildings. However, one personal beef I have with the LEED standard is that at present they only recognize one forest-certification standard, that of FSC (Forest Stewardship Council, an arm of WWF, the World Wildlife Fund). While I respect FSC's standard and believe they have done some great work, they are certainly not the only good standard out there for forest products. SFI (Sustainable Forestry Initiative), ATFS (American Tree Farm System, a certification program for family forest landowners that has been around since the early 1930s that is run by AFF, the American Forest Foundation), and PEFC (Programme for the Endorsement of Forest Certification schemes), an established European entity, are all excellent forest-certification programs and should be recognized by LEED and all other respectable building standards. An interesting point is that ATFS, SFI, and PEFC all have mutual recognition, that is to say they respect and recognize each other's standards. It would be, in my opinion, the right thing to do if FSC would join hands with these other fine entities with mutual recognition. Discussions to this end have begun and are ongoing, but so far FSC seems to have a desire to avoid this path, which I think is unfortunate. In any case, I believe it would behoove everyone if LEED and similar entities should open their arms to the other existing standards as well as recognizing the fine work of FSC.

Another more regional "green" certification is the Southeast Environmental Certification for residential houses, called EarthCraft. The entire maverick community of Serenbe, Georgia, has been EarthCraft certified. I will explore the model of Serenbe later, but Garnie Nygren, the community's director of operations, explains: "EarthCraft is under the Southface organization out of Atlanta. As a house is being built, there are certain points that builders can achieve, from the insulation they use to how they zone the house with heating and air. So EarthCraft comes in when the house is almost done to do an air test to make sure that air is flowing evenly throughout the house, so you have the highest energy efficiency possible. Our residents, once they move into their houses, see anywhere from a 20- to 40-percent reduction in the energy they use to heat and cool and run the house."

The North Carolina based company Enertia is a great example of a constructor of residential housing that takes into account all aspects of energy efficiency while using creative and attractive design concepts. They begin by taking into consideration the location of the house or structure to be built, and how to properly position it, then use geo-thermal, solar, special techniques of wood insulation properties, and other concepts to build a house that can conceivably make more energy that it uses. Enertia makes common-sense use of daytime heat and cooler nighttime temperatures. Along with other special construction systems, they build homes that are incredibly beautiful and among the most energy-efficient in the world. Their website, enertia.com, explains in depth how they do it and shows how attractive these amazing homes are. Enertia is a fine example of how the construction of a home using innovation, science, nature, and creative design can make an amazing place to live with virtually no energy costs and very little, if any, carbon footprint.

Seeing industries changing from the inside is a nascent sign of hope that the sleeping giant America is waking up to sustainability. The list of terrific examples alone could take up a book, but I'd like to point out a few businesses that one might not otherwise believe had much of a carbon footprint, or other negative effects on the environment yet are doing—or have said they're going to do—something about it.

When thinking of carbon footprints, one tends to think of coal-burning electric plants, or mines, steel mills, even airlines. Not about Wall Street. Yet the investment firm Goldman Sachs surprised a lot of people, both in the corporate world as well as the world of conservancy, in 2005. The year before, it had a acquired a portfolio of mortgages in default in Tierra del Fuego, Chile, consisting of 680,000 acres of bio-diverse, ecologically important land. Employees at the investment firm didn't know what to do with it: Break it up and sell it, log it? Then someone suggested they purchase it and protect it. Senior management agreed, and the company endowed the land to the Chilean government in a partnership with the Wildlife Conservation Society. Some extreme criticism followed, particularly from the Free Enterprise Action Fund, a right-wing mutual fund that "confronts CEOs who participate in the 'liberal-industrial complex'—the alliance of left-wing investors and corporate managers, special interest groups and politicians—who collaborate to advance the liberal agenda." The FEAF, which is defunct and had merged with what is now the Congressional Effect Fund, was of the opinion that a bank shouldn't be concerned about the environment.

The criticism didn't stick, and Goldman Sachs went further, releasing an eight-page environmental policy framework. In it, the company said it would disclose the greenhouse gas emissions of all its operations; make $1 billion available for investments in renewable energy; create a think tank to seek out lucrative green markets; work on public policy measures relating to climate change; conduct rigorous assessments of how any of its new projects may impact the environment or indigenous people; and refuse to finance extractive projects in World Heritage sites or any projects that violate the environmental laws of a host country. The policy also declares that "We believe that companies' management of environmental and related social risks and opportunities may affect corporate performance."

As one freelance business writer said, "This is not a case of Goldman pretending its job is to save the world, or forsaking its primary mission to make money for its investors. Self-interest is in full effect here. Goldman Sachs is positioning itself to be a leader in the green energy sector."

The company is basically looking far ahead, and saying: "There are real financial costs to ignoring the environment and the people who depend on it for their survival, and we don't intend to get stuck paying them."

It definitely IS smart business being green. As Brian Dumaine points out in *The Plot to Save the Planet*, it's reasonable to assume that environmental issues and climate-change-related contentions may be one of the next big legal battlefields. According to Dumaine, the state of California filed suit against six automakers in 2006, with the contention that greenhouse gases from their vehicles caused billions of dollars in damage to the environment, damage that taxpayers would have to pay to reduce. Also, eight state attorneys general filed a lawsuit against the nation's largest electric utilities. The suit is an attempt to force power plants to cut emissions of gases linked to global climate change. The claims draw on science, century-old nuisance laws, and a decision by state officials to circumvent federal agencies.

"More and more big institutional investors believe that those corporations that fail to adapt to global warming will soon see their shares pummeled. The first companies to respond to climate change could not only protect their share price but also create a long-term competitive advantage," Dumaine writes.

* * *

Another company that has taken a great deal of criticism for its green efforts is Walmart, the world's largest retailer, and, according to *Fortune* magazine, one of the largest greenhouse gas producers in the nation.

Walmart made the pledge in 2005 to work only with suppliers who embrace non-polluting manufacturing processes, sustainable farming, fishing and forestry practices, and to reduce waste and energy use in its stores and transportation fleet.

The company has built "green" supercenters in Arkansas and Colorado that are designed to eventually cut electrical usage by up to 80 percent

Harsh critics describe it as "greenwashing"—a public-relations exercise to mitigate a record of controversy. But if the company even comes close to delivering on their promises, the motivation doesn't matter. So far, it hasn't met its goals but issues quarterly reports that it is making progress and is seeking ever-more innovative ways to achieve its intention to drastically lower its carbon footprint. To Walmart's credit, it has stayed the course and continues to make in-house improvements as well as pushing its providers to follow their lead. In any case, such a large retailer taking even baby steps to sustainable business practice sends out shockwaves through the retail world.

In September 2008 Walmart announced it was teaming up with the Environmental Defense Fund in the Global Plastic Shopping

Bag Waste Reduction Commitment, with the goal of having a one-third reduction in plastic bags by 2013.

But, like Goldman Sachs, Walmart is not in the business of saving the world; it's in the business of making money—and taking steps to be more environmentally friendly is good business sense. Ultimately, of course, Walmart has had a huge impact on how people live, shop and even decide on housing, which has not been smart and sustainable, and which I'll address in a later chapter.

* * *

Steve Bing comes pretty high on my list of admirable conservationists and environmentalists. His political activism might be as well known as his forays into the entertainment business but what's less known is that he's foot the bill for the world's first and only LEED Platinum-certified airplane hangar, Hangar 25 at Bob Hope airport in Burbank, California, which is the headquarters for the Avjet Corporation. I won't get into all the specifics, but the building includes, according to Bing's Shangri-La Construction company, "a solar-powered roof system that supplies at least 110% (and often double) of all necessary power needs, including clean powering of aircraft auxiliary power units in use while aircraft are on the ground, electric tow and maintenance vehicles and office operations."

It's part of Steve's—and his company's—conviction that "sustainable design and construction are achievable at a cost comparable to traditional construction" and he's out to prove it. I have great admiration for him and his accomplishments.

* * *

Vermont-based ice cream maker Ben & Jerry's is one of the most innovative "green companies," I think.

Their Dairy Stewardship Alliance has been, since 2003, a collaborative effort between Ben & Jerry's, the University of Vermont's Center for Sustainable Agriculture, the St. Albans Cooperative Creamery, and the state of Vermont Agency of Agriculture. Its goal is to foster knowledge and practice of sustainable diary farming.

In the fall 2008, the company started trials on new hydrocarbon freezers, which use alternative refrigerants that do not contribute to the loss of the ozone layer. They claim that they'll share the technology if, and when, they gain clearance from the Environmental Protection Agency.

The company takes considerable effort to catalogue and consider its carbon footprint, and targets energy reduction in its factories, among other green practices.

Years after it took the step of buying unbleached paper packaging, Ben & Jerry's began buying its new containers from a company whose paper supply came from sustainably managed forests, and now boasts a certification by FSC. While I would again point out that there are other equally good standards for forest certification out there that the company could choose, I think it's a wonderful thing that Ben & Jerry's has taken the steps to engage in a certification program.

Ben & Jerry's supports foundations and environmental groups annually with grants and has one of the most admirable mission statements I can think of:

"Product mission: To make, distribute and sell the finest quality all natural ice cream and euphoric concoctions with a continued commitment to incorporating wholesome, natural ingredients and promoting business practices that respect the Earth and the Environment.

"Economic mission: To operate the Company on a sustainable financial basis of profitable growth, increasing value for our stakeholders and expanding opportunities for development and career growth for our employees.

'Social mission: To operate the company in a way that actively recognizes the central role that business plays in society by initiating innovative ways to improve the quality of life locally, nationally and internationally."

The company's founders and managers clearly understand that environmentally sensitive business is the best business.

* * *

The high-end clothing retailer Patagonia has, for years, been a leader in sustainable business practices. It was the first major retailer to begin using only organic cotton, the first to begin making fleece from recycled bottles, and turn a portion of its annual revenues to environmental causes and organizations. In 1989, it co-founded the Conservation Alliance and encouraged other similar companies to become involved.

According to the gogreen.ae website, "The Alliance now boasts 155 member companies, each of which contributes annual dues to a central fund. Patagonia gives to the alliance each year, and maintains a permanent seat on the board of directors. Twice yearly, the Alliance donates 100 percent of its membership dues to grassroots environmental groups working to protect threatened wildlands and biodiversity. In 2007, it granted $800,000 to 29 organizations. Grants since 1989 total over $6.5 million."

Granted, the retailer still has a negative environmental impact in that much of its manufacturing is done overseas in places with standards that most would say are low. But when it built a 171,000 square-expansion of its distribution center in Reno, Nevada, Patagonia set out for a Silver LEEDS rating. It won the even higher Gold standing. The company has prompted other manufacturers such as Gap, Levi's, Nike, and Timberland to take steps to minimize their environmental impact.

* * *

3M has made a comprehensive effort to embrace sustainability and reduce emissions, and made its top three goals—according to its website—to "Manage our environmental footprint. Develop solutions that address environmental and social challenges for our customers and society. Assure our products are safe for their intended use through their entire life cycle."

In April, 2009, the company was again recognized by the US Environmental Protection Agency and Department of Energy for the sixth year in a row by receiving its fifth Energy Star Award for Sustained Excellence in Energy Management—a record for an industrial company, according to 3M.

The list, thankfully, of companies taking similar approaches is growing—even in a difficult economic climate.

* * *

Former US Vice-President Al Gore didn't just change the way people think about climate change with his Oscar Award-winning film *An Inconvenient Truth*, he got many people to START thinking about it. At a conference in San Francisco, Gore declared that the late-2009 United Nations Climate Change Conference in Copenhagen "is the Gettysburg for the environment. We are radically changing the relationship between the human species and the rest of the earth. It is the time we have the opportunity to change." In Gore's more recent book, *Our Choice*, he offers hope that we can make the changes necessary to curb global warming and solutions to reach reasonable goals to do so.

Many people were disappointed with the results of the 2009 Copenhagen meetings, and there is no doubt that there was much disagreement, turmoil, finger pointing, and head shaking going on during the conference. There is also no doubt that lesser goals were set concerning climate change and our environment than we would all like to have seen as an outcome. However, while one may see the glass as half full, there was some progress made. Still, I believe the majority of the world (including yours truly) has a difficult time understanding why more and better results can't be attained in these kinds of summits. I almost wish that we could lock the main world leaders into a room with no food or drink until they come out with something substantial that makes sense and that can be monitored for results.

But minor progress is definitely better than no progress at all.

There has always been a contingent of people, of course, thinking toward the next generations and what challenges they'd face as a result of what decisions are being made now.

Lester Brown, a former president of WorldWatch Institute—a Washington, D.C.-based group that advised leaders on sustainable living practices, said "Building an environmentally sustainable future requires nothing short of a revolution, restructuring the global economy, dramatically changing human reproductive behavior and altering values and lifestyles."

The Club of Rome, which consists of former and current heads of state, UN officials, diplomats, scientists, economists, and business leaders from all over the world, was formed in April of 1968. An independent, not-for-profit organization, it published *The*

Limits to Growth, a study by a group of scientists at the Massachusetts Institute of Technology, back in 1972. Eventually selling millions of copies, the work "demonstrated the contradiction of unlimited and unrestrained growth in material consumption in a world of clearly finite resources."

The message from the club—whose members include Al Gore, most of the heads of state of, and royal families in, Europe, and Dr. Ashok Khosla, one of world's leading experts on the environment and sustainable development—has become far more grave than it was in the year of its release, however.

More recent warnings include the club's contention that "Modern industrial civilization is fast outstripping the Earth's natural regenerative and life-supporting capacity ... at current rates of resource depletion and environmental degradation a near collapse of ecological integrity will occur within the next 100 years." The latest declaration is that we're much closer to a "point of no return."

Whereas Al Gore asserted in *An Inconvenient Truth* that we had roughly a decade, the Club of Rome believes "The acceleration of critical trends and cross-impacts among them indicates that the "window of opportunity' for pulling out of the present global crisis and breaking through to a more peaceful and sustainable world is likely to be no more than four to five years from the end of 2008."

While there are ongoing arguments about "how long we have" to turn things around, and even some of the very people that are writing the books on these matters change their minds and predictions on these time frames, it still seems to me that it's long overdue for us to take a long, hard, and serious look at what we are doing to ourselves and our planet. Surely we can agree that we are putting tremendous pressure on our natural resources, our atmosphere, and other aspects of our environment?

Many believe that our biggest threat is also our most controversial: Global warming from the buildup of greenhouse gases. (It has its disbelievers; I'll address that shortly.)

Prior to the 2009 Copenhagen summit, the 1997 Kyoto Climate Change Conference set forth the objective of the "stabilization of greenhouse gas concentrations in the atmosphere at a level that would prevent dangerous anthropogenic interference with the climate system."

The plan was to establish a legally binding, international agreement, whereby, all the participating nations would commit themselves to tackling the issue of global warming and reduce greenhouse gas emissions. The US proposed, in an article on the global issues.org website, "to just stabilize emissions and not cut them at all, while the European Union called for a 15-percent cut. In the end, there was a trade off, and industrialized countries were committed to an overall reduction of emissions of greenhouse gases to 5.2 percent below 1990 levels for the period 2008–2012. Disturbingly, the Intergovernmental Panel on Climate Change said in its 1990 report that a 60-percent reduction in emissions is what was needed."

While a signatory to the agreement, and despite a compromise, the House and Senate, during the last Clinton administration and the first Bush administration, failed to ratify the agreement, so it has remained unbinding in America. Instead greenhouse gas emissions continue to rise, despite some welcome advances.

For instance, according to the EPA, it would take twenty of today's cars to release the same toxins as a single vehicle made in the 1960s. There is 98 percent less lead being released into the environment, while carbon monoxide release is down, as is nitrogen oxide (contributing factor to smog-causing ozone) and sulfur dioxide (contributing factor to acid rain). In all, the EPA says, total motor vehicle emission reduction stands at 48 percent less than it was in the 1970s, which is quite an accomplishment considering how many more vehicles there are on the roads and urban areas have multiplied in size.

Yet worldwide, the rate of increase of greenhouse gas emissions continues at roughly 2 to 3 percent a year. From 338 parts per million of carbon dioxide in our atmosphere, we now have 387 parts per million, according to the government's National Oceanic and Atmospheric Administration. In more tangible numbers, according to the US government's Energy Information Administration (EIA), the world dumped 29 billion metric tons of carbon dioxide alone into the atmosphere in 2008; by 2030—unless there's a change in how we live our lives and run our industries—we will dump 40.4 billion metric tons into the atmosphere every year. And let's not forget that there is the accumulative effect of year after year of this.

The US had an increase of 1.6 percent in 2007, but, thankfully, had a remarkable 2.8 percent reduction in emissions in 2008. Part of this is credited to regulation and governmental efforts but is also generally acknowledged to be as a result of a slowing economy and demand for energy.

We can hardly feel good about the big picture, though. China has passed the US as the world's biggest polluter, according to the Netherlands Environmental Assessment Agency, and now is responsible for 24 percent of the world's global emissions. America stands at 22 percent. The EU produces 12 percent, India eight percent and the Russian Federation 6 percent.

However, based on per-head of population, China is still far behind the US, which remains the biggest polluter per person by a large margin. US citizens produce an average of 19.4 metric tons of carbon dioxide each year, while those in China produce just 5.1 metric tons each. Sadly, that's likely to rise. Much of the growth in pollution levels is expected to come from developing countries such as China and India, which burn a great deal of coal.

"With strong economic growth and continued heavy reliance on fossil fuels expected for most of (the developing) economies, much of the increase in carbon dioxide emission is projected to occur among the developing … nations," the EIA said in the report, its annual International Energy Outlook.

It's one of the reasons American administrations failed to ratify the Kyoto Accord. First, lawmakers said to reduce emissions in the US would harm the economy and the American workforce. They also proclaimed that loose restrictions placed on China and India, the two largest, and most-populated, developing countries, would render the treaty ineffective in the long run for the international goal of lowering emissions.

Officials from 194 countries gathered in Copenhagen in late 2009 with the goal of drafting a new accord to replace the Kyoto Accord, and tackle global emissions into the next decade. It was an acrimonious conference, often deadlocked on procedure, and tense in part because of the opposition to emission-reduction measures related to fossil fuels in light of the struggling US and, indeed, world economy.

An accord was passed, with the United States, China, and 108 other countries accounting for nearly 80 percent of the world's greenhouse gas emissions signing onto a voluntary agreement to curb climate change.

While that sounds like good news, the voluntary accord falls short of a binding treaty sought by many nations, and sets a goal of limiting global warming to below 2 degrees Celsius (3.6 Fahrenheit) above pre-industrial times.

Yvo de Boer, former head of the UN Climate Change Secretariat that compiled the list, said pledges for cutting greenhouse gas emissions so far fell short of that goal.

"It is clear that while the pledges on the table are an important step toward the objective of limiting growth of emissions, they will not in themselves suffice to limit warming to below 2 degrees Celsius," he said in a statement.

On one hand, some environmental groups were optimistic, considering the number of nations signing on, along with the amount they pledged in reductions.

"What we now know that we did get out of Copenhagen was clarity of what countries are going to be doing to fight climate change," said Keya Chatterjee, US Acting Director of the World Wildlife Fund's Climate Change Program. The situation is "much better than we had a couple months ago. But it's still not where we need to be."

But others were vocally disappointed and declared the accord a failure. "Given where we started and the expectations for this conference, anything less than a legally binding and agreed outcome falls far short of the mark," said John Ashe, chairman of the Kyoto Protocol talks.

In addition to the United States and China—the two largest emitters of greenhouse gases—the countries that formally joined the Copenhagen Accord included India, Japan, and the nations of the European Union. The accord has no enforcement provision, though it does require participants to allow international scrutiny of their efforts. Still muddying the waters is the fact that a number of the countries' pledges are contingent on internal legislation. The

US, for instance, will not set a concrete target until Congress passes a climate bill, and Canada's pledge is linked to that of the US. Even at their most stringent, the pledges do not meet the accord's goal of holding warming to 2 degrees Celsius (3.6 degrees Fahrenheit) above pre-industrial levels, climate scientists and environmental groups say.

There was a lot of politics and posturing by both third-world, and first-world nations, and the United States received the brunt of a lot of the criticism for historically being the world's worst polluter. That's understandable, and shortsighted; we need to focus on the future, not the past.

Because planet Earth is getting warmer, our weather is becoming less stable and more extreme—winters are getting more severe in some parts of the world while summers are getting hotter. Some years are cooler, others hotter, but overall the planet is getting warmer. To boil it down to one statistic from the US government's own National Environmental Satellite, Data, and Information Service, seven of the eight warmest years on record have occurred since 2001 and the ten warmest years have all occurred since 1995.

In a survey compiled by the Environmental Defense Fund updated in February, 2009: There has been a 100-percent increase in intensity and duration of hurricanes and tropical storms since the 1970s, according to a 2005 MIT study.

The damage caused by hurricanes hitting the US coast in 2005 alone cost $100 billion, according to the National Climatic Data Center. By the year 2030, Glacier National Park will have no glaciers left, according to the US Geological Survey.

In the past thirty years, four hundred thousand acres of Arctic sea ice has melted, according to the Arctic Climate Impact Assessment, a project run by the Union of Concerned Scientists, which began as a study organized by students and scientists at MIT in 1969.

For about two hundred years, we have been pumping carbon dioxide into the atmosphere. The US government's National Oceanic and Atmospheric Administration says, "Human activity has been increasing the concentration of greenhouse gases in the atmosphere (mostly carbon dioxide from combustion of coal, oil, and gas; plus a few other trace gases). There is no scientific debate on this point. Pre-industrial levels of carbon dioxide (prior to the start of the Industrial Revolution) were about 280 parts per million by volume (ppmv), and current levels are greater than 380 ppmv and increasing at a rate of 1.9 ppm yr-1 since 2000. By the end of the twenty-first century, we could expect to see carbon dioxide concentrations of anywhere from 490 to 1260 ppm (75-350 percent above the pre-industrial concentration)."

The debate is whether the two are linked.

Former Vice-President Al Gore is probably the leading figure in the call to reduce man-generated greenhouse gases, of course, with his film, *An Inconvenient Truth*, his books and lectures. However, he and those who believe in a link between global warming and man-introduced carbon have staunch detractors.

Colorado State University climatologist Dr. William Gray is among the scientists who do not believe in global warming being caused by humans. In fact, in 2009, he told the *Denver Post*, "This scare will also run its course. In 15 to 20 years, we'll look back and see what a hoax it was." Gray is only one of the leading scientists to think so. In December 2008, a UN climate conference in Poland was told by 650 researchers that they believed man-made global warming was a hoax, offering alternative theories, most prominently that it's the sun's nuclear cycles, not carbon dioxide in the air.

Senator James "Jim" Inhofe of Oklahoma is a well-known naysayer of global warming. Inhofe is a staunch Republican known for quoting the Bible as the source for his positions on a range of issues. He is one of the most vocal skeptics on climate change and often states his opinion in his comments on the Senate floor. In one such speech in 2003, he stated that there was "compelling evidence that catastrophic global warming is a hoax. That conclusion is supported by the painstaking work of the nation's top climate scientists." In the same speech, he went on to say that "satellite data, confirmed by NOAA balloon measurements, confirms that no meaningful warming has occurred over the last century." But the fact is that the satellite temperature record corroborates the evidence that there is a warming trend in surface temperature measurements.

One can run in circles looking at the statistics, but it is well documented that the majority of scientists are in agreement that global warming and climate change is a reality.

But even as the debate rages, why not improve the way we live and the way we treat the earth for its own sake? Again, isn't it obvious that we are putting a tremendous amount of pressure on our planet and our natural resources? Regardless of what side of the fence one stands on in terms of whether humankind is responsible for this warming trend, shouldn't we just do the right thing when it comes to energy use, growth, pollution output and the like? Can't we all use our common sense and realize that we need to be kinder to our planet and smarter in how we go forward? Isn't all this a no-brainer?

As Timothy Wirth, the president of the UN Foundation and the Better World Fund put it, "We've got to ride this global warming issue. Even if the theory of global warming is wrong, we will be doing the right thing in terms of economic and environmental policy."

Aside from emission control, some scientists have been trying to tackle the problem of carbon dioxide more head on. As Brian Dumaine points out, scientists discovered marine algae and other phytoplankton capture vast quantities of carbon dioxide from the oxygen as they grow, and take it with them to the bottom of the sea when they die, perhaps forever locking that carbon out of the atmosphere. However, to greatly increase algae or plankton growth requires seeding designated ocean areas with some form of iron, a process known as "geoengineering."

The National Academy of Sciences describes geoengineering as "options that would involved large-scale engineering of our environment in order to counteract the effects of changes in the atmosphere."

While I believe these kinds of options should be explored, one can't help but think that manipulating the environment even more could turn out to be a dead end, especially when it wouldn't directly tackle the cause of the problem, which is where we should be focused.

We need to be thinking further ahead: If we stop breaking the earth, we needn't worry about trying to fix it.

Ebb and Flow

An Evolving American Landscape

"What is the use of a house if you haven't got a tolerable planet to put it on?"

Henry David Thoreau

"Welcome to Flint, Michigan. Looking for a townhouse? We have some here, right across from a pasture where cows and horses are grazing. A detached family home in a village, surrounded by parkland? We've got that, too."

No, this utopian conversation isn't real—yet. But it may be a reality sometime soon. Flint is in rapid decline, which has been accelerating for several decades, with the slow collapse of the auto industry and, some argue, flawed urban planning from the beginning.

It's not alone. According to Dr. Justin Hollander, Assistant Professor of Urban and Environmental Policy and Planning at Tufts University, "Over the last fifty years, 370 cities throughout the world with populations over 100,000 have shrunk by at least 10 percent."

In the United States, a country that has always equated rapid growth with success and the "American dream," a new reality is setting in as cities are downsizing, in some cases stopping water and sewer service to abandoned areas, bulldozing and turning concrete jungles back into parks, wildlife refuges and bike trails. For years, efforts were focused on stemming the decline of Flint. Once a city of 200,000 anticipating growth that would take it over 350,000, it has fallen to less than 110,000, a quarter of whom live in poverty. Now, a newer idea is taking hold: Speed up the decline. Instead of waiting for houses and commercial buildings to go into foreclosure, become abandoned and then demolishing them, planners are talking of tearing down whole blocks and even whole neighborhoods. There is a saying among farmers and forest landowners that "asphalt and concrete are the last crops." It is indeed very difficult to turn back to natural lands after development has taken hold, but apparently not impossible.

The population will be condensed, as will stores and services and some jobs. Areas that are currently concrete-covered strip malls might be returned to nature, to forests, natural pastures, and parklands.

Former Genesee County treasurer Dan Kildee was a main innovator in the charge to change Flint. With twenty-five years in Flint county government and his successful vision of transition being implemented there, Kildee is now taking his talents to a higher level, having been tapped to lead a Washington, DC-based think tank on land use around America.

"The real question is not whether these cities shrink—we're all shrinking—but whether we let it happen in a destructive or sustainable way," said Kildee. "Decline is a fact of life in Flint. Resisting it is like resisting gravity. We need to control it instead of letting it control us."

"Everybody's talking about smart growth, but nobody is talking about smart decline," says Terry Schwarz, senior planner at Kent State University's Cleveland Urban Design Collaborative. The center runs the Shrinking Cities Institute in Cleveland, a city that has lost more than half its population since 1950. "There's nothing that says that a city that has fewer people in it has to be a bad place."

It's a contentious idea: Not all people will want to abandon their neighborhoods, even if they're the only family on the tattered street. And who's to choose which neighborhoods are torn down and which are preserved?

According to the 2000 US census, the abandonment and deterioration of large areas of Detroit in the wake of the collapse of the American auto industry, Detroit qualifies as the most-ruined city in the country, as illustrated by this collapsing mansion. *Photo courtesy seedetroit.com*

"Not everyone's going to win," Flint's Kildee said. "But now, everyone's losing. If it's going to look abandoned, let it be clean and green. Create the new Flint forest—something people will choose to live near, rather than something that symbolizes failure."

Since 2002, Kildee's land bank program has taken ownership of four thousand unoccupied land parcels in the county. In addition, one thousand abandoned houses have been demolished, and nine hundred empty lots have been turned over to adjacent neighbors. Kildee has been quoted by local media as saying that the growing number of communities that have formed local land banks are evidence that the program of some foreclosed property in trust and using it for public good like community gardens is better than the old system of automatically reselling foreclosed properties to the highest bidder. "For 35 years that system was in place, all you have to do is drive through Flint to see how that works."

He's had strong critics from Republican commentators (especially since he began consulting for the Obama administration), but points out that the law that created the Genesee County Land Bank Authority was bipartisan, and the idea of exporting the Flint model was adapted by the former Bush administration. Kildee says he's now been approached by officials with the Federal Reserve, the Federal Deposit Insurance Corporation, and the Department of Housing and Urban Development about bringing the land bank program to other cities. Among the fifteen towns considering such measures are Syracuse, New York; Cleveland, Ohio; Baltimore, Maryland; and Pittsburgh, Pennsylvania. Of the twenty largest cities at mid-century, all but four have shrunk.

Detroit, Cleveland, Pittsburgh, St. Louis, and Buffalo, New York, have all lost more than half their population over the past fifty years. Philadelphia lost nearly a third of its residents, slipping to about 1.4 million people in 2006, according to estimates by the Census Bureau.

Indianapolis, Indiana, and Little Rock, Arkansas, have established land banks for those cities' governments to take control of their geographical future. Richmond, Virginia, has lost a quarter of its population since its peak of 250,000 residents. Since 2006, however, it's had an active program to bulldoze abandoned homes and turn the properties into green space, and to replace cinder block apartments with single-family dwellings with green space.

Flint may be in the news most prominently because of the collapse of the nearby US auto industry, but Youngstown, Ohio, has been grappling with its decline ever since the demise of the domestic steel industry in the 1970s. Youngstown counts itself as the first American city to embrace its shrinkage.

"You look at the facts and come up with solutions," chief planner Anthony Kobak says. "The first step the city has come to terms with is being a small city."

Youngstown approved a 2010 plan. The goal: "A safe, clean, enjoyable, sustainable, attractive city," Kobak says.

The city has preserved 260 acres of land for green space. It's relaxing its zoning rules so that people can have small horse farms or apple orchards in the city, and it's offering financial incentives for people to move out of abandoned areas. "If you had three or four square blocks that at one time had forty homes per block and now have maybe five homes total, we could relocate those people across the street and convert the vacant area into a large city park," Kobak says, describing the much more attractive idea of people living across the street from a park than across from decrepit houses. "If we're looking to preserve an area for green space, we may offer that person relocation money rather than rehab money," Kobak says.

St. Louis has suffered a similar fate due to declining industry and the now-minimal importance of the Mississippi River as a transportation corridor, and is taking a look at its abandoned commercial zones to assess whether they might be suitable for residential use. "We had a lot more people here," says Rollin Stanley, former director of St. Louis's planning and urban design agency. "We had a lot more need for commercial strips. That need isn't here today. We have to rethink where we house people," Stanley said. "We're rethinking land use allocation to meet the needs of the population we're going to see," he says. "We're not shrinking. We're rethinking."

And it's going to require some lucid, long-term "rethinking" because urban shrinkage has implications beyond lost jobs and empty houses.

In a June 2009 paper, Dr. Hollander asserted that: "Another problem with population decline is that only those urban residents with means can relocate, leaving behind the poorest and most destitute residents. With fewer middle- and upper-income residents in a neighborhood, there are fewer role models available to youth and prospects for upward mobility are dimmer.

"Widespread past and present discrimination in hiring and in the housing market have systematically limited relocation options for African Americans and Latinos. As such, when a neighborhood loses jobs, African Americans and Latinos have fewer choices for places to move to, which causes a further racial concentration in ghettos."

Some say we shouldn't be surprised at the decline of some American cities, that the American dream of the suburban nation was flawed from the start. Back in 1961, in fact, American-born

Canadian writer, urbanist, and activist Jane Jacobs published *The Death and Life of Great American Cities*, in which she made a powerful argument against the urban planning policies of the 1950s—the ideas of zoning industrial, commercial, residential, and building ever-more out from the center of towns and cities. It was the first and most influential book against urban sprawl, hated by planners when it came out and now required reading in universities around the world.

Notably, she counted Manhattan and Toronto as models for the way cities should be: interconnected "villages" with green spaces, excellent public transit, vibrant downtowns that haven't been carved up by freeways—places that, by their very nature, encourage a sense of community.

Nearly fifty years ago, Jacobs predicted the "death" of cities. And clearly, the health of many of them is failing. In fact, the University of California, Berkeley, now has a Shrinking Cities faculty studying this very trend.

"Shrinkage is moving from an idea to a fact," says Dr. Karina Pallagst, director of the Shrinking Cities in a Global Perspective Program. "There's finally the insight that some cities just don't have a choice."

Today, Berkeley says, every sixth city in the world can be defined as a "shrinking city."

In 2004, the university's program formed the Shrinking Cities International Research Network (SCiRN), a group of academics tracking the shrinking cities trend, and looks at urban development implications and solutions. As of this writing, SCiRN is comprised of some thirty members from fourteen countries around the world. Since their inception, they have made studies of suburbs, cities, towns, and regions that are investigated through a common comparative framework. Their goal is to produce both theoretical and methodological tools for analyzing shrinking towns and cities in different national contexts.

"There's a new movement to reclaim urban areas by clearing parts of them and even letting them go back to nature," the program proclaims. "Why fight for more growth, they argue, when downsizing and re-greening would make a city more viable and more livable for those residents who remain? It would be a reversal of urban sprawl."

It's being called "smart decline."

Dr. Frank J. Popper, a professor of Planning and Public Policy at Rutgers University, and City University of New York's College of Staten Island political science and economics professor Deborah E. Popper define smart decline as "planning for less—fewer people, fewer buildings, fewer land uses."

In fact, in a 1987 paper the two researchers began considering the future of the Great Plains region, "North America's grassland and breadbasket, is a vast, beautiful, charismatic place with a volatile settlement history. Since the end of the Civil War, the Plains has suffered three large cycles of population, economic and environmental boom and especially bust."

In an area roughly the size of Montana, 130,000 square miles, the Poppers envisioned "Buffalo Commons," in which private lands return to public use and wilderness.

As Dr. Hollander explains, "The Buffalo Commons proposal is based on the assumption that human interaction with the environment, as it has existed since European settlement, cannot continue on the Great Plains. The Poppers hypothesize: Over the next generation the Plains will, as a result of the largest, longest running agricultural and environmental miscalculation in American history, become almost totally depopulated. At that point, a new use for the region will emerge, one that is in fact so old that it predates the American presence. We are suggesting that the region be returned to its original pre-White state, that it be, in effect, deprivatized."

While they are concentrating on a rural environment, the model of smart decline applies to urban areas in the same way, "planning for less—fewer people, fewer buildings, fewer land uses … ecologically and economically restorative possibilities."

According to the SCiRN: "This alternative model could include the demolition or dismantling of under-utilized housing and other building stock, the removal of redundant streets, and downsizing of municipal infrastructure to correspond to declining population. Once unneeded components of the built environment are removed, opportunities may arise for restoring native landscape ecologies and reconstituting a new kind of city, where pockets of development are surrounded and connected by natural areas. Planned shrinkage can identify opportunities to establish lively and attractive development clusters that take advantage of the best the region has to offer, while improving air and water quality, enhancing wildlife habitat, and establishing exciting new recreation opportunities"

Urban services such as fire departments, police departments, water and water treatment services and even garbage collection would be markedly more efficient and less expensive, Flint's Kildee argues. "Much of the land will be given back to nature. People will enjoy living near a forest or meadow," he said.

Kildee acknowledges that some Americans call his actions "defeatist" but insists it's "no more defeatist than pruning an overgrown tree so it can bear fruit again."

Alan Mallach, senior fellow of the National Housing Institute, says of smart decline: "In a way, think of it as a 21st-century version of a traditional country pattern." He warns, however, of decline without being "smart" as just as wasteful as the last century's urban sprawl, saying that without planning, "It's happening in a sloppy, destructive fashion where you get areas that are essentially abandoned, but they're not useable open space, they're not environmentally sound, so they're basically wasteland."

Of American cities, St. Louis, Pittsburgh, Philadelphia, Newark, Detroit, Cleveland, Buffalo, and Youngstown, Ohio, have suffered population losses ranging from 26.7 percent in Philadelphia to as high as 59.4 percent in St. Louis. In fact, no city in American history has slid so far as St. Louis; once the fourth largest city, hosting both the World's Fair and the Summer Olympics in just one year (1904), St. Louis now doesn't rate in the top 50 cities for population.

As Colin Gordon, a history professor at the University of Iowa College of Liberal Arts and Sciences says in his book, *Mapping Decline: St. Louis and the Fate of the American City*, "St. Louis, Missouri, is now a ghostly landscape of vacant houses, boarded-up storefronts, and abandoned factories. The Gateway City is, by any measure, one of the most depopulated, deindustrialized, and deeply segregated examples of American urban decay."

He, and many others, point to bad urban planning and zoning practices, which have negatively affected nearly every urban center in America.

"As the strained city neighborhoods went downhill, whites fled to suburbs. During the 'white flight'—which began in the 1950s and picked up steam in the '60s and '70s—each suburb developed its own zoning code, typically providing for only single-family houses on large lots and prohibiting industrial, commercial, multifamily housing or small-lot development," he writes.

"Those codes guaranteed that people who lived in the suburbs were of a certain income. They barred poor and working-class people in the central city from ever moving to the suburbs. So the city got a larger share of the area's poor, while the county got all the wealth. The demands on the city in terms of fighting crime, maintaining infrastructure and schools and providing public housing steadily increased, but its ability to earn money through property taxes collapsed."

St. Louis may be the most glaring example of where urban sprawl took its toll on the traditional city, but it bears witness to more than just the past.

* * *

As I've illustrated, while a few unique urban centers are in some cases declining, the basic fact is that America is growing and will continue to grow—soaring past 400 million around 2040—and while there needs to be, obviously, "smart decline" in the areas that are now experiencing these historical population losses, "smart growth" is still the main challenge we face and is crucial to the many cities, towns and states to which the American population is fleeing, and where most immigrants seek to live.

Let's face it, the world is growing, America is growing, and most of our communities are going to continue to grow. The question is: Will these areas embrace "smart growth" or continue our country's fifty-year trend of environmentally reckless, unsustainable "urban sprawl?"

If I can simplify the two models, sprawl is universally a negative, and, until recently, perhaps a necessary negative without alternative. It is continued outward expansion of communities, consuming farmland and forestland and, in general, green space. Smart growth at its most basic means the promotion of development within existing areas, and in a way that takes into account the convenience, health and longevity of the buildings and people who live within. That is not to say, however, that we can't have smart growth by using some lands that might be better suited for development but at a minimum we need to better use what we already have.

In 1973, George B. Dantzig and Thomas L. Saaty published *Compact City: A Plan for a Livable Urban Environment*, which is still cited as the spark for what's become known as smart growth for both opponents and advocates of the movement.

I find it amusing, however, that back in the late 1960s, researchers from the University of Moscow wrote *The Ideal Communist City* in which they described suburbs as "a chaotic and depressing agglomeration of buildings covering enormous stretches of land." They also described, as very vocal smart-growth opponent Randal O'Toole has written that "monotonous stretches of individual low-rise houses" is excessive.

O'Toole, an accomplished economist and director of the Oregon-based Thoreau Institute as well as a scholar at the Washington, D.C.-based Cato Institute, became the leading critic of smart growth policies—and supporter of urban sprawl—with the publication of his book *The Vanishing Automobile and Other Urban Myths* in 1996. He is also highly critical of public transportation and President Barack Obama's plans for high-speed rail in the US. In my opinion, O'Toole would seem to be stuck in the wrong "American dream."

Of course, every reader will form his or her own opinion, but I wanted to make it clear that while I, and many others, believe smart growth is necessary and urban sprawl an unsustainable mistake we've been making for the past fifty years, there are those who oppose smart growth.

However, in a survey done by the Pew Center for Civic Journalism in 2000, 18 percent of Americans said sprawl and destruction of rural lands were the most important issue facing their local community—above crime and violence.

By 1960, according to national census figures, more than half the US population lived in either rural or densely populated areas, with only 15 percent living in suburbs. Thirty years later, more Americans lived in suburbs than in metropolitan areas, with more than half the population living in suburbs. From 1982 to 1997, figures indicate, Washington, D.C., grew in population by 30 percent, though the number of residents per square mile decreased by 12 percent. The city of Chicago grew in size by 46 percent between 1970 and 1990, though the population increased by only 4 percent.

Frankly, it doesn't make sense. Suburbs require the same infrastructure of roads, water, sewer, electricity, police, and fire service that metropolitan zones do, yet by the nature of their lower density, suburbs don't have the tax base to independently support these services, so municipal governments end up leeching tax from the city dwellers to help pay for the suburbanites. That's when the inner cities sometimes begin their decline—businesses chase the suburban residents to the outskirts, further watering down the urban tax base, leaving the remaining city residents with fewer shopping options.

More seriously, urban sprawl is widely seen to have negative health and environmental impacts. As Andres Duany, Elizabeth Plater-Zyberk, and Jeff Speck point out in their book *Suburban Nation: The Rise of Sprawl and the Decline of the American Dream*, residents of sprawling areas emit more pollution per person, suffer more traffic fatalities, are more prone to obesity as walking and bicycling are not viable commuting options. Of course, this isn't the leading cause of obesity, but Barbara McCann, a former director of information and research at the Washington, D.C.-based Smart Growth America, and co-author (with Dr. Reid Ewing, a research professor at the National Center for Smart Growth at the University of Maryland) of *Measuring the Health Effects of Sprawl*, contends that: "While certainly not the leading explanation for America's growing obesity epidemic, sprawling communities encourage Americans to drive more and walk less. In turn, this leads residents to more inactive lifestyle, which increases risk for health complications such as cardiovascular disease and stroke. A common denominator of modern sprawling communities is that nothing is within easy walking distance of anything else. Houses are far from any services, stores, or businesses; high-speed roads are perceived as dangerous and unpleasant for walking; and businesses are surrounded by vast parking lots."

One of the goals of McCann and Ewing is "getting decision makers to consider how the billions spent on transportation and development can make communities more walkable and bikeable is one avenue to improving the health and quality of life of millions of Americans."

The effect of sprawl has serious impacts on the environment, even though part of the appeal is for "greener" spaces in terms of larger lots and lawns.

According to the American Farmland Trust, from 1982 to 1992 America lost an average of 400,000 acres per year of "prime" farmland to urban and suburban development. "This translates to a loss of 45.7 acres per hour, every single day."

Expanding sprawl is putting a third of America's endangered species at heightened risk of extinction as a result of habitat loss, according to *Endangered By Sprawl: How Runaway Development Threatens America's Wildlife*, written by researchers at the National Wildlife Federation, Smart Growth America, and NatureServe.

Sprawl is also at the root of increased pollution from air emissions from cars, more paved roads and concrete, which does not absorb water, instead causing runoff which eventually carries toxins to streams, rivers, lakes and the oceans.

What's also defeating about the model of urban sprawl, many researchers agree, is that it also affects the very suburbs it begot. As the initial areas of suburbs become increasingly urban, developers build new suburbs further out on open areas and the cycle continues.

Smart growth has its opponents and critics. Some say sprawl is good, that it's the American dream and has given people their choice to live in larger houses with larger yards. Yet it's bound them to the automobile and indeed limited their mobility choices, and, during the last fifty years, suburban living hasn't necessarily been what people want—it's been the only thing offered to them. Polls often conflict, but I haven't seen one were Americans didn't list traffic congestion traveling to and from suburbs at the top of the list of what wasn't satisfactory about life in America.

A simple truth, whether it's fair or not, is that the environment simply cannot afford to house everyone in low-density suburbs. We'd run out of land. That's just a fact.

Author Douglas Farr, an architect and urban designer, who wrote *Sustainable Urbanism: Urban Design with Nature*, argues that the supposed "American dream" is a hoax.

"It may sound heretical or revolutionary but the demographic trends suggest otherwise," he said in an interview. He continued: "The baby boomers who at this stage in their lives are empty-nesters (couples whose adult children moved out of the family home) do not want to live in suburbs any more. Many prefer to live in the urban environment close to restaurants, culture and shops. So do their kids when they get their first job. They want to be close to other young professionals, meet people and go to bars. Americans also are becoming more sensitive to environmental issues. This influences their consumer choices. As to cars, in light of uncertainty over oil exporters, skyrocketing gasoline prices and climate change concerns, our dependence on the car as the primary mode of transportation is just not sustainable."

I'm generally concentrating on developments in America, but there's a community in Denmark that I am compelled to mention. It's not new—the area of Sonderborg on the country's southwestern tip has been inhabited for centuries. But in 2009, officials and residents came together to create "ProjectZero," which aims to have the area on track to be carbon-zero by the year 2029. According to officials, "The ZEROfamily program started early 2009 and more than 100 families with 406 family members have participated in the learning process. The families have been inspired to improve energy efficiency in their homes, transportation, cooking and other habits. Special programs and events have been organized to engage kids and teenagers in the learning process.

"No later than 2029 the Sonderborg-area should be a ZEROcarbon growth area. This will be achieved through substantial energy efficiency improvements and a change of energy supply to the area's own renewable energy sources. We will create a living exploratorium of dynamic energy systems. When we succeed in these ambitious goals, we will experience growth and attract great attention to our area. The Sonderborg-area will be a pioneer for sustainable climate mindset. Being ahead of the external demands will be of benefit to us and will strengthen our businesses.

"The world around us will change radically in the coming years. Due to the climate change, we will experience increased political focus on climate solutions, increasing demands and tougher measures for individuals and companies. New high carbon taxes, increasing energy prices, will most likely be a result of this."

Very wisely, I believe, the Danish officials and residents are adhering to the reality that, as they say, "In the longer term it is estimated that the rising prices for coal, oil, natural gas and the future carbon quotas can justify further investments in energy efficiency, wind turbine parks and the change to a carbon-neutral transport system."

And it's working: According to www.uk.brightgreen business.com "In January 2010 the final evaluation took place based on 35 families' data and remarks. The average saving for 2009 was approximately 20 percent on heat/power and water with the best practice in the range of 40 percent. After one year of learning the families now recommend a consultant to review their home as the next step."

Smart Growth is making urban areas more appealing, encouraging people to move back into the city, where abandoned factories or warehouses have been turned into condos and apartments, shops and offices, for instance. But it's not as easy as the idea might suggest, and in many cases, it's illegal.

One of the many challenges to smart and sustainable growth is that our zoning laws are not just outdated, but are fundamentally flawed. I think that's been illustrated pretty well with what's been happening to many urban areas, such as Flint, Detroit, Buffalo, Philadelphia, and most strikingly, St. Louis. And if that's just my opinion, consider this: Those cities we all love—San Francisco, Charleston, Boston's Beacon Hill, D.C.'s Georgetown, Nantucket, Santa Fe, Carmel—much of Paris, London and historic towns in most European countries—couldn't be built today. As Duany,

Plater-Zyberk, and Speck write in *Suburban Nation*: "All of these well-known places, many of which have become tourist destinations, exist in direct violation of current zoning ordinances. Even the classic American main street, with its mixed-use buildings right up against the sidewalk, is illegal in most municipalities." And they write, "Somewhere along the way, through a series of small and well-intentioned steps, traditional towns became a crime in America."

Duany and Plater-Zyberk are among the founders of the Congress for the New Urbanism (a collective which the *New York Times* calls "the most important collective architectural movement in the United States in the past 50 years") and designed the acclaimed Florida community Seaside, a mixed-use development with densities greater than conventional suburbs.

Time magazine described Seaside as "the most astounding design achievement of its era and, one might hope, the most influential." It has been used as a model for other new urbanist developments in the United States and abroad. Modeled on diverse neighborhoods found in such cities as San Francisco and Manhattan, Seaside is cited as the first of the New Urban developments.

I'll get deeply into these "new" community designs in the next chapter, but let me briefly explain: It's a trendy phrase, but New Urbanism is more like a return to the past. For the first quarter of the last century, cities and towns were built around a center, where people shopped, socialized, worked and lived.

That's true mixed-use urban planning. When the automobile took over our lives in the second half of the twentieth century, we cast our urban planning history as obsolete and embraced suburbs —which are entirely dependent (without high-speed rail service) on automobiles to get us to our work, to stores, to leisure activities such as movies or live entertainment. It has consumed vast amounts of farmland, forestland and pastures to make way for cookie-cutter box housing, strip malls, fast-food restaurant and vast tracks of concrete and asphalt.

Sprawl, as defined by the American Institute of Architects, is "a low-density development that rigorously separates residential

The heart of Northwest Florida's Emerald Coast, the maverick, yet old-fashioned design of the community of Seaside is meant to "reflect a simpler time, when meals were shared, stories entertained and walking was how people got around," according to the community's marketing efforts. *Photo courtesy Seaside, Florida*

uses from other land uses, and that relies entirely or almost entirely on automobile transportation to connect the separate uses."

As environmental author James Howard Kunstler of *The Geography of Nowhere and Home from Nowhere* says, "The project of suburbia is the greatest misallocation of resources in the history of the world. America has squandered its wealth in a living arrangement that has no future."

As dozens of companies and individuals began to coalesce their theories about urban development and voice their disapproval of sprawl, the movement came to a head in 1994 in a book by Peter Katz called *The New Urbanism*, in which more than a dozen leading architects and designers, including Duany and Plater-Zyberk, came up with a template for a return to a more sustainable and proper urban development.

Their 13-point Criteria

The neighborhood has a discernible center. This is often a square or a green and sometimes a busy or memorable street corner. A transit stop would be located at this center.

Most of the dwellings are within a five-minute walk of the center, an average of roughly a quarter mile or 1,320 feet.

There are a variety of dwelling types—usually houses, rowhouses, and apartments—so that younger and older people, singles, and families, the poor, and the wealthy may find places to live.

At the edge of the neighborhood, there are shops and offices of sufficiently varied types to supply the weekly needs of a household.

A small ancillary building or garage apartment is permitted within the backyard of each house. It may be used as a rental unit or place to work (for example, an office or craft workshop).

An elementary school is close enough so that most children can walk from their home.

There are small playgrounds accessible to every dwelling—not more than a tenth of a mile away.

Streets within the neighborhood form a connected network, which disperses traffic by providing a variety of pedestrian and vehicular routes to any destination.

The streets are relatively narrow and shaded by rows of trees. This slows traffic, creating an environment suitable for pedestrians and bicycles.

Buildings in the neighborhood center are placed close to the street, creating a well-defined, outdoor room.

Parking lots and garage doors rarely front the street. Parking is relegated to the rear of buildings, usually accessed by alleys.

Certain prominent sites at the termination of street vistas or in the neighborhood center are reserved for civic buildings. These provide sites for community meetings, education, and religious or cultural activities.

The neighborhood is organized to be self-governing. A formal association debates and decides matters of maintenance, security, and physical change. Taxation is the responsibility of the larger community.

As proponents of Smart Growth point out, saving our wetlands, forestlands, pastures, and farmlands is not the only reason to reconsider our growth models. And neither is the price of gasoline.

Over the past half-century, most Americans have spent increasing time isolated in cars and suburban homes where there's little social contact as previous generations enjoyed in pedestrian-friendly streets and public spaces; we're less involved, generally, with our communities. We spend nearly 30 percent of our income on car payments, gas, maintenance and insurance. And we spend increasing amounts of time in stressful traffic.

As we pointed out earlier, the lazy suburban lifestyle with little or no walking has been a contributing factor to obesity and related health issues in the country.

Urban planning professor Jonathan Barnett, in his book, *The Fractured Metropolis: Improving the New City, Restoring the Old City, Reshaping the Region*, outlined ten adverse effects of sprawl:

Sprawl development contributes to a loss of support for public facilities and public amenities. In economic terms, sprawl encourages market failure; residents of sprawl communities have access to public facilities that they do not support with their tax dollars, and residents of older communities subsidize the existence of these facilities. Sprawl communities typically lack parks, museums, civic spaces, libraries, and the like. This frequently occurs either because some of these amenities are privatized and made available only to a small segment (owners of large lots have less need for public open space), or because sprawl dwellers can be "free riders" on urban facilities supported in substantial part by others.

Sprawl undermines effective maintenance of existing infrastructure. Existing developed areas—cities and older suburbs—have sewers, water systems, city streets, bridges, schools, transit systems and other hard infrastructure to maintain. But exurban development draws population away from areas with existing infrastructure and into new areas where new infrastructure must be constructed or where some infrastructure costs are avoided, at least temporarily, through the use of wells and septic systems, or by reliance on undersized roads that are upgraded at great public expense long after the developments have been constructed. The frequent result is a shift of population regionally, leading to a decline in the urban and older suburban tax base. This decline in turn prompts increases in urban taxes and rates (needed to support the existing infrastructure across a smaller population), and/or to deferral of maintenance activities.

Sprawl increases societal costs for transportation. Costs rise largely because of the need for expensive retrofits. Typical scenarios include the conversion, after sprawl has occurred, of exurban two lane roads to four lanes or six lanes, adding signals, construction of grade separations for intersections, and building county or inter-county connector highways and metropolitan belt roads. This invariably occurs at great expense and disruption—because of increased right-of-way costs, difficulties in maintaining traffic flow during the construction period, and often-substantial community opposition. This retrofit dilemma is a spin-off of the problem of traffic. People hate traffic—in fact, part of the reason for sprawl is the elusive promise that commuters and commercial offices can outrun traffic by continually expanding into lower traffic areas. And, at least initially, average commute times are generally lower within sprawl areas than commutes from sprawl areas to the center city. But traffic is, in general, extremely bad in sprawling metropolitan areas—often worse on weekends when travel is more diffuse and timing strategies intended to avoid peak travel times do not work. Catch-up transportation expenditures have to be made. Unfortunately, often they can't be made. The retrofit problem is a perennial feature of sprawl, as any sprawl dweller can personally attest, and its costs are high.

Sprawl consumes more resources than other development patterns. Because homes, offices, utilities, and other features are farther apart (requiring more asphalt, more lengths of pipe, more conduits, more wires), because each commercial and institutional structure requires its own acres of parking, and because much of the utility infrastructure is duplicative of the "stranded" infrastructure in nearby older communities—society's overall consumption of metal, concrete, asphalt, and energy is higher.

Sprawl separates urban poor people from jobs. Ownership of an automobile and the resources to maintain it are essential for work in the suburbs, the site of most new jobs in the modern economy. However, the prevailing sprawl model of development drastically separates different price levels of housing from one another, as well as separating job areas from residential areas. These characteristics of sprawl mean that locating new affordable homes near jobs is quite difficult, and sprawl consequently reduces the availability of jobs for those in urban areas that lack reliable automobile transportation.

Sprawl imposes a tax on time. Sprawl development requires that we spend more time on the road. Exurbia, including most post-war suburbia, rigorously separates residential housing, food stores, other retail establishments, warehouse and transfer facilities, industry, schools, and office buildings. This has adverse effects on neighborhoods, and leads to more automobile travel. In exurban areas, commercial establishments can be accessed only when people drive to each location. Non-work automobile trips now comprise more than 80 percent of all daily trips. Residents of sprawl areas do not forego the benefits of mixed uses of land, but they pay a price in time, and they lack choice in their mode of travel. Sprawl also makes it take much longer for the one-third of Americans who reside in central cities and inner ring suburb to get to green fields areas for recreation and enjoyment. Sprawl, in effect, imposes a hidden tax on time by making certain amenities more remote and harder to reach.

Sprawl degrades water and air quality. Sprawl development is hard on streams, wetlands, and runoff quality. It reduces the resilience of streams and other waters by degrading headwaters and impoverishing habitat. For example, in the Chesapeake Bay region, sprawl is the largest threat to water quality. It increases the area of impervious surface, decreases retention time for rainwater and diminishes its infiltration into the soil and water table, and it leads to rapid erosion and structural degradation of streams and rivers, which therefore receive runoff in much greater volumes in a shorter period of time.

Sprawl results in the permanent alteration or destruction of habitats. Sprawl development converts large areas to asphalt, concrete, and structures, altering the landscape hydrology and reducing the biological productivity and habitat value of the land. While any conversion of open lands to developed uses can impair the prior environmental values, sprawl development does so at a high rate of land conversion per unit of development. A related problem is the loss of productive farmland near metropolitan areas. This feature of sprawl development has been documented by the American Farmland Trust through repeated studies under the rubric of Farming on the Edge. Farmland contributes at least incidentally to wildlife habitat and potential for future restoration. Although there is, at least in the near term, no threat to the nation's total food production given the amount of remaining farmland, as well as farmland currently fallowed under federal conservation, the loss of prime farmland is not desirable in the long term.

Sprawl creates difficulty in maintaining community. People do have communities in their suburban neighborhoods, workplaces, and in their organized activities. Modern day exurbs are not the places of alienation described by some "new urbanist" writers, many of whom draw upon affection for the older urban neighborhoods of the early and mid-20th century. But these new sprawl communities require more driving, and more complicated arrangements to maintain social connections. This also means that children are at the mercy of scheduled activities and "play dates" rather than neighborhood interactions, and exercise becomes an isolated activity on the schedule, rather than a natural consequence of walking, biking, or using public park facilities.

Sprawl offers the promise of choice while delivering more of the same. In America, choice is not only a cherished value, it is also something that our market economy claims as its highest achievement. But, paradoxically, we have lost choice in our system of development. Sprawl constrains our choices. If you want a new house, you can have one on a half acre in the suburbs with no retail around. If you want to locate a store or an office, the arterial strip or highway interchange is for you. If you want transportation, you can use your car. If you are poor you can live in substandard housing in the inner city or manufactured housing on the farthest fringes of the metropolitan area. This lack of choice is why every part of exurban America resembles every other part.

In 2009, *Time* magazine reported: "The American suburb as we know it is dying. The implosion began with the housing bust, which started in and has hit hardest the once vibrant neighborhoods outside the urban core. Shopping malls and big-box retail stores, the commercial anchors of the suburbs, are going dark—an estimated 148,000 stores closed last year, the most since 2001. But the shift is deeper than the economic downturn. Thanks to changing demographics, including a steady decline in the percentage of households with kids and a growing preference for urban amenities among Americans young and old, the suburban dream of the big house with the big lawn is vanishing. The Metropolitan Institute at Virginia Tech predicts that by 2025 there will be a surplus of 22 million large-lot homes (on one-sixth of an acre or more) in the US."

In addition to abandoned industrial parks and suburbs marked for bulldozing and a return to greener use, some cities, such as New York, Washington, D.C., New Orleans, Buffalo, Portland, San Francisco, Milwaukee, Toronto, and other cities are taking the unusual step of studying the ultimate benefit of tearing down elevated freeways. Once thought a panacea for ballooning traffic volume, the freeways cut swaths through cities, dividing neighborhoods and upsetting the quality of life for local residents.

Now, designers are reconsidering the approach. Congress for the New Urbanism and the Center for Neighborhood Technology assert that replacing aging elevated freeways with more neighborhood-friendly boulevards is not only more cost effective than trying to maintain aging highway infrastructure, but it restores urban areas choked off for decades by the highways.

The Southern Bronx River Watershed Alliance has proposed the removal of the Arthur V. Sheridan Expressway, a poorly connected one-and-a-quarter-mile stretch that mars the waterfront along the Bronx River. The alliance has suggested replacing the freeway with a surface street which would better connect to the traffic grid, and reclaim twenty-eight acres of waterfront land for residential, commercial and open-space development.

It's this re-imagining of our cities that will constitute the best of smart, strong, and sustainable growth. "As much as possible, we need to redirect development to existing communities and infrastructure," Kaid Benfield, director of the smart-growth program at the Natural Resources Defense Council, told *Time*, "otherwise, we're just eating up more land and natural resources."

Whereas some areas in Flint, Michigan, for instance, are being torn up and returned to green space, other communities, such as Long Beach, California, have embraced abandoned malls and retail centers and turned them into offices and apartments and shops, creating a "town center" where there wasn't one before.

"All of these projects are developer-driven, because the market wants them," says Ellen Dunham-Jones, co-author of the book, *Retrofitting Suburbia.*

Of course, there will be failures where housing prices have dropped too harshly or where there is no employment.

"Though creative cities will grow more attractive for empty-nest-retirees and young graduates alike, we won't all be moving to New York," *Time* asserts.

There are some cities in America that have, for years, been embracing smart growth with urban zoning laws that try to inhibit suburban expansion: Portland, Oregon, for instance.

According to SprawlCity.org, which garners much of its research from environmental authors Leon Kolankiewicz and Roy Beck based on government census data: "In 1973 the Oregon legislature passed its landmark urban growth boundary law, requiring each municipality in the state to draw a line in the sand (or through forests and farms, in the case of western Oregon), beyond which urbanization could not march—at least, in theory. Today, each of Oregon's 241 cities is surrounded by an urban growth boundary (UGB). Portland's was first established in 1979.

Greater Portland not only stayed aesthetically pleasing but met the Smart Growth goal of increasing density greatly. In the decade prior to the imposition of the Urban Growth Boundary, new population was added at the density of 2,448 per square mile. In the decade after the imposition of the Boundary, it was added at the density of 3,744 per square mile. That was a 53 percent increase in density, a major achievement."

When most American cities were busy building multi-lane freeways through neighborhoods, Portland tore down a six-lane expressway to construct a waterfront park. Now, the city has a greenbelt boundary to protect 25 million acres of farmland, forestland, and natural lands.

As I've already said, growth is going to happen in some parts of the country no matter what, and the data show that despite the best intentions and regulations, much of Oregon still lost natural lands. "The discouraging news after all that effort is that the Portland Urbanized Area still sprawled out across 39 additional square miles (25,000 acres) from 1980 to 1990. In its first decade of vigorously applied Smart Growth techniques, Portland could not stop the urbanization of rural land. The reason? The population grew by 146,000 during the decade," the researchers reported.

However, when growth is compared between Oregon and the state of Washington, there's a striking difference in the two approaches to growth according to a 2002 report. In fact, Portland would have lost an additional fourteen square miles of farmland and open space without its growth restrictions, despite adding nearly three hundred thousand new residents, according to the Seattle-based research center Sightline Institute.

Among the findings:

In the 1990s, greater Portland's total population grew at a faster pace than many developing-world megacities, such as Cairo, Egypt, and Jakarta, Indonesia.

In the Oregon counties, total population increased by 270,000, and the number of people living in compact, transit-oriented neighborhoods (defined as 12 or more people per acre) increased by 141,000. By 2000, 28 percent of residents in the three-county region lived in compact neighborhoods.

In contrast, Clark County sprawled, Seattle-style. The population grew by 106,000, and the number of residents of low-density, car-dependent areas (defined as less than 12 people per acre) increased by 78,000. By 2000, only 13 percent of Clark County's residents lived in compact communities.

Per capita, Clark County converted about 40 percent more land from rural to suburban population densities than did the Oregon counties. If the Oregon counties had grown in a pattern similar to that of Clark County, suburban development would have overtaken an extra 14 square miles of farmland and open space.

Person for person, Clark County's sprawling residential development fully or partially covers 23 percent more land with pavement, rooftops, and other human-made "impervious" surfaces—which are harmful to streams and salmon—than Oregon's more compact residential neighborhoods.

Said Sightline research director Clark Williams-Derry, "Few areas in North America provide such a stark illustration of different approaches to planning."

Portland's planning discourages driving, supporting pedestrian-friendly, transit-oriented neighborhoods that offer easy access to jobs, shopping, recreation and entertainment.

"The big success of our land-use policies is developing communities where people can meet most of their needs locally," Rex Burkholder, a council member of Metro, the regional government, told the US State Department's America.gov information website.

"At the time most other US metropolises were pushing out farms and devouring open spaces to build suburban developments, Portland became a magnet for Americans who appreciated sustainable living more than one popular version of the 'American dream'—a single-family house with a front lawn and backyard and a car or two to get to work or a shopping mall," the State Department says.

Said Erin Flynn, director of economic development at the Portland Development Commission, "It is genuinely the ethos of the city to live sustainably and care about the (natural) environment."

As the city's population is expected to increase to 2.3 million in 2010, a 50-percent increase over 1990 figures, property prices have skyrocketed—as they do everywhere there's demand. The city refurbished a warehouse district into a neighborhood of condominiums and lofts and that area, too, became expensive.

This is one of the principal complaints of opponents of smart growth, but Portland is addressing the issue with subsidies for developers and other incentives to develop affordable downtown housing for people of all income levels. "Everybody has to have an opportunity to live his or her values," Flynn said.

Besides, and though I'd rather not be too harsh about it, but, when critics bemoan the cost of living in cities such as Boulder, Colorado, or Portland, Oregon, they blame high housing prices on smart growth. Well, maybe smart-growth cities, with their lack of dreary suburbia, green spaces, pedestrian-friendly streets, bike paths and excellent public transportation are nicer, higher-in-demand places to live when compared to cities where urban sprawl goes unchecked.

Which is pretty much the point: smart growth needs to be smart. That means including affordable housing without subsidies, the revitalization of blue-collar and industrial areas for multi-purpose use, and bicycle access and public transportation.

Boulder, Colorado, is another city that began protecting itself from sprawl with an open-space tax in 1967 and an ordinance in 1976 called the Danish Plan (named after the city councilman who designed it) that enacted a greenbelt around the city and an annual growth restriction of 2 percent. The city and Boulder County now have more than one hundred thousand acres of open space and mountain parks. It's a place where more than 90 percent of residents recycle, where new water meters are not allowed above certain elevation, thus protecting ridgelines and peaks, and where,

Boulder, Colorado, is another city that began protecting itself from sprawl with an open-space tax in 1967, and an ordinance in 1976 called the Danish Plan (named after the city councilman who designed it), which enacted a greenbelt around the city and an annual growth restriction of 2 percent. *Photo from Wikipedia public domain image repository*

when recent federal tax cuts gutted city budgets, residents voted themselves a third sales-tax hike to raise $51 million to buy and protect even more open land.

Austin, Texas, is another city cited as a success in having arrested urban sprawl and, like Portland and Boulder, is among the most popular of the smaller cities in the country with high qualities of life. In the late 1990s, Austin adopted its Smart Growth Initiative to ensure that the city's long-term growth management minimized damage to the environment and exploited all opportunities of building a "more livable city." Among the goals were to protect the city's water supply in the west, limit growth to the east, and protect its popular Barton Creek Greenbelt to the north.

It's worth noting that because of these efforts, National Geographic Adventure calls Austin the number one adventure town in America "because of its ability to combine the great outdoors with its unique culture." Austin has 205 parks, fourteen nature preserves, and twenty-five greenbelts. (Incidentally, the city's efforts don't stop at urban planning; it currently leads the country in wind power and biodiesel production, and in 2007 announced its Climate Protection Plan with the goal of making all its buildings, operations, and vehicles carbon-neutral by 2020.) Now that's what I call sustainability!

The city has devised a Smart Growth Matrix to help its planners and politicians assess developments to ensure they meet location criteria in terms of desired growth, proximity to mass transit, desired urban design characteristics, compliance with neighborhood plans, increase in tax base, and other factors. In terms of housing, the city has a SMART Housing ordinance, which stands for Safe, Mixed-Income, Accessible, Reasonably-Priced, Transit-Oriented Housing.

Austin's moves, as of 2009, according to the EPA, have been copied by some forty other cities around the country.

Denver, Colorado, also deserves mention for its smart-growth efforts. The city has adopted a general plan to look at future development and revitalization as "pedestrian-friendly, human-scale communities comprised of housing, office, neighborhood retail, and civic uses. They are sustainable communities where pedestrians are prioritized over automobiles, and residents can work and play close to home."

A great example of Denver's efforts is the redevelopment of Stapleton Airport. Built in 1929 and originally called Denver Municipal Airport, it was re-named Stapleton in 1944 and served as Denver's main airport until 1995 when the new Denver International Airport was built. The last flight out of Stapleton was on 27 February 1995, and huge yellow Xs were painted on the runways indicating they were no longer to be used; Denver International took over operations that same day. Stapleton's entire airport infrastructure was eventually removed except for the control tower and a parking structure, which remain standing as a reminder of the site's former days. A master plan for what to do with the old airport was developed beginning in 1990 by a private group consisting of civic leaders from the city of Denver called the Stapleton Development Foundation. In 1995 the plan was unveiled, and redevelopment of the site began in 2001 by Forest City Enterprises as the most ambitious and largest new urbanist project in the US. The intention was to build "a network of urban villages, employment centers, and significant open spaces, all linked by a commitment to the protection of natural resources and the development of human resources. The master plan emphasizes environmentally sound development, walkable neighborhoods, and lifelong learning. It rests on the principles of economic opportunity, environmental responsibility, and social equity." To date some 3,200 single-family houses, condominiums, and other for-sale housing, as well as 400 apartments have been built. When all is said and done, Stapleton is slated to house some 30,000 residents, have four schools, and two million square feet of retail space.

When Denver's Elitch Gardens amusement park closed, the city took the 27-acre site and transformed it into Highlands' Garden Village, "a compact neighborhood that provides housing, office, retail, parks, and entertainment. The site contains 291 homes, as well as 200,000 square feet of commercial and live/work space, while still preserving and restoring 140,000 square feet of open space."

In Santa Fe, New Mexico, a run-down complex in the city core was saved rather than torn down. The Second Street Studios was envisioned as a place where younger artists and creative people could live, work, and sell their goods. It's now a tourist destination.

One of the most remarkable examples of smart growth is Suisun City, north of San Francisco. Established in the mid 1800s, the area went through various phases of development, but in the 1960s and '70s growth accelerated due to the San Francisco Bay Area's suburban ring expansion to formerly rural Solano County. Another influence was the construction in the 1960s of Highway 80 just outside the city, in effect moving commercial traffic away from railways and water conveyance. In 1989, the "heart" of Suisun City—the downtown waterfront—began to decline and deteriorate. In that same year, an aggressive redevelopment program was initiated centered on the Old Town Waterfront and Historic Main Street district. Within 20 years, Suisun transformed itself from a boarded-up, rundown, crime-ridden downtown with an oil refinery polluting its waterfront to one of the EPA's model towns—"diverse, walkable, and picturesque. Its crime rate is low and its housing affordable," according to the EPA.

According to the EPA: "Suisun City's residents, businesses, and elected officials agreed on a common vision for their town's future: Clean-up polluted Suisun Channel and make the waterfront a focal point of their town.... Re-establish historic Main Street as a social and retail gathering place.... Strengthen municipal finances by encouraging tax-generating commercial development such as retail shops and restaurants along Main Street and the waterfront. In its rebirth, Suisun City avoided large-scale redevelopment projects such as shopping centers and industrial parks that would have obliterated its historic, small-town character."

Santa Cruz, California, has shed some of its traditional zoning restrictions and created the Accessory Dwelling Unit Development Program, which allows homeowners to convert garages into apartments or add second structures on properties, increasing density and adding more affordable housing.

In Orlando, Florida, the abandoned Naval Training Center could have become an eyesore; instead, the community banded together and envisioned a plan consisting of mixed housing, a main street, access to lakes and integration with existing neighborhoods.

San Diego, California, also took advantage of a Naval center closing when its Naval Training Center shut down, by creating Liberty Station, an area of parks and waterfront access for the public for the first time in nearly a century.

Greensboro, North Carolina, is very smartly revitalizing a downtown neighborhood—rather than tearing it down. The ten-acre project sits a block-and-a-half from the town's main street and has been a run-down area but will soon see its historic buildings and open spaces transformed into a social district.

The capital city of my own state, Atlanta, Georgia, deserves special mention for the changes it has seen since its reconstruction after the Civil War. As I mentioned in my introduction, Atlanta has grown by leaps and bounds and has been ranked many times as one of the fastest-growing cities in America. To put things in perspective, in 1870 Atlanta and its surrounding area had a population of just over 20,000. Today, while the core city itself has an estimated population of about 520,000 (making it the thirty-third-largest city in the US), the metropolitan area stands at well over 5 million, the ninth highest in the country.

Like many American cities, Atlanta has experienced a lot of ups and downs through its history. While the mushrooming expansion has slowed somewhat in recent years, Atlanta has been familiar with growth pains for a long time. Much of Atlanta's growth spurts have been rampant and reckless, but there have been some bright spots. One is the development called Glenwood Park, the brainchild of Internet entrepreneur Charles Brewer, founder of MindSpring (now more commonly known as EarthLink). Glenwood has been the recipient of many awards, and stands as a great example of smart inner-city development. Brewer invested about $8 million in the early part of this century to buy twenty-eight acres in the metro-Atlanta area. Before construction, Brewer had many challenges. First, clean up of extensive industrial residue was undertaken and removal and recycling of some 40,000 cubic yards of concrete as well as 40,000 cubic yards of wood chips was dealt with. Recycling of 700,000 pounds of granite block was done, and eventually used in the development's parks. Installation of new sewer lines and an innovative storm-water system that reduced runoff by two-thirds was put into place, and the landscaping was irrigated with the reclaimed groundwater, not potable city water.

Next he had to have a state highway civilized by getting it transferred to the city's jurisdiction and then instituting traffic-calming measures that allow it to serve as the development's sociable main street, lined by trees and shops. All of that took a little more than a year. Brewer and his associates had to work with the city on adoption of Traditional Neighborhood Development street standards, with narrower widths and tighter corners. That effort ate up another seven months, and finally construction began.

Interestingly, and to his advantage, Brewer and his development arm, Green Street Properties, did not borrow any money for the project. Because of this, they were not pressed to compromise on any of the design principles.

When completed, Glenwood instantly became a model of environmentally conscious urbanism, and was also a financial success. The team planted more than one thousand trees in the area, many of them in the streets, between parking spaces to reduce the "heat island" effect of pavements and to make pedestrians more comfortable. He built under the EarthCraft standards, stressing energy-efficient design, water conservation, and ways to eliminate soil erosion. A great balance of housing, office space, restaurants, retail shops, and green space were installed. One of the goals Brewer attained was to introduce "a really great townhouse ... something that is sorely lacking in Atlanta."

Glenwood Park is a wonderful example of what can be accomplished within a populated metro area, converting what was once a derelict property to a beautiful and eco-friendly mixed use.

In a weird twist of fate, Atlanta became a unique study for scientists after March 2008 when a tornado ripped through the downtown core of the metropolis—something most common to rural areas. In fact, according to one report from The National Oceanic and Atmospheric Administration, there have been only twenty-three so-called downtown tornadoes in the last 130 years.

Causing a quarter-of-a-billion dollar path of destruction, the Atlanta tornado was analyzed over the following year and, in 2009, Purdue University climatologist Dev Niyogi announced that Atlanta itself was partly to blame.

"The conditions that brought in the storm were the hammer, but local features were the chisel. They pinpointed the severe weather," he said.

Working with University of Georgia climatologist Marshall Shepherd, Niyogi discovered that the sprawl of heat-trapping concrete "caused the storms to intensify, and that came to a final punch in the urban area. All of this is consistent with our understanding of the physical processes of tornadoes."

Says Shepherd, "Atlanta is a classically sprawling city. As we move towards more smart-use, mixed-use and dense urban development, we should explore how it impacts the weather system."

In one study by the scientists, they discovered that a devastating storm in Mumbai, India, was brought to a boil, as it were, by the city itself—the storm couldn't escape the microclimate coming from below, and ended up dropping thirty-seven inches of rain in a single day on the area.

"One way we can start developing a resilience to some of these climate changes is by thinking how we should plan our urban and non-urban landscapes, and what environmental setup could help buffer us from some of these extremes," said Niyogi. "It's the very initial stages of the science, but we're going to hear more."

And now, something I personally find really cool and with a wow factor that is going on in Atlanta. In the face of all the outward growth in Atlanta, the city has also been working on a plan called the Atlanta BeltLine, a twenty-two-mile loop around the downtown core that will incorporate green development, varied housing, transit, 1,200 acres of new green space, and more. It's mostly abandoned industrial property, railway and scrubland, and the city describes it as "the largest, most wide-ranging urban redevelopment currently underway in the US."

With a budget of $2.8 billion, the city faces considerable funding problems but work is ongoing, and I'm thrilled to see this kind of urban renewal in one of the places in America that has been considered a "sprawl city" for so many years!

A similar project, and one that has, in part, influenced and inspired the BeltLine project is the High Line project in New York City. Built in the 1930s as part of a large-scale, public-private infrastructure project called the West Side Improvement, it lifted freight traffic thirty feet in the air, removing dangerous trains from the streets of Manhattan's largest industrial district. But as we know, times change and now no trains have run on the High Line since 1980. An inspired community-based non-profit group called Friends of the High Line was conceived and formed in 1999 when the historic structure was slated to be demolished. Friends of the High Line works in partnership with the city of New York to preserve and maintain the structure as an elevated public park.

So as we can see, there are dozens of wonderful examples of smart growth that have started happening in America—and one I find particularly interesting is the opposition to "big-box" stores. In fact, it's becoming a haves and have-nots situation, only the have-nots are the ones fighting to keep it that way.

Walmart, Target, Lowe's, Home Depot, and their like are undeniably popular for their low-cost philosophy. Yet, according to researchers at the National Trust for Historic Preservation, communities across the country are learning the cost of such

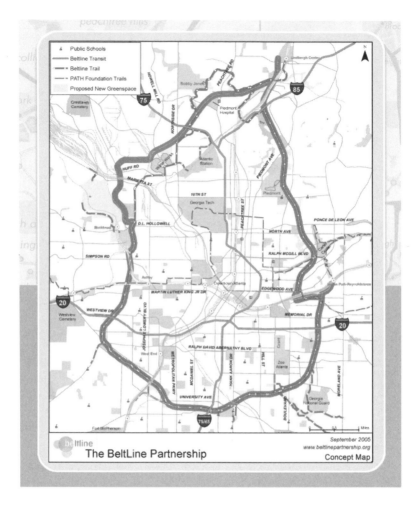

developments and residents are rising up to stop them, basically embracing the "not in my backyard" mentality:

"At any given moment, hundreds of grassroots organizations across the country are fighting tooth and nail to keep these retail behemoths out of their communities. 'Is the worst of the suburbs the best we can hope for?' asks a flier distributed by citizens in New Orleans protesting a proposed 199,000-square-foot Walmart store in the historic Lower Garden District. 'We're not gaining a store; we're losing our community,' laments a citizens' group in Decorah, Iowa, in an ad placed in *USA Today*. What's behind these battles? In the view of many, big-box stores impose hidden costs that don't appear on the price tags of the products they sell: traffic congestion; loss of trees; open space and farmland; displaced small businesses; substitution of jobs that support families with low-paying jobs that don't; air and water pollution; dying downtowns with vacant buildings; abandoned shopping centers; a degraded sense of community; and sprawl. The list of problems linked to big-box stores is long. Whether one loves or hates big-box stores, it is indisputable that their effects are long-term and significant."

However, there are some bright spots among this controversy. My good friend Carlton Owen, who is also the president and CEO of the US Endowment for Forestry and Communities, was instrumental in getting Walmart into a program called "Acres For America," which was quite an interesting and positive concept.

As Carlton tells it: "The idea for Acres for America came as I listened to a group of local environmentalists complain about rapid growth—one of those sessions where everybody complains about 'the weather' but doesn't do anything about it. I got to thinking about ways that we could actually use the down side of growth in the urban/suburban areas to catalyze conservation in areas where functioning landscapes were still available ... but wouldn't be in time. I literally began scribbling an idea of looking at the poster children of sprawl (the big box stores) and trying to get a handle on impact.

"I took two chains—Lowe's and Walmart—and used a local GIS program to guesstimate the footprint of the 'average' store (including parking lots, etc.). Then I went to their websites and looked at total numbers of stores, and through projections in annual reports got a look at expected growth and started 'tallying the acres.' While one store might be 12-20 acres, when one does the math times 3-4,000 we begin to talk about 'real habitats.'

"Then, the concept emerged as 'acre for acre.' Take funds for each local acre and areas that were already losing environmental values due to being near other development and even if 'saved' would become only woodlots for a few sparrows and squirrels. The concept began to gel. Go for acre-for-acre off-sets but in ways that really looked to the future and ensured large functional landscapes. The premise was to put the focus on using conservation easements to protect lands from development but would still be available for recreation, sustainable forestry, grazing, etc.

"I then thought about 'the proper size of ask' and other sweeteners we could add to the deal. What if we said, let's do the deal over ten years to lower the impact and what if we said for every dollar you invest (Walmart) we'll invest at least another dollar. After getting the concept roughed out on paper I shared it with a number of leaders in major conservation groups across the nation. After being rebuffed several times, I turned to my friend Peter Stangel of the National Fish & Wildlife Foundation (NFWF) where I served as a board member at the time. Peter 'got it' instantly."

Eventually, through the efforts of fellow NFWF Board Member, Kirk Dupps (and a former Walmart executive—Carlton quickly adds, "Acres for America would never have happened without Kirk.") a meeting was arranged with Walmart execs and our group. The big pitch: "You are the biggest corporation in the world and Walmart is the poster child for sprawl—you are having trouble in individual towns that are fighting you. While we can't change local politics, we do think we can help you enhance the climate by putting you in a leadership position on conservation issues."

Carlton continues: "After presenting some cold hard facts to them and suggesting some numbers, we asked for $35,000,000 to be paid over 10 years—$3,500,000/year—AND, with the commitment that NFWF would match at least dollar-for-dollar for another $35,000,000 and that at a minimum we'd achieve the world's first ever acre-for-acre offset for a business' development footprint. Today, the program continues to roll along, now in its sixth year and total lands impacted are at more than 600,000 acres.

A couple of years later, NFWF honored Rob Walton and Walmart for their conservation commitments—going well beyond Acres—at an all-star dinner in New York's Central Park. The quiet Walton told the crowd of his initial skepticism about Acres. And too, how it had helped the company as a whole embrace the role that it could play in global sustainability. He noted that their new plans to double the fuel efficiency of their trucking fleet (they are the largest in the world); and to reduce energy consumption at stores, and to see more sustainably produced products, all were founded in their early experience in Acres. This is also the night that Rob secretly bid $38,500 for a guitar that Chuck Leavell provided, signed by the Rolling Stones ... as Rob told me later, "I'm a big Stones fan ... and would have paid more if necessary!"

Later, on an odd twist, one US senator attacked me for "doing a deal with a company that was so insensitive to workers rights and health care issues." I said, "Senator, I sleep very well at night on this one. Walmart just did more for conservation than any private company in history and they did it all voluntarily. Besides, I don't write health care and wage laws, you do."

While a highly successful program, my biggest disappointment comes in that my vision and hope (and one that Walmart shared) was that Acres was not to become a national movement with other companies following suit. We wanted to extend the gains to Target, Lowe's, Home Depot, Kroger, etc., but it was not to be. However, the potential was and is clearly there. What we were able to do in Acres is to get a company to acknowledge that it has a role and an obligation beyond that in law of dealing with its 'other' impacts."

Well done, Carlton! And it is certainly heartening that a huge company like Walmart would acknowledge their footprint and do something about it. Let's hope that in time, other big-box stores will indeed follow suit. (For more on this program, see: Walmartstores.com/Sustainability/5127.aspx).

While it's encouraging to see programs like Walmart's "Acres For America," which in effect helps to offset their footprint, it is undeniable that these big box stores still eat up a lot of natural lands, disrupt some neighborhoods and communities, and we should be careful of what we allow these behemoths to do. One bright spot is that some of these giants are beginning to take a hint and develop smaller satellite stores, more along the lines of the mom and pop stores they have put out of business.

There are some amazing smart-growth models in America (and elsewhere), as I've illustrated, they are small developments compared to the sustainable housing that the country is going to need over the next thirty years. While some cities have been shrinking, others have embraced smart growth and sustainability, while others are growing at alarming rates.

According to authors and leading researchers Leon Kolankiewicz and Roy Beck, over the twenty-year period from 1970-1990, "the 100 largest Urbanized Areas sprawled out over an additional 14,545 square miles. That was more than 9 million acres of natural habitats, farmland and other rural space that were covered over by the asphalt, buildings and sub-divisions of suburbia. And that was just for the half of Americans who live in those 100 cities."

Ever-expanding suburbs and roadways to curb congestion just don't make sense. As authors Andres Duany, Elizabeth Plater-Zyberk, and Jeff Speck joke, "Trying to cure traffic congestion by adding more capacity is like trying to cure obesity by loosening your belt."

According to Census Bureau statistics found online, the worst centers for urban sprawl in America traditionally are Atlanta, Georgia (701.7 square miles of natural land lost to sprawl between 1970–1990); Houston, Texas (638.7 square miles lost); New York City/New Jersey (541.3 square miles lost); Washington, D.C. (and adjoining parts of Maryland and Virginia, 450.1 square miles lost); and Philadelphia, Pennsylvania (412.4 square miles lost). Coming in at number six, maybe to some surprise, is the city that would otherwise seem to be the poster child for urban sprawl, Los Angeles, California, which lost 393.8 square miles of wilderness.

But some researchers have discovered an alarming trend with this sprawl: It's not necessarily tied to population growth.

Associate professor Rolf Pendall of Cornell University studied 282 urban centers over the course of the 1980s, finding that population increase accounted for a 31-percent loss of natural lands, while in cities where there was no increase in population, natural lands were still lost at an average rate of 18 percent.

Former Albuquerque mayor and author David Rusk's study of 213 cities over the 1960–1990 time period found a population increase of 47 percent, while land lost to urban development increased 25,000 square miles to 51,000 square miles (107 percent).

The US Department of Housing reported in 2000 that the country's urban areas are, on average, expanding at twice the rate of the population. As the Sierra Club claims, since there are multiple causes of urban sprawl, "their impact is multiplied together, so that if population increases by 50 percent, and density decreases by 50 percent, land consumed will increase not by 100 percent, but by 300 percent."

And here's pretty blatant validation of smart-growth policies: In the same time as these studies, Portland's population ballooned 50 percent, but its land area increased by only 2 percent, according to the Natural Resources Defense Council and Surface Transportation Policy Project.

I'm quoting 1970–1990 statistics because they're the broadest: Cities make the fastest-growing list depending on criteria used that year: For instance, in 2008 New Orleans was the fastest-growing city, based on percentages, as it was getting an influx of people returning there from the exodus caused by Hurricane Katrina, but New York City had nearly twice as many people relocate into its city limits in the same year, so we could run in circles with year-by-year statistics.

No matter how you crunch the numbers, however, these are the facts: America's population continues to grow. Parts of America are shrinking, parts are undergoing urban renewal, and other parts are growing at record rates.

Let's hope we're smart about how we handle each scenario.

The Community Concept

Changing the American Dream?

*"We have squandered a great part of what we
might have used, and have not stopped to conserve the
exceeding bounty of nature, without which our genius for
enterprise would have been worthless and impotent."*

Woodrow Wilson
(First president of a fully United States, in 1913)

Among all the great qualities that makes America who she is,
is that we have what's been called "The American Dream."

It's been interpreted in many ways—expressed, at least,
in the Declaration of Independence ... the recovery from the
Great Depression and the boom after the Second World War.
The Dream was founded during the Cold War, and was fueled
by the industrial and military machine ... and has been
represented by quite a number of very strong cultural symbols
and goals. For most folks, "The American Dream" means
something like: a nice home in the suburbs where the kids all
got along, a new car every few years, the latest kitchen
appliances ... job security, regular raises and a nice pension
with some major corporation.

Professor Stanley K. Schultz, head of the Department of
History at the University of Wisconsin-Madison, in one of his
many excellent lectures, said:

"In large part, the "American Dream" was supported by expanded military investment. The federal government increased military spending after the "fall" of China and the Korean War. Companies that had never been involved in the military came to see the Department of Defense as their best customer. By the mid-1950s, there were over 40,000 defense contractors working for the federal government. By the 1960s, more than half of all government expenditures went to the military. By the 1970s, the Department of Defense had more economic assets than the 75 largest corporations in America."

According to Schultz, Americans constituted just six percent of the human race yet consumed a third of the planet's resources. Few worried. This was the "American dream."
If I may quote Schultz again:

"If we consider an annual income of $10,000 a middle-class income, then, in the 1940s, 9 percent of families fit that definition. By 1960, however, more than 30 percent of the population was middle class. Changes in education and housing further demonstrated the growth of the middle class. The year 1960 marked the first time in United States history that a majority of high-school aged people actually graduated from high school. Aided by the GI Bill, college enrollments also increased. Owning a home also became a tangible reality for more and more Americans, as the availability of housing increased and veterans could secure low-interest mortgages. By 1960, 25 percent of all housing available had been built in the prior decade. "

By the 1960s, television was in nearly every home—preceded by rock 'n' roll. More than a third of Americans lived in suburbs; the "American dream" was consuming raw materials and precious farm and forestland at an alarming rate—as I mentioned in my introduction, seeing the rate of growth of Atlanta on our family's trips from Alabama.

Even Woodrow Wilson saw it happening so fast that he himself said, "There has been something crude and heartless and unfeeling in our haste to succeed and be great."

Three months after he was elected president, Barack Obama somberly said of the economy he'd inherited and was now charged with rescuing (a gross domestic product that shrank 3.8 percent in the final quarter of 2008, the worst contraction in almost thirty years), that this is a "continuing disaster for America's working families," a disaster that amounts to no less, he says, than "the American Dream in reverse," according to a report by the Associated Press.

As David Kamp pointed out in a 2009 *Vanity Fair* article, "Along with millions of jobs and 401(k)s, the concept of a shared national ideal is said to be dying.... American Dream came to mean fame and fortune, instead of the promise that shaped a nation."

The "American dream" was, and is, probably different to every American, and the phrase has moved beyond our country and gone global. It seems that almost everyone in the world wants to live "The dream"; isn't it interesting that there is, to paraphrase Kamp, no "Canadian dream" or "Albanian dream?"

"These are tough times for the American Dream," Kamp wrote: "As the safe routines of our lives have come undone, so has our characteristic optimism—not only our belief that the future is full of limitless possibility, but our faith that things will eventually return to normal, whatever "normal" was before the recession hit. There is even worry that the dream may be over—that we currently living Americans are the unfortunate ones who shall bear witness to that deflating moment in history when the promise of this country began to wither. This is the "sapping of confidence" that President Obama alluded to in his inaugural address, the "nagging fear that America's decline is inevitable, and that the next generation must lower its sights."

Call them misguided, call them drug-induced—both, in many cases—but the "utopian" commune models of the 1960s and through into the '70s (some of which have matured into admirable self-sustaining mini-societies) actually had their start as far back as the early 1900s. In fact, the very admirable Mennonite and Amish communities have maintained a sustainable, respectable way of life for centuries. Unfortunately, the modern world—more specifically, the government—are guilty of stepping on to their turf. Literally.

As the *New York Times* recently reported, more than 50 percent of the five thousand, or so, farms in Lancaster County, Pennsylvania, are owned by Amish farmers. And while common sense would consider the Amish "model environmental citizens," as the paper called them, there's just one problem: Manure from their farms washes into streams and then into the environmentally troubled Chesapeake Bay.

Like farmer Matthew Stoltzfus told the *Times*, "We are supposed to be stewards of the land. It's our Christian duty."

Unfortunately for the Amish farmers, under the direction of President Obama, the Environmental Protection Agency has been ordered to restore the bay to health: That means the Amish must change the way they farm, or face stiff penalties. The EPA's man leading the agency's move in the county, David McGuigan, told the newspaper that "I don't think the full community understands."

Chesapeake Bay has, for decades, been polluted by fertilizers such as nitrogen and phosphorus, as well as by manure. The *Times* reports, quoting EPA data reads that, "the county generates more than 61 million pounds of manure a year. That is 20 million pounds more than the next highest county on the list of bay polluters, and more than six times that of most other counties."

Of course, by their very cultural nature, the Amish and many Mennonites steer as clear from "outsiders" and particularly the government, as they are able.

"They feel they should take care of their own," says Donald Kraybill, a professor at Elizabethtown College in Pennsylvania whose special area of study is the Amish history and way of life.

"It's been an issue over the last 30 years," Dr. Kraybill said. "We have too many animals here per square acre—too many cows for too few acres."

If the government agency can't find a way to work with the farmers individually, the government says it will resort to fines and penalties. According to the *Times*, the majority of Amish farms inspected by the EPA was not in environmental compliance and, in fact, had contaminated wells.

Some farmers are angered by the intrusion, while others already have systems in compliance, and the agency is certainly doing what it can to lessen the cultural impact. But it has certainly generated controversy. Sam Riehl, a farmer in the area, told the *Times*. "We wonder whether we are being told what to do, and whether the EPA will make it so that we can't even maintain our farms."

Getting back to the '60s and '70s era, what many thought of as a "commune" of drugs, free love, nudity, and that whole scene was, in part, a response to a significant number of young Americans that became disillusioned with the war in Vietnam and what they saw as runaway commercialism. Calling themselves flower children or hippies, or what have you, they began experimenting with a return to the land, nature and nurture, and a self-sustaining lifestyle. They grew their own food, made their own clothing and, indeed, a number have "matured" and are by what just about anyone would describe as "respectable" custodians of their land, their families and their communities. Far from being isolationists, many are influential and important members of the larger "communities" they are involved with.

Now understand that I am by no means suggesting we go back to that era, or that they "had it right." But I do think there are a few things we can learn from taking a look at the true intentions of the folks that engaged in these communes. Some of the survivors of those times have gone on to succeed in life and business, and to do quite a lot of good things for others through their outreach.

One that comes to mind is the wonderful Wavy Gravy and his Hog Farm, with its headquarters in Berkeley, California, and a two-hundred-acre farm known as Black Oak Ranch that is home to his Camp Winnarainbow, which plays host to numerous music festivals and charitable causes, and is home to a performing arts camp for children every summer.

"Our camp provides the opportunity for children (and adults) to discover new realms of personal achievement, communion with nature, and have BIG FUN at the same time. For over thirty years kids (and adults) have run away to join our circus in beautiful Mendocino County, in Northern California," Wavy said over the phone from his spread in California.

"Drawing from our knowledge of circus and performing arts, we teach timing, balance and a sense of humor. Kids learn respect for themselves, others and the environment. We honor the creative spirit of each child in an atmosphere of approval and mutual encouragement. Our goal is to provide a training ground to nurture future leaders for a harmonious and sustainable world."

Of course, the consummate performer as well as promoter, Wavy explained he's got a lot more on the go than just Camp Winnarainbow for kids—he's deeply involved in sustainable environmental issues and more. There's www.campwinna rainbow.org and, of course, there's www.wavygravy.net. There's also an interesting website called www.seva.org, which Wavy and others have supported, such as fellow rocker Bob Weir who is also an advisor on their board. In addition to partnering with Native American communities to address the deadly rising epidemic of diabetes among various tribes, they work for sustainable agriculture in areas of Mexico and, remarkably, in conjunction with locally run sight programs in India, Nepal, and Tibet, provide more than eighty thousand eye surgeries a year.

It's worth mentioning, too, the Lama Foundation in New Mexico—"a sustainable spiritual community and educational center dedicated to the awakening of consciousness, spiritual practice with respect for all traditions, service, and stewardship of the land." (www.lamafoundation.org) In fact, the very spiritual Ram Dass stayed with the foundation founders after his life-changing trip to India and, with the help of the community's residents, assembled the book *Remember Be Here Now*. Not only still in print, the book has sold more than a million copies and is one of the standard-bearer texts for people wishing to make a transition to a more spiritual lifestyle.

The community was one of the first of—let's say—European descent, to experiment with entirely natural building techniques using straw bale, adobe brick, and straw clay structures, though sadly many of the first were destroyed in a massive forest fire in 1996. The community has thrived, however, and was one of the early innovators in New Mexico with "pit greenhouse" designs, which permit year-round cultivation of the community's crops and can even provide passive solar heat to nearby homes.

The meals at Lama are primarily, but not always, vegetarian. The electrical power comes entirely from solar panels. Another key to Lama's survival, in my opinion, is also due to its longstanding anti-drug policy and commitment to personal spiritual practice.

The reason I wanted to mention a couple of examples of successful "commune-style" communities is that some of the examples of their practices are not just some hippy-dippy-freaky concepts at all, in fact, they're based in part on something that makes sense and, believe it or not, is returning to some areas of America.

I think there is some value in examining these things, as they present some community concepts that can be applied to smart growth. Having a tight-knit community that works together can have positive effects on modern societies, both poor and rich.

Two of the most prominent movements in smart growth are New Ruralism and New Urbanism. The former is a large part of that this book is about: Giving a great deal of thought to aspects of growth such as organizing towns and cities around compact neighborhoods and having highly efficient and non-polluting transportation and also having a sustainable agriculture—growing food that requires little transportation, and that is cultivated in an environmentally sound manner. New Urbanism meanwhile, is the continued desire for traditional neighborhoods, the classic American dream, basically, though modified for more ecologically sound planning than has seen runaway urban sprawl.

The organizing body for New Urbanism is the Congress for the New Urbanism, founded in 1993. Its foundational text is the Charter of the New Urbanism, which says:

"We advocate the restructuring of public policy and development practices to support the following principles: neighborhoods should be diverse in use and population; communities should be designed for the pedestrian and transit as well as the car; cities and towns should be shaped by physically defined and universally accessible public spaces and community institutions; urban places should be framed by architecture and landscape design that celebrate local history, climate, ecology, and building practice."

The first "New Urban" town built was the aforementioned Seaside, Florida, on which construction started in 1981. It has its supporters but is largely seen as an example of a utopian town for only the very wealthy.

Other prominent New Urban developments include Stapleton outside of Denver, Colorado; the site of the former Stapleton airport, planners intent on creating a town for thirty thousand, complete with schools and shops within walking distances of most of the homes. Another is Mountain House in California—a development ultimately to consist of twelve villages, each with its own elementary school, park, and commercial area—all linked by light rail and walkable streets.

Mesa del Sol is a planned city-within-a-city south of Albuquerque. Developers had wanted it to be a series of four villages each with schools, retail, and recreation within walking distance. According to the developer, Forest City, "the plan calls for 100,000 residents to occupy 37,500 green built units over 40 years in four separate villages."

People across our country are beginning to consider and explore these kinds of well-thought-out communities, and developers are re-thinking what has historically worked, and what has been proven not to work. And, what has surfaced is that often

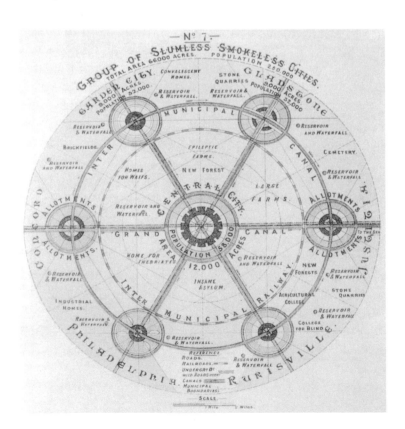

what has not worked is the "traditional" American dream city model. We've already explored how some cities grew too fast and without careful though, resulting in challenges that were completely unexpected down the road. Cities like Detroit and Flint, Michigan, are being forcibly dismantled and re-designed. From Jackson, Mississippi, to Birmingham, Alabama, both of which have lost roughly 5 percent of their populations in the past ten years, to the Detroit and St. Louis, which are less than half as populated as they once were.

In these and other cities that are experiencing extreme downsizing, whole neighborhoods sit empty, buildings are abandoned, derelict and crumbling. On the other hand, we see cities that grow so fast that they can't keep up with the necessary infrastructures that are essential to controlling traffic and providing comfortable spaces in which to live and work. With so much wasted space, it is evident that growth was certainly not smart, nor strong, nor sustainable.

So, what has worked?

The traditional English village model, for one. In fact, in the late 1800s, an English writer named Ebenezer Howard was disturbed by what he saw as the merging of rural and urban environments in basically what has turned out to be unsustainable and definitely not smart growth. He wrote a book called *To-Morrow: A Peaceful Path to Real Reform* (it was reprinted as *Garden Cities of Tomorrow* in 1902.

His vision was an alternative called the Garden City.

According to the Wikipedia entry on Howard, his "book offered a vision of towns free of slums and enjoying the benefits of both town (such as opportunity, amusement, and high wages) and country (such as beauty, fresh air, and low rents). He illustrated the idea with his famous Three Magnets diagram, which addressed the question "Where will the people go?", the choices being "Town," "Country," or "Town-Country"—the Three Magnets.

It called for the creation of new suburban towns of limited size, planned in advance, and surrounded by a permanent belt of agricultural land. These Garden cities were used as a role model for many suburbs. Howard believed that such Garden Cities were the perfect blend of city and nature. The towns would be largely

Serenbe's charming inn and cottages. *Photo courtesy Serenbe*

independent, and managed and financed by the citizens who had an economic interest in them.

In 1899 he founded the Garden Cities Association, now known as the Town and Country Planning Association and the oldest environmental charity in England. Howard's ideas were hugely influential in Europe and, indeed, Letchworth Garden City is a suburban garden city north of London. A second garden city, Welwyn Garden City, was started after World War I, and offers a combination of town and country life. Medium-sized agriculture to serve the communities' needs protects wildlife and habitat.

Howard believed that land should be kept in as natural a state as possible and that "novelty" landscaping should be avoided.

I have seen probably the best modern example of this in the community of Serenbe, just outside of Atlanta. Only thirty minutes from the metropolis is what many designers and planners cite as possibly one of the best neighborhoods ever designed and built.

And it pretty much happened by accident.

Founder Steve Nygren was a prominent Atlanta restaurateur, with thirty-four popular eateries in eight states. In 1991, he and his wife Marie bought sixty acres in the Georgian countryside about thirty miles southwest of Atlanta so they and their three daughters would have a weekend getaway from the city. It transformed their lives. Three years later, Steve retired and the family sold their Atlanta home and relocated full time to the country, to what they dubbed "Serenbe," a morph of the words "serenity" and "be."

Within two years they'd turned the 1930's horse barn next to their house into guest rooms and in 1996 opened the Serenbe Bed & Breakfast. They planted a garden thick with tomatoes and zucchini and dug a pair of swimming pools, along with a fishing pond. They populated the property with llamas, donkeys, rabbits, and goats, and added a croquet lawn, an open-air pavilion for weddings, miles of hiking trails and a labyrinth made of stones cleared from the organic fields.

"We invited people to come and simply unfold and relax," Steve says.

As reported in a 2009 *New York Times* story on Serenbe, "In 2000, while jogging through the pastoral countryside, Steve and his daughter Garnie noticed bulldozers on adjacent farmland and panicked that Atlanta's sprawl was about to consume his solitude. In fairly short order, he managed to purchase nine hundred acres adjacent to the farm and, feeling it was inevitable that land so close

Steve and me on one of my several tours of his family's Serenbe community in Georgia. *Photo by Jeff Craig.*

to the city would be developed, determined to set an example."

"My first reaction was to buy as much land as I could to protect us (from development)," says Steve. "But then I realized this was not practical. I didn't have enough money to buy enough land to really, truly protect it."

So he rallied his neighbors to push through zoning changes aimed at limiting development to self-contained clusters, surrounded by wilderness. Under the plan, 80 percent of the 40,000-acre Chattahoochee Hill Country region must be preserved as green space, and that which is developed is limited to building clusters capped at 220 homes, including live/work spaces, and commercial buildings.

Steve and Marie then set about to turn their Serenbe retreat into a small town modeled on centuries-old English country villages—which he says are a perfect model of sustainability, proven for centuries—so-called "farm-to-table" communities. Even today, many of those English villages have butchers, farmers, blacksmiths, and carpenters—workmen of each required trade as members of the community.

"That's the model," Steve says. "It was easy to just consider what is clearly not working and what has worked for centuries, and what has worked for centuries is a community founded on principles of farm-to-table cooking and environmentally conscious building techniques, where people shop and dine locally, helping to sustain each other's business while also creating less waste.

"People are looking for what's important, quality of life, for them and their children. Many of the residents want to know their neighbors, and we're creating public spaces where they can interact," Steve says.

Steve envisioned an eventual development of four individual communities on the nine hundred acres, a return to a simpler, smarter and healthier way of life—back to the days when everyone in the village knew everyone else, exactly the opposite of the growth patterns of urban sprawl. By merging ecologically sound sustainability principles with the design philosophies of walking neighborhoods made up of both homes and shops, Steve and Marie envisioned real communities with a range of economic and cultural diversity that exist in a truly green and sustainable way, where people are drawn together over gardening, over cooking and over art of every kind. "We're intentional in the way that we respect the environment. It's about the way you live, the way you interact, the way you eat," says Marie.

"I thought I was going to be a gentleman farmer," Steve says. "Never did I guess I'd be working as hard as I'd ever worked in my life, as a land developer"—especially as the developer of one of the most acclaimed twenty-first-century high-tech eco-villages on the planet.

Serenbe's first two high-density hamlets have risen, (the master plan for the settlement calls for three hamlets), based on what's called "sacred geometry" principles—very loosely explained as living in harmony with the Earth—with buildings clustered along the rolling hills and hollows of the land rather than developments built on land that has been bulldozed into squares for cookie-cutter homes in a manner that so defines one of the ugliest aspects of what we know as urban sprawl. Steve points out that the entire development is based on disturbing the land as little as possible—the streets and houses aren't on neat grades or in a grid block.

"We eliminated the need for mass grading," he says.

Mirroring what Steve says in Serenbe literature, he says "Each Serenbe building project is designed to flow with the terrain, disturbing our natural landscape as little as possible. The entire community is laid out with accessible pathways to encourage walking. Native plants and organic landscaping techniques are used exclusively throughout Serenbe, eliminating the need for chemicals and expensive lawn maintenance. Conventional lawns require both chemicals and excessive watering—neither of which is smart or sustainable. At Serenbe, there are no green, manicured lawns. Instead, each home faces a village street and backs on to forest, wildflower meadow or gardens or horse trails.

Garnie Nygren, one of Steve and Marie's daughters, and one of the top managers of Serenbe, explains in their development literature that "all the homes are built to the standards of the EarthCraft House Program. These standards include energy efficiency, low maintenance, air quality, water conservation, and resource-efficient building materials and systems. An EarthCraft

House is a healthy, comfortable home that reduces utility bills and protects the environment."

In July 2010, Serenbe unveiled its new "Nest Cottage" concept. The first model cottage, which is one of the cluster of fifteen cottages, was built in partnership with Southface and the US Department of Energy and is equipped with measuring devices that will give data on real energy savings and cost savings of things like solar, geothermal, WaterSense appliances and other energy uses. The Nygren's builders and architects estimate that energy bills will total $200 for the YEAR for these homes.

On one of the many beautiful hiking trails throughout Serenbe, is one of the most incredible tree houses I've ever seen. It was designed for the most part by all the children that were involved in the community early in its existence. Cleverly placed within several large hardwood trees, it sprawls through them with grace and provides a wonderful spot for the kids to play and adults to enjoy watching them.

According to Serenbe brochures, "using newly designed, yet inexpensive, reuse-water techniques, treated effluent water is reused for irrigation and future water supply for toilets. Other wastewater is treated in a two-stage, chemical-free passive system that incorporates non-disruptive filtration and dispersion.

Rather than creating concrete spillways that concentrate storm runoff, Serenbe storm water runoff is directed into natural systems of vegetated filter strips and shallow channels of dense vegetation. These natural filters remove pollutants while dispersing water flow.

Residents and tourists mingle on the "main street" of the Serenbe community, which includes acclaimed restaurants, shops and art galleries. *Photo courtesy Serenbe*

There's a "main street" area of retail shops, restaurants, art galleries, and services, and Serenbe Farm, a twenty-five-acre

Rolling hills and horse pastures make it difficult to believe that the Serenbe community is only 30 miles from Atlanta. *Photo courtesy Serenbe*

organic farm that provides residents and the local restaurants with fresh produce and now grows enough organic food that it's selling produce to outlets and restaurants in urban Atlanta.

The founding of Serenbe and the land conservation efforts that came about through Steve and his family's tenacity has had an unexpected bonus. As the rapid growth of Atlanta has, for decades now, consumed hundreds of acres of forested land in and around the metropolis, the increasing loss of trees has left the area more vulnerable than ever to pollution.

In a study commissioned by Serenbe and conducted by Atlanta-based Arborguard Tree Specialists, it has become apparent that the whole forty-thousand-acre Chattahoochee Hill Country tract that has now been protected in part by land trusts initiated by Steve and his neighbors, contains the trees that are, essentially, the lungs of Atlanta. The study showed that the trees at Serenbe store 1,333,840 tons of carbon and sequester, or remove, an additional 52,660 tons of carbon per year. The trees also remove 1,484.01 tons of pollution a year from the air. In layman's terms, that means that Serenbe's trees store the equivalent of the carbon emissions of 182,717 cars for a year, or the equivalent of the emissions of 106,792 single-family homes for a year.

"As Atlanta has grown, so has the challenge to our air quality," said Spence Rosenfeld, president of Arborguard, which uses its ArborScout tool to measure the condition of trees on a given property tract.

Steve and other eco-conscious developers are hoping this provides tangible evidence that they are doing things right after decades of growth that was NOT right, and that it inspires more balanced and sustainable growth throughout metro Atlanta.

"People are looking for what's important, quality of life, for them and their children. Many of the residents want to know their neighbors, and we're creating public spaces where they can interact," Steve says.

"With an agriculture component, a sense of community, where all the houses are close together, and everyone knows everyone, it's very much like small towns of sixty, eighty years ago," Steve says.

"We break a lot of the current development rules. From the ground up, we're devoted to the environment and being respectful to nature. A community with private homes, restaurants, original boutiques, and art galleries, Serenbe was created as an example of how development doesn't have to occur at nature's expense—of our thousand acres, a maximum of 30 percent will be disturbed."

The success of Serenbe is tangible: Even in the downturn economic climate of the past two years, Steve and Marie's vision is thriving. In the last three years, Serenbe has grown to a community of more than two hundred residents, mostly young families who work in the Atlanta area, the self-employed, or retired. So far, 102 freshly built, environmentally friendly homes and business spaces have been rented and sold, a small collection of boutiques and galleries has popped up, and at the heart of the community, three restaurants are thriving.

It's far from what you'd describe as a "commune," but Serenbe is just one among a growing trend of "Cottage Neighborhoods," and a suburb and shining example of a beautiful, well-thought-out community that is thriving, and truly born out of smart growth. For more on Serenbe, see: www.serenbe.com.

Also outside of Atlanta is Peachtree City (www.peachtree-city.org), which has been around for more than fifty years and was one of the country's first eco-friendly twentieth-century communities.

In the 1950s, developers decided to turn twelve thousand acres of farmland twenty-nine miles southwest of Atlanta into a community of four villages and two man-made lakes. Each village has its own retail area, parks, and schools, but the ten thousand families in Peachtree City are all neighbors, connected by eighty-eight miles of winding paths made for golf carts, which can be found in almost every garage.

"Life is a lot sweeter at 18 miles per hour. It forces you to slow down," explains resident and former mayor Steve Brown.

The whole idea from the start was an oasis from the concrete and glass of the big city, a comfortable place to raise a family away from the pollution and crime that marks "city" life.

Atlanta is one of the poster cities for everything negative about runaway development and urban sprawl, but this is not to say the place doesn't have its eco-proponents! In fact, it's worth mentioning that there are some newer developments within the urban limits, which are embracing sustainable and green principles. Among them is East Lake Commons, a cohousing community built on twenty partially wooded acres, located four miles east of the downtown core. Cohousing is a relatively new form of intentional community that places emphasis on resource sharing, community involvement, sustainable living, and diversity.

As the community advertises to prospective residents, "Our family-friendly village is built around pedestrian paths ... 67 townhouse residences and a large community center used for community meals, meetings, and social events, and including two guest rooms."

East Lake Commons also proudly boasts having a three-acre organic garden, an orchard, greenhouse and pond.

"We are part of a much larger urban renewal/urban pioneering effort involving unprecedented cooperation between government, private commercial enterprise, and local neighborhood associations to revitalize the historic East Lake district of Atlanta. Ongoing educational and outreach programs, including summer camps for kids and yearly neighborhood festivals," the community's website proclaims.

Georgia's neighbor to the north, South Carolina, is also concerned about the urban sprawl and low-density development that has been pushing the boundaries of Charleston out into the green rural areas on its northern, western, and southern boundaries.

While the city's complex "Century V Plan" does not include specific protections for forests, parks, and wetlands from future conversion to urban use, there are numerous environmental groups that are politically active in bringing about change and ensuring smart and sustainable growth, which is encouraging, and the Century V Plan is, at its heart, the wish of the city's administrators and elected officials to improve the quality of life, long-term, for the residents of the community.

Minutes away from Myrtle Beach, South Carolina, is the "green" community of Southbury, which prides itself on being "the community where neighbors wave when driving by and friends catch up at the mailbox. The neighborhood is designed to bring people together with its lighted sidewalks, front porches, and paired mailboxes.

The community features tree-lined streets, and houses include rear garages for curb appeal. Plans for houses vary as to prevent Southbury from becoming a cookie-cutter neighborhood. When completed, the entire neighborhood of Southbury will be green. All houses will be both LEED and Energy Star certified, according to www.greenecocommunities.com/South-Carolina/Southbury-south -carolina-green-homes.html.

Also in South Carolina, not far from Charleston, is the ambitious and incredible development called Poplar Grove. The brainchild of my friend and master developer Vic Mills, Poplar Grove (www.poplargrovecharleston.com) is located on an historic 1697 former rice plantation just twelve miles from Charleston, yet it seems as if it were a hundred miles from any urban center.

Originally a 500-acre project, Vic's company acquired a further 5,400 acres, and local zoning laws would have allowed him to construct seven thousand homes on the site. But Vic has long been a bit of a contradictory man—a conservationist and environ- mentalist who's also a developer. He was involved in the first conservation community on the Savannah River, the nine-

Poplar Grove founder Vic Mills: A developer with a clear vision for conservation and quality of life. *Photo by Jeff Craig*

hundred-acre River Island in Augusta, Georgia. More than 30 percent of that project is part of a conservation easement and the development is bisected by many nature trails—hardly the strip-mall and cookie-cutter box homes we've come to associate with urban sprawl.

At the South Carolina Poplar Grove site, Vic initially planned for 3,500 homes rather than the 7,000 he could have set out to build. But after meeting with Ducks Unlimited about the project being a much-lower-density development, he put 3,100 acres into a conservation easement called the Ashley River Plantation District and lowered his plans for that part of the property to just 50 homes. This commitment inspired surrounding property owners to jump on the conservation bandwagon and resulted in the preservation of more than 12,000 acres, including adjoining Middleton and Millbrook plantations.

In total on the nearly 6,000 acres, Vic is constructing only about 800 residences, ranging from cottage homes to plantation home sites of up to 100 acres each.

"As the developer, our returns are less than had we sold it," he admits. But Vic is focused on the long term and the quality of life of the residents of his development, as well as preserving the wetlands. He likes the idea of creating a place where people can enjoy a simpler lifestyle closer to nature. Plus, in working with Ducks Unlimited, the conservation easement resulted in a substantial reduction of what Vic would have had to finance for the project, which makes it a win-win-win all the way around. Now that's smart.

"People want the opposite of what they have at work," he says. "They want passive activities: walking trails and canoe rides. I've tried to develop a community with an eye toward how it lives. We hope our children who grow up here will know the difference between a wood duck and a mallard and between an egret and a crane."

When I visited the site and met with Vic, he proudly showed off the hundred-acre equestrian facility, part of more than fifty miles of riding and hiking trails, a green barn, a community pool, a boat landing, a town square, and kayak outposts that were under

One of the first stages of the Poplar Grove community development.
Photo courtesy Poplar Grove

construction, in the planning stages or already completed.

"The barn will exhibit efficient use of energy, water and materials. Even the grasses and fertilizers used in the pasture areas will be environmentally friendly," he says. A windmill will pump water and a cistern will catch rainwater—even natural fly spray will be use on the horses.

Residents cycle along a street in Poplar Grove. *Photo courtesy Poplar Grove*

"Our vision is to take this natural wonderland, these 6,000 acres of marshland, woods, canals, ponds, open waterways, nature trails, along with the thousands of flowers, plants, trees, birds, fish, and animals that live here, and respect every leaf, every droplet of water, and every living, breathing thing," says Vic.

Before any construction took place, Vic had consultants survey the entire property, identifying all

One of the many excellent examples of a home built around old-growth trees in the exceptionally well-designed Poplar Grove development. *Photo courtesy Poplar Grove*

the major old-growth trees. Pines and vegetation that were choking the oaks were removed, the major trees were treated with fertilizer, and food plots were installed for the animals. Now, Vic says, the place is "wildlife on steroids!"

It is impressive that Vic has designed all of the development around old-growth trees—the streets, the houses, the man-made ponds and streams, all are designed to accommodate the trees, rather than cutting them and bulldozing to make way for subdivisions.

Vic says that the vision of Poplar Grove "calls for careful land planning and responsible building with a bias toward ecologically friendly materials. If we remain true to our vision, one hundred years from now those who live here should see very much what we see today. This is a gem, an invaluable jewel of nature that demands, deserves, and expects protection."

He's right—it's a very special place, and it's heartwarming to know that a developer with Vic Mills's environmental sensibility is in charge.

My friend and a master developer from Texas, David Hill, takes a different approach. He has developed numerous successful projects in and around Austin and San Antonio. Instead of using tools like conservation easements and designating high-density areas in order to preserve open space, he takes a more economic view of developing land while still preserving wildlife and natural elements of the landscapes he works with.

One of his latest projects is called Cordillera Ranch, an upscale development in the Hill Country around San Antonio that is comprised of 8,700 total acres with more than 4.5 miles of the magnificent Guadalupe River. David and his development team have put a strong emphasis on maintaining a beautiful natural landscape with plenty of wildlife and outdoor activities available, but in a way that gives him more flexibility without the restrictions that come with easements and certain building standards. It is sort of a "self policed" approach to developing.

As David tells it: "It is my opinion that any development approach that has a primary objective of being a "conservation" development (that term has a lot of different interpretations in the environmental or development community) or preserving open space must still be economically viable. If they aren't economically viable then there will be very few that will be done that way. For a variety of reasons I am not a big fan of using tax credits or write-offs related to conservation easements to make the numbers work. When we were starting this project we analyzed the conservation easement/tax benefit approach and ultimately decided there was too much risk and uncertainty about possible changes in IRS regulations or with Congress regarding the valuations and tax implications of conservation easements.

"When we started the planning process on this unique and beautiful property my mission statement to our staff was "we must be good stewards of this land, it is a very unique and special property," To accomplish that, the objectives that we set forth for

The native vegetation around homes in Cordillera Ranch is left as undisturbed as possible. *Courtesy Cordillera Ranch*

the project were to: (1) create a very low density, upscale community that is economically sustainable with unique outdoor lifestyle opportunities, (2) preserve open space and minimize disturbance of the native vegetation, (3) protect and promote wildlife and their habitat, (4) preserve and protect the incredible 20-plus mile views, and (5) preserve the night sky with comprehensive "dark sky" exterior lighting restrictions. Cordillera Ranch is such a large landmass that we truly can have a positive, dramatic impact on our "starscape" vista if we protect it.

"Our development plan has included lot product that generally ranges from 1 acre up to 13 acres with very stringent architectural controls particularly in establishing minimal areas of disturbance for a home site and requiring that the majority of each lot is left undisturbed and kept in existing native vegetation. We have currently developed a little over 1,000 home sites on about 4,900 acres (out of the 8,700 total acres) and when that area is fully built out with homes more than 80 percent of the land will remain as undisturbed native vegetation.

"I have also looked at a number of developments (or attempted developments) that tried the concept of clustering all of the development on a small percentage of a property (say 10 to 15 percent) and leaving the remainder of 85 to 90 percent as permanently restricted, commonly owned open space land (with or without a conservation easement). Although I like the intent and objective, unfortunately the economics don't seem to work on that approach around here and I have not seen many in Texas that were economically successful. Case in point is that Cordillera Ranch initially started with approximately 4,200 acres and it was immediately very successful using the large lot development concept we came up with. An adjoining landowner that had approximately 4,400 acres watched our success and decided they would do a "conservation" development that would cluster approximately 500 home sites on several hundred acres and leave the remaining approximately 4,000 acres as restricted open space. That approach was unsuccessful and after over a year of marketing it with zero sales they threw in the towel. I ultimately made a deal with them and merged that property into Cordillera Ranch and our development scheme with immediate success. Under our development concept we will achieve similar results as to open space that they were trying to get, i.e. 80 to 85 percent of total land area will remain as undisturbed native vegetation and wildlife habitat. The difference is that a proportionate amount of that

A resident enjoys a vista of open space across Cordillera Ranch.
Courtesy Cordillera Ranch

A fly fisherman at the property owners park on the Guadalupe River at Cordillera Ranch.
Courtesy Cordillera Ranch

native vegetation and habitat is included with each lot under our concept rather than in one large, restricted commonly owned tract.

"It seems to me that most Texans have not embraced the idea of paying for the cost of all that open space land left in one large contiguous tract unless it is actually a part of the individual property they own. Our concept also included a variety of amenities such as a private club, with a golf course and outdoor lifestyle amenities (equestrian, sporting clays, fishing lakes and Guadalupe river access and activities) that would drive the desirability and price point up for the development to make the overall economics work. Those amenities sit on less than 2 percent of the total land area so not really much impact given the overall size of the project. All of that land that is ultimately left undisturbed still has a cost associated with it and if it is going to be left as-is rather than developed then those costs have to be recovered somewhere/somehow in the development economic model. This may not be the perfect purist approach but again, the economics have to work otherwise low density/low impact developments won't get done. The end result of our approach to developing Cordillera Ranch will result in almost 7,000 acres out of 8,700 remaining in native vegetation and habitat at full build out of the project."

Cordillera has been a very successful development, and during my visit there I saw plenty of beautiful natural land with well-constructed and carefully placed homes and the clubhouse, recreational buildings and landscaping fit in nicely with the lay of the land. So it just goes to show what can be accomplished with a good ethic, common sense and a good master plan.

All over America, there are eco-villages and eco-friendly, large-scale developments being built or already in existence, and while it would take a book in itself to discuss all of them, I would like to highlight the very successful Prairie Crossing development outside of Chicago (www.prairiecrossing.com).

In their online literature, Prairie Crossing boasts that the community "was designed to combine the preservation of open land, easy commuting by rail, and responsible development practices. It is now considered by many a national example of how to plan our communities to enhance the environment and support a better way of life.

Prairie Crossing's land was purchased to safeguard its open spaces. Prairie Crossing is part of the Liberty Prairie Reserve, more than 5,000 acres of publicly and privately held land that includes nature and forest preserves, farms, and trails. At Prairie Crossing itself, greenways have been constructed and houses placed to

The Salt Lake Valley Daybreak development is among one of the increasing number of well-designed, sustainable communities in America. *Photo courtesy Kennecott Land*

protect the environment, native vegetation, and wildlife of the Midwest. Three hundred and fifty of its acres are legally protected from development.

More than ten miles of trails, a stable, and a large lake with beach and dock provide opportunities for healthy outdoor exercise. The farm supplies fresh organic vegetables, flowers, and fruits to the community, and individual garden plots are available at a small cost. In the belief that community and conservation can go hand in hand, the trails and gardens of Prairie Crossing are designed to be places where people can meet to enjoy and care for the land. The Homeowners Association has taken responsibility for the community amenities, design review, and other aspects of community life at Prairie Crossing. Volunteer stewardship activities are organized by the Liberty Prairie Conservancy, which conducts environmental programs throughout the Liberty Prairie Reserve.

Prairie Crossing is approximately an hour from Chicago by train or car. There is rail service to Chicago and O'Hare Airport from two stations adjoining the site.

Homes at Prairie Crossing have been constructed with techniques that reduce energy consumption by approximately 50 percent in comparison to new homes in the area. Community-wide recycling and composting programs are in effect. Prairie Crossing is designed to encourage walking and biking as alternatives to short trips by automobile. A wind turbine provides power to the farm,

The Salt Lake Valley Daybreak community features more than 20 miles of walking and biking trails and more than 250 acres of parks and open spaces. *Photo courtesy Kennecott Land*

and the new buildings of the Prairie Crossing Charter School are designed to Leadership in Energy and Environmental Design (LEED) standards.

"Prairie Crossing is being developed by families who wish to see the conservation community concept replicated elsewhere. They have made every effort to ensure that the project is economically feasible and have carefully budgeted for long-term success."

One of the more unlikely developments is that of mining giant Rio Tinto's Kennecott Utah Copper company, which is building a community called Daybreak at the foot of its Salt Lake Valley mining operations.

At first glance, the idea of a centuries-old mining company volunteering to not only clean up its waste, its impact on the environment after decades of operations, and reclaim the land is laudable. But in the case of Rio Tinto's Kennecott, I think it's pretty obvious that the Daybreak Community is, in fact, not just a public-relations exercise. The company's land division has been cleaning up its evaporation ponds and ensuring groundwater is safe and there are no toxins left behind, returning the land to natural grasses and even wheat fields.

Don Whyte is CEO of the project and has been a friend of mine for a decade or so. He has hunted with us at Charlane Plantation, and we've had many conversations about smart and cautious

Unlike the cookie-cutter urban sprawl model that has plagued American development for the last half-century, communities such as Daybreak are being constructed with even the notion of the biodiversity of which trees attract which birds. *Photo courtesy Kennecott Land*

development. Don left his home and successful business in Florida a few years ago to take on the Rio Tinto Daybreak project, and he says the company had a broader vision that indeed drew him to the company from his life in Florida: reclaiming the land to establish a sustainable living community nestled in the valley between two mountain ranges: "Urban encroachment was already a reality, so when it came closer to us looking at post-mining use of the land, urban development became something to be considered. But also, working for such a large mining company, we have the resources to do the things other developers can't. Somebody new to the asset would have problems. It's one thing to return the land to the standard for wheat, but a much higher standard for people living on property. By doing it ourselves we did the clean up and took responsibility and it made sense for us to develop it ourselves, and make sure it's done right."

As he points out, Daybreak is the mining company's first residential development.

Don says concerns over environmental impact have been "a core value of this company, but admittedly it's a tough story to tell the public, as open-pit mining takes up a lot of land and the general public perception of mining. But we looked at the big picture and, looked at all of our land not impacted by operations, and came to the conclusion that by staffing up with the appropriate expertise we could do something that would be remarkable."

And that would be a sustainable residential environment that's well planned and well constructed with the long-term in mind.

"Since 2004 Daybreak has become one of the Salt Lake Valley's great success stories: home to over one thousand families so far, and a showcase for sustainable ideas and technologies. In fact, everything we do has to pass the sustainability test: Is it good for you? Is it good for our community? Is it good for the planet? Is it good for our economy? You can see from these questions that sustainable thinking is just as down-to-earth practical as it is blue-sky philosophical," Don said in an interview.

As the company proclaims, "sustainability is no passing fad. It's here for the long haul, and when properly understood and put into practice it can benefit us all in profoundly important ways. We don't mean to sound overly dramatic, but our ability to live sustainably today will determine, in large part, the kind of future we leave for our children. Fortunately, a sustainable lifestyle is also a rewarding lifestyle."

Don says Daybreak was designed, and is being constructed, to offer something for everyone—lofts, town homes, single-family dwelling and mansions, priced from the low six figures to more than $1 million.

With more than twenty miles of walking and biking trails, more than 250 acres of parks and open space "so far," he says, and a 65-acre, man-made lake well stocked with fish and ideal for sailing, canoeing, kayaking, as well as many other fitness and recreation facilities either in place or in the planning stages, Daybreak is a model community, Don says.

Every home is built to EnergyStar guidelines, and the use of renewable wind and solar energy is at the forefront of the development's planning he says. By the middle of next year, a light rail system will tie the valley's community together.

"One of the remarkable things is that Daybreak is not a cookie-cutter designed community," he says. "I had been concerned about traditional urban development. We're doing this so that the streets are lined up with the mountain ranges. Nearly every home is nestled on a street in a fashion by which there are incredible views of one of the mountain ranges. Walkability of neighborhoods is very important; the streets twist and turn, using natural grade to give us interesting views; it's hard to find a place without a mountain view. Sitting on my front porch, for instance, I see the tram at top of a mountain."

He said that by taking advantage of the mining company's water rights, they've been able to use non-potable water to irrigate the landscaping—which itself has been designed with groups of plants that need to be irrigated together. The streets have a mixed biodiversity of trees, "we've carefully selected a broad selection which supports a variety of birds."

With a long-term plan of mixed use residential and 14.5 million square feet of commercial space planned in five to ten office complexes, planned medical and mining teaching university facilities, the Daybreak community, Don says, is intended to provide "truly the luxury of living and working in the same community, without long commutes and all the conventional urban problems.

Yet, he points out the valley remains just thirty minutes from downtown Salt Lake City and the airport, which will also be connected by light rail.

"So Daybreak is exceptionally close, on world scale."

Around the world, eco-villages have been sprouting, just as most of the world, developed and undeveloped, has aspired to what has been known as the "American dream." Ireland, Wales, Australia, New Zealand, even wealthier locations in India are aspiring to eco-friendly development.

Higher-profile sites include Melrose Arch in Johannesburg, South Africa; Alta de Lisboa near Lisbon, Portugal; and Jakriborg in southern Sweden. All prove that a smart, strong, and sustainable future can be found by looking to the past—which is interesting if one considers that the only way for the American dream to still be a reality is if it is pursued in the more ecologically sound ways of the days in which it was founded.

Drive and Desire

Transportation Without Devastation

"The best, the most exquisite automobile
is a walking stick; and one of the finest things in life
is going on a journey with it."

Robert Coats

I've often thought that if aliens were to land here and take stock of what they saw around them, they'd probably have a long list of things they'd think were nuts about the human race. Somewhere very close to the top of that list would be the way we've transported ourselves around over the past century, particularly the last sixty or so years.

Hey, I love my truck and my tractors here on Charlane Plantation, and I can't imagine trying to get the necessary work done on a place like ours without them. But I don't like to think about the pollution output and the carbon footprint they create when I'm out enjoying myself riding the back roads of the plantation checking on our forest, hauling farm materials, or working in the woods and pastures. The EPA asserts that pollution from our cars, trucks, buses, trains and planes is one of the largest sources of air pollution in the country. And, don't forget that there's also a large, cumulative addition of air pollution from recreational vehicles such as motorcycles, ATVs, boats, forklifts, generators, and even my gasoline lawnmowers, trimmers and leaf blowers—and yours. The good news is that many of our American manufacturers are beginning to address these issues and are making all this equipment better, more fuel efficient and cleaner burning. I've been working with two companies in particular that have made great strides in improving their products. New Holland, for instance, is one of the first heavy-equipment companies to embrace biodiesel and has led the way in this field. At present it is the only one to have made its products capable of running on 100 percent biodiesel (B100). The Stihl company has been making its products—chain saws, brush cutters, trimmers, blowers, and the like—with the lowest emissions of anyone on the market, far exceeding EPA standards. Companies that are taking their responsibilities seriously, like New Holland and Stihl, are to be commended for their efforts, and hopefully others will follow their lead.

While Toyota has been the leader in hybrid-car technology, GM has now introduced the Chevy Volt, and no doubt other hybrids and electrics are on the way. Companies like UPS and FedEx that use fleets of big trucks are experimenting with hybrids and electrics as well, and we'll get into some of this in further detail.

But let's face it, America and many other nations, are still addicted to oil, and when you put it all together—just in America—our traditional choices of transportation and use of the internal-combustion engine are, simply, devastating for our health.

While studies vary, it is believed that the US uses about 19.5 million barrels of crude oil a day to fuel its cars and other vehicles. China's oil use is growing rapidly, but is far below that of the US at present. Estimates are that China is using about 8.5 million barrels a day now and is on pace to using some 12 million barrels a day by 2020. The US Energy Information Administration (EIA) forecasts that by 2010, world oil consumption will grow to 85.2 million barrels per day. Any way you look at it, that's a lot of oil and a lot of pollution. Whether we're talking about the US, China, or anywhere else in the world, according to the EPA, a gallon of gasoline produces about 19.4 pounds of carbon dioxide seeping into the atmosphere, and a gallon of diesel produces about 22.2 pounds.

But our oily, greasy, gassy vehicles have a far more reaching and lasting impact: Water from rain, storm drains and ditches flows

The annual cost of fighting traffic smog from vehicles such as these in a daily jam on a Los Angeles freeway is estimated by the California state government to be as much as $28 billion.

directly to streams and bays, polluting them and their banks. We all live in watersheds of some kind, and our massive use of traditionally powered vehicles also has a less obvious impact than what's coming out of your car's tailpipe: oil and antifreeze leak onto our highways and eventually end up in our streams and rivers.

Not to be too extreme about all this, but the fact is that even washing your car in the driveway is not environmentally friendly as the soap ends up in the storm drains and in our streams. I'm not saying it's bad to wash your car, but commercial car washes do not expel their waste water directly into storm drains.

According to a report in the *Los Angeles Times*, citing statistics provided by the California Air Resources Board, 24,000 people in California annually—three times more than previous estimates— die each year as a result of exposure to smog caused by vehicles and factory smoke stacks. The state now considers the annual cost of smog to be roughly $28 billion.

Compiling data from several sources, including the National Automobile Chamber of Commerce, US Bureau of Transit Statistics, and the EPA's Office of Transportation and Air Safety: There were about 8,000 cars in the US at the turn of the twentieth century (1900). In 1960 the number was 74 million. By 2006 there were 251 million—and more than 600 million in the world. By 2030, that number is expected to double unless we change the way we get around.

Thankfully, we have choices. And these choices are becoming more embraced all the time. I'll address two: alternative vehicles and alternative fuels to make them run.

Perhaps the one innovation you've seen on the news the most—and, most importantly that you've seen on the road the most—is the hybrid car. The most successful ones to date, which you've more than likely seen on the roads, have been the Toyota Prius and the Honda Insight. Ford introduced its Escape Hybrid in recent years and now makes several hybrid models. Most car manufacturers have now jumped on the bandwagon and are making various models using hybrid technology.

A hybrid is basically an ordinary car, except that it has two motors, an electric one and a gasoline-powered one. A hybrid also generally employs the technology of capturing the energy that comes from applying the brakes to store in on-board batteries. The reason for the two motors is to embrace the strengths of each while also mitigating the weaknesses of each. For instance, gas is polluting and not efficient, but it is generally more powerful than electric, which is not polluting and is, generally efficient. Tesla Motors, which went public in 2010 (the first American car manufacturer to do so since Ford in 1956) initially made an extraordinary electric sports car called the Roadster that sells for more than $100,000. Tesla now makes other models that sell for less, and it is yet to be clear how successful they might be going forward.

In big cities, where heavy traffic is a leading cause of smog, the wide use of hybrids would have a beneficial effect on air pollution as much of the commuting time is in bumper-to-bumper traffic, during which an electric motor is sufficient and produces no exhaust. At speeds greater than 40 miles per hour, the gas motor kicks in. Given this hybrid use of energy, both from the batteries and the gas or diesel engine, mileage can be up to 30 percent greater than other vehicles.

I guess you could say those are the upsides. The downsides are that this technology—while explored since the first patent in 1905—is relatively new. The first large-scale production of hybrid cars, in Japan, didn't become available to the public until 1997. That means it's still more expensive than traditionally powered vehicles. And owing to its complexity, owners could experience larger repair bills. So prospective buyers need to calculate the financial economy of a higher-priced vehicle with lower fuel costs, based on current and projected gas prices, the number of miles driven a year, and the expected length of ownership. For many, it doesn't make economical sense, even if it makes environmental sense—although in the future, uncertain costs may come into play, such as "congestion" fees. It's something implemented in London, England, in 2003 and which many other cities either have or are considering, often based on vehicle type, penalizing those with gas guzzlers—in some cases to the tune of $50 a day. Britain is also bringing in a plan to charge cars for distances traveled on the nation's roads, not only as a tool to raise revenue and encourage car buyers to consider hybrid or alternative vehicles, but also to, as they suggest, lower congestion and pollution. According to London's mayor's office, compared to 2002, traffic congestion is 22 percent lower, carbon emissions have decreased 16 percent, nitrogen oxide pollution has declined 13 percent, and particulate matter is down by 15 percent.

Perhaps less constrained by personal financial options, corporations are increasingly considering hybrid options, also realizing the public relations benefit of "being green."

One of the first companies to embrace hybrid vehicles for their delivery fleets was FedEx which, as of this writing, operates more than 170 hybrid delivery vans around the world.

Hillary Evans, one of our researchers and writers at the Mother Nature Network (mnn.com), discovered some interesting statistics where American businesses have, in some cases, been working to help themselves by saving on fuel costs—and helping the environment as a nice side effect—by switching to hybrid vehicles.

As she wrote in an article on MNN, "Walmart looks to save $10,000 per truck every year with its new hybrid tractor-trailer designed by Eaton Corp. and Peterbilt. UPS expects a fuel savings of 176,000 gallons of fuel each year now that it's added 200 new hybrid delivery trucks to its fleet. Carbon emissions may or may not present a business expense in the future, but even without these costs figured in, commercial vehicles recoup their investment within just a few years."

As Hillary discovered from the Environmental Defense Fund, "medium and heavy-duty trucks account for 6 percent of carbon dioxide emissions. Delivery trucks idling in traffic burn unnecessary fuel and kick extra emissions into the air. These particles have been tied to respiratory problems like asthma, heart conditions, cancer, and even lower IQ scores in children.

According to Hillary's research, Coca-Cola's New York fleet of hybrid vehicles has resulted in a 32-percent reduction in emissions.

Another "green" contender in terms of transportation is the electric car. Again, like hybrids, they have been the subject of experimentation since nearly the beginning of the automobile. They produce zero emissions, but their range is limited, and they require frequent and inconvenient recharging, which has always been one of their biggest challenges. Without advanced battery technology, many believe, the cars will never come into widespread use and success.

It isn't that it hasn't been tried.

In 1996, General Motors unveiled the EV1. The company never offered the vehicles for public sale, but instead allowed special lease agreements in a select few states. A second-generation was also introduced, but the vehicles suffered serious design flaws, including sixteen cases of the cars catching fire due to faulty electric wiring. In 1999, the company discontinued making the vehicles, and in 2003 the company officially cancelled the program and recalled all the vehicles and destroyed most of them, aside from a few for museums and universities. Former GM chairman and CEO Rick Wagoner told *Motor Trend* magazine in 2006 that his worst decision during his tenure at the company was "axing the EV1 electric-car program and not putting the right resources into hybrids. It didn't affect profitability, but it did affect image."

By 2009, GM had returned to the electric car and began production on the Chevy Volt. Chevy has put a price tag of $33,500 for the current models.

But already on the streets are the aforementioned boutique Tesla Motors' sedan, which has remarkable specifications for running and recharging times, and the company's high-performance Roadster, which is far more like a Ferrari than anything else (and so is its price).

However, there is an interesting trend in electric vehicles that fits exactly the model of smart growth, as I've learned and appreciated from experts such as Ray Anderson and others: It's called the NEV, which stands for Neighborhood Electric Vehicle. Instead of designing a car for all forms of use, the NEV is designed explicitly for short drives in urban environments where, of course, emissions are of greatest immediate concern in terms of people's health and that of the environment.

They're light, not very powerful or fast—think of a really grown-up golf cart. But they are street-legal in most states, on roads with speed limits of 35 miles per hour or less, and can travel from thirty to sixty miles on a single charge—more than enough for the local store or commuting to work, especially in a smartly designed urban environment (which, as I've said, is what we need to do for the future; we can't redesign the past but we can properly design the future).

There are actually too many NEV producers to list here and, unfortunately, some exciting ones have come and gone in short periods of time. But there are more established manufacturers, such as those of conventional golf carts who are expanding their businesses.

It's been regarded as something we wouldn't likely see in our lifetime, but the mass-produced, private hydrogen fuel-cell vehicle might not be that far off. There have been, basically, hydrogen fuel-cell buses and vehicles on our roads as experiments, but Honda has been touting its very limited edition FCX Clarity as a success, while other manufacturers such as Hyundai say they will start mass production of vehicles by 2012.

Most manufacturers have either announced hydrogen fuel-cell lines or have rolled out prototypes, but as the economy has failed, the programs seem to be ever in flux. Ford, for instance, announced it was dropping its fuel-cell research and development, and in May 2009, the Obama administration officially dropped the funding of fuel-cell technology development. Energy secretary Steven Chu said the technology and finding a way to transport and make widely available hydrogen is not practical for the next ten to twenty years.

I am thrilled to say, however, that agricultural equipment manufacturer New Holland has released an innovative NH2 hydrogen-powered prototype tractor, which is part of its Energy Independent Farm program. As mentioned earlier, New Holland is also a leader in biodiesel use for agricultural equipment, and to date it is the only manufacturer of its kind to have the capability of using B-100 (100 percent biodiesel) in all their tractors.

It's worth mentioning again that efforts in biodiesel manufacturing are also being made by other companies that make power tools, and the like, used for landscaping and maintenance applications. Stihl, for one, is to be applauded for going far overboard to make their products energy-efficient, quiet, and low-emission. Many companies engaged in making lawn mowers, such as Scag, are starting to use propane or natural gas instead of only petroleum-based fuels. These are all admirable steps, and every little bit helps.

But in this chapter I want to get into options for our general transportation, in particular, alternative fuels, fuels that have for some time, or may in the future, be usable in conventional vehicles without requiring a retrofit.

The most prevalent is ethanol. It's been around for centuries, mostly in the form of alcohol for human consumption, but over time it has been used as lamp fuels and from 1908 onward, Ford Model T cars were able to be adapted to run on ethanol. Ethanol's use came to a stop with Prohibition in 1920 and didn't pick up again until the energy crisis in the 1970s, when ethanol began to be added to gasoline. It now constitutes fifteen to 85 percent of what we put in our tanks.

Traditionally made from sugarcane, corn or other grains, ethanol as a gasoline supplement or replacement has been made primarily from corn crops. Today, according to authorities, 97 percent of ethanol is made from products traditionally used for food production. This has caused quite a lot of controversy: The federal government's Congressional Budget Office estimates that the increase in ethanol production and the rising cost of corn is, in part, responsible for food prices rising 2 percent in 2006, 4 percent in 2007, and more than 5 percent in 2008. What's worse, from an environmental standpoint, is that to produce more corn in order to lower food prices and meet demand, we need more cornfields, more fertilizer, and more irrigation. While ethanol showed promise in helping us to get away from foreign oil dependency—certainly a noble purpose—it has caused the great "food vs. fuel" debate.

In addition to affecting the prices of corn, soybeans, and other food products, using ethanol for fuel could cause conversion of forestlands to open fields for production of these crops. Forests and grasslands are our most important "carbon sinks," soaking up carbon dioxide from the environment. Getting rid of these sinks increases the carbon footprint of making ethanol. Besides, corn requires a lot of energy to distill into nearly pure alcohol. The environmental impact of growing corn is not sustainable; the largest input of nitrogen into our land, and eventually, water, is fertilizer (which itself is made from nonrenewable resources). Corn also requires heavy use of herbicides and insecticides. According to the EPA, corn accounts for a quarter of the total acres of crops in the country, yet consumes nearly two-thirds of total herbicide used.

Thankfully, the government itself has admitted that ethanol from corn and some other similar crops is not a long-term goal.

"Corn-based ethanol is a bridge, an extremely important one, to the next generation of ethanol and biofuels," EPA Administrator Lisa Jackson in a public speech on May 5 2009, the day the agency announced its proposed ethanol policy.

"Why should we take two very limiting factors for human quality of life—food and energy—and convert one into the other?" asks professor David Tilman, from the University of Minnesota.

In fact, he thinks that biofuel created from diverse prairie grasses is more efficient and better for the environment than fuel made from food crops such as corn and soybeans.

So, basically, the best way to grow crops for ethanol production is not to grow them at all: harvest natural prairie grasses, he says.

"We have a vision of restoring a lot of prairie throughout the Midwest, and having something that will be mowed every year for

The most efficient and easiest manner in which to not use feedstock such as corn and soy for fuel production is to go even more natural, some experts say: We should be using natural, wild, diverse prairie grasses. *Photo Copyright © FreePixels.com*

hay and then either pelletized and burned, or converted into ethanol," says Tilman.

According to a study by Tilman, producing "cellulosic" ethanol from diverse plots of perennial grasses promises several advantages over corn-grain ethanol: greater yields, more ethanol, less pollution, and fewer greenhouse gases—and all without diverting a food source.

According to Tilman's study: "Perennial biomass such as native grasses would need little in the way of chemicals, energy, or even work—just mow it once a year. It wouldn't even need to be planted. "What we've seen is that we can get a lot of biomass produced in plots with no input of fertilizer, no irrigation, no input of pesticides, almost no energy input at all," says Tilman. With low energy inputs, cellulosic ethanol might produce four times more energy than the fossil fuel it consumes. "With little need for fertilizer or pesticides, native grass production produces little polluted runoff. Since the soil is never bare or plowed, little erosion occurs.

"Diverse grasslands, such as native prairie, produce 51 percent more energy per acre than corn, even though corn grain produces more ethanol per weight. "After 10 years, diverse plots produced 238 percent more energy than monocultures, such as switchgrass. Multispecies plots are more resilient too. And Tilman's past research has shown that diverse grasslands outproduce monocultures during drought.

"Prairie grasses' massive root systems sequester carbon, actually reducing greenhouse gases in the atmosphere. Raising prairie grasses for biofuels would not only produce less greenhouse gas than burning fossil fuels, it would actually remove and store 1.2 to 1.8 tons of carbon dioxide per acre per year over the course of a century.

"The researchers estimate that growing mixed prairie grasses on all of the world's degraded land would produce enough bio-energy to replace 13 percent of global petroleum consumption and 19 percent of global electricity consumption."

Production of ethanol has always been relatively standard, but there are some maverick companies close to producing fuel for vehicles from biomass material, such as waste wood from sustainable forestry practices—which as a forest landowner, certainly gets my attention.

When tree farmers like me have a harvest and are left with the debris of branches, bark, cut off end pieces, twigs and foliage, in the past we have had to either burn that waste or pay to have it dealt with. But nowadays, there is a better solution. In some areas of the country, we can actually get paid to have it processed into electricity or even liquid fuel products. Even overgrown understory within forest stands that are causing competition among the trees in the stand can now be harvested and used for this purpose. That's what I call smart, strong, and sustainable.

Take a look at Utah State University researcher Dallas Hanks: he's heading a study to determine if the ditches at the sides of the nation's southern roadways should be used to grow oil seed crops for biofuel production. He says there are ten million acres lining four million miles of road.

Far-fetched? Perhaps not—and possibly even a wise use of areas that are, for the most part, not being used productively. Or how about filling your tank with what was once household garbage that went to the local biofuel plant rather than a landfill? Even your old car tires, ground finely and turned into material that can be converted to a biodiesel.

One such company not only exploring these options but close to making them a reality is Broomfield, Colorado-based, Range Fuels (www.rangefuels.com).

Their technology has been in development since the early 1980s. The company is way beyond the experimental stage, and in 2010 completed the first phase of a new commercial cellulosic biofuels plant near Soperton, Georgia. They are on line and in production, with plans to begin phase two in 2011. The plant, according to Range, is taking material that was formerly discarded, "such as timber harvesting residues, corn stover (stalks that remain after the corn has been harvested), sawdust, paper pulp, hog manure, municipal garbage, and more, including highly productive grasses and trees, such as switchgrass, eucalyptus, miscanthus (elephant grass), and hybrid poplar" according to Bob McDonald, Senior Vice President of Engineering, and turn it into low-carbon biofuels and clean, renewable energy. Range says it will produce approximately 10 million gallons of ethanol, methanol, and higher alcohols a year, with a goal of eventually achieving production of 100 million gallons of ethanol and methanol annually after 2012. Additionally, the company says, it will be able to change its process if market conditions demand DME (a diesel blend or substitute), gasoline, diesel, and power.

Range Fuels began a first-of-its-kind, fully integrated, thermo-chemical-conversion pilot plant in the first quarter of 2008 at its development center in Denver, where it successfully converted wood from Colorado pine-beetle kill and Georgia pine and hardwoods into renewable fuels. But the decision to build their first commercial plant in rural Georgia was made because the state has an abundant supply of renewable, sustainable non-food feedstock in its forests, and it makes economic and environmental sense to be as close to those raw materials as possible; Range hopes it will be able to sell the fuel it creates as locally as possible, so that the carbon-footprint balance sheet balances in favor of the environment.

"Our focus on efficiency goes beyond how we produce biofuels and energy—it also extends to where we produce it," Range Fuels' Bob McDonald says.

The company declares on its website: "Our distributive design lets us bring systems to sources where biomass is most plentiful, instead of having to transport biomass to a central processing site. This reduces transportation costs and related transportation fuel consumption. Our modularity also allows the system to grow as more biomass becomes available. Simply adding another module— which is easy to ship and install—immediately doubles the output. We put our systems where they are needed, in just the size that is needed."

Supported and financed in part by well-known venture capitalist Vinod Khosla, co-founder of Sun Microsystems, the company started its unique, proprietary method of converting woods into renewable fuels in 2008 using a two-step process. The first step is turning the biomass into a synthetic gas using heat, pressure, and steam, and then passing the syngas over a proprietary catalyst that yields cellulose-based biofuel of just about any specific configuration, be it a replacement for gasoline, diesel, or even aviation fuel or compressed-gas-based fuels.

Range Fuels' process has a zero carbon footprint, has low emissions, and is thermally self-sustaining.

The company has a pretty cool outlook on energy, co-opting the classic "miles per gallon" and translating it into what Kevin Biehle, Range Fuels' Vice President of Production, calls "miles per tree." Hey, ya gotta love that!

Says Mike Cate, Range Fuels' Vice President of Procurement and Fabrication, about the company's motivation to be so innovative and ahead of the curve in an entirely new industry that itself is far ahead of the conventional energy curve: "We can convert a variety of materials, including waste material that serves no useful purpose ... we call this conversion 'waste to value.'"

I've been particularly excited by Range Fuels' prospects—no surprise considering my family and I live on a forested plantation not too far from where they've chosen to build their first commercial plant. Still, there's just nothing but positive out of a science directed at turning waste into value (energy).

Other leading companies in the industry, though they are each embracing different technologies to achieve the same results, include Coskata, in Warrenville, Illinois, and Verenium, based in Jennings, Louisiana.

Coskata is developing the efficiency of a three-step process for converting just about any carbon-containing materials into syngas—including crops such as switchgrass and miscanthus; wood chips, forestry products, corn stover, bagasse and other typical agricultural wastes; municipal waste and industrial organic waste such as petroleum coke—which is then fermented into ethanol and separated from the solid residue. The microorganisms (rather than chemicals) the company is using to break down the base carbon materials also consume carbon monoxide and carbon dioxide released in the process. They do this at low pressure and temperatures, so the actual process is energy-efficient and carbon-neutral.

The company claims that its aim is to be able to create ethanol at the lowest possible cost—in a process that will make it a direct competitor and, indeed, a replacement for petroleum-based gasoline. Coskata (www.coskata.com) has the potential to yield more than a hundred gallons of ethanol per ton of dry carbonaceous input material, the company claims, while also using less than half the water required to refine a gallon of petroleum-based gasoline.

While Coskata'a pilot facility is in Illinois, just like Range Fuels, the company has constructed a commercial facility in Madison, Pennsylvania, south of Pittsburgh.

"With feedstock flexibility, Coskata can build plants in almost any country around the globe," the company says on its website. "Coskata will be able to reduce dependence on foreign oil in regions of the world such as North America, Latin America, Asia, and Australia." The company believes its process gives it the ability to build plants of varying scales near local source material supply—be it wood biomass, agricultural waste, sustainable energy crops, or construction waste—and sell the ethanol directly to nearby population centers.

Meanwhile, the Illinois lab continues to work on new and improved microorganisms that can more efficiently break down carbon-based materials.

The Verenium Corporation (www.verenium.com) is taking yet another approach, creating new and more efficient enzymes to break down carbon-based materials. The company, which was purchased by BP in mid-July 2010—news that was missed due to the massive BP oil spill off the Louisiana coast—basically focuses not so much on energy creation as it does on the development of enzymes aimed at the creation of next-generation cellulosic ethanol, as well as high-performance, specialty enzymes that make soybean and sunflower seed oil extraction more efficient.

Janet Roemer, Verenium's president and COO explains that the company is developing enzyme strains allowing "for the simultaneous increasing of oil yields and improving the efficacy of meal production without requiring major changes to the existing plant layout."

The company's technology has been most widely embraced by Argentina's leading soybean and sunflower processor, Molinos Rio de la Palata, which reports a significant increase in oil yields using the new Verenium enzymes.

"The ability to squeeze extra yield from the same plant without increased chemical usage is critical to our philosophy of minimizing the overall environmental impact of our processes," said Luis Palacios, Molinos' Industrial Manager.

Verenium claims its enzymes can be used on nonfood feedstock, such as dedicated grass-energy crops, agricultural waste, and wood products.

This technology of finding the right enzymes to break down cellulosic material is also being researched in several institutions of higher learning. Georgia Institute of Technology has been involved in this for several years now, and programs all over the country have begun to investigate and experiment with ways to improve the process. Programs exist in states from New York to California, and in between, and it's encouraging to know that talented, capable minds are working on the challenges.

I find all this exciting, and one of many things I like about all three companies is that they have stemmed at least one traditional criticism of ethanol production: The use of feedstock.

The POET company (www.poet.com)—the largest ethanol producer in the US—has twenty-six plants all over middle America, each one consuming about 21 million bushels of corn to produce 60 million gallons of ethanol a year. But the company is actively pursuing a change from using food sources such as corn and soy to its next-generation cellulosic ethanol plants, which will produce fuel from corncobs, algae, wood chips, switchgrass, and other common resources. "The technology," the company's website says, "will allow us to produce cellulosic ethanol from any plant material."

Interestingly, and even more encouraging, is that ethanol is not the only fuel companies such as these, and others, are proposing to produce.

Biodiesel is, I think, one of the bright lights on the horizon and isn't the only fuel to come from plants; biodiesel is another exciting front that, I think, is perhaps even more exciting than sustainable ethanol production because not only is it sustainable, but it's also recycling at its finest. Imagine no more landfills. Your non-recyclable garbage (that is stuff that's not paper waste, cans and bottles, and plastics) no longer goes to the dump. Even your old car tires are hauled off to the local biomass fuel plant, where they're converted into biodiesel. Restaurants sell their old vegetable oil to companies that collect it and in turn sell it to biomass fuel plants.

Not only is it not that far-fetched, but it is actually old technology to a degree. In fact, the inventor of the diesel engine, Rudolf Diesel, ran his invention on peanut oil. Recognizing that the time was far off for what has become known as biodiesel fuel, he said in the late 1800s that, "The use of vegetable oils for engine fuels may seem insignificant today, but such oils may become in the course of time as important as petroleum and the coal tar products of the present time," according to online resources on Diesel.

And that's the primary difference: Biodiesel is not a petroleum (unless using recycled tires, of course) product. It's truly an alternative fuel, made from biomass sources rather than a fossil

It would take the area of a football field for corn or soybean to produce the same amount of oil that algae can produce in the area of a two-car garage using water-and-plastic tubing photobioreactors such as this one. *Photo courtesy solar.calfinder.com*

fuel pumped from the ground. As such, it is a renewable energy source. It can be made from soybeans, but of course like the corn used to manufacture ethanol it's not desirable to be turning our food sources into fuel. Biodiesel can be made from flax, mustard, rapeseed, sunflower, palm, hemp, and it can also be made from animal fats and waste vegetable oil.

In many cities, there are now small-scale operations reclaiming restaurant deep-fry oil and turning it into biodiesel—though there has been wide criticism that there is no federally mandated or industry-wide standard of quality—even if it is kinda cool that your diesel exhaust smells like french fries! So, the consensus I've heard first-hand and read from many people with experience in the field—both those making biodiesel from cooking oil and those buying and using it—is that one needs to be certain of the quality, and consistent quality, of the "mom-and-pop"-sized biodiesel operations.

According to University of Minnesota researcher and assistant professor Jason Hill, biodiesel is a more responsible fuel source than even ethanol from any source. It yields 93 percent more energy than is required to produce it, and compared with soy, uses

1 percent of the nitrogen, 8 percent of the phosphorus, and 13 percent of the pesticides—and less toxic chemicals too. During my 2007 "Green Leaves and Blue Notes" tour of Germany, which resulted in my *Live In Germany* CD released in 2008, I was not only touring and playing concerts, but also doing public relations and media events for forestry interests in Germany.

In the process, I had the opportunity to stay with several private forestland owners and tour their lands, learning of some of their methodologies and practices. One of the most interesting experiences I had was on the lands of Matthias Graf von Westphalen, who owns forests and agricultural lands in Bad Wünnenberg, Wasserplatz in East Central Germany. Matthias has quite a unique setup, and is experimenting with several concepts of sustainable energy. He has planted a range of fast growing tree species including hybrid poplar, eucalyptus and others as an experiment to see which ones grow fastest and strongest for cellulosic energy purposes. This will help determine the best species to use for making electric energy and liquid fuels from biomass.

But even more interesting, Matthias grows rape (a plant similar to sunflowers) as part of his agricultural operation, and takes some of the rape seeds from his harvests, crushes them and processes them in a facility on his property into a biofuel that he uses to run his tractors, trucks and other farm equipment.

Therefore, he is practicing true sustainability … growing his own fuel to run his operation. Additionally, he has several wind turbines on his property that create electrical energy that is sold to the "grid." I found this fascinating, and believe it is a wonderful model for others that might want to engage in this kind of self-sustaining farming.

Obviously, there are substantial costs to the equipment needed to press the seeds and convert into biofuels, as well as some costs to convert the machinery so that it can run on this type of fuel. And it takes some time to recoup those costs, therefore it's not something that every farmer could afford.

But if there were incentives offered through government programs that would encourage such efforts, I believe we would see much more of this kind of sustainable farming. The addition

Matthias Graf von Westphalen (at left) grows his own fuel. *Courtesy Chuck Leavell Archives*

of the wind turbines and experimental forestry make it even more interesting and intriguing. Hopefully in the future we will see such incentives for our farmers here in America so that we can follow Matthias' lead.

One of the most exciting biomass sources for biodiesel, I think, is algae, though it's proved to be a very volatile and inconsistent industry, with companies coming and going faster than our ability to accurately and reliably cite their progress and research here. Researchers have been working on the concept for years, but there are now plants growing algae—which can double in weight three to four times in a single day, and eat up a lot of atmospheric carbon while doing so.

I'm not certain there is a more unstable—or let's say inconsistent, corporately speaking—form of alternate energy than bioalgae. During the course of researching and writing this book there were some relatively high-profile industry leaders which despite years of promising research and development

Wind turbines on Matthias' land. *Courtesy Chuck Leavell Archives*

efforts, suddenly hit financial brick walls and vanished. So instead of talk about who's doing what, I'd like to just highlight the very apparent fact that there is clearly massive allure, if not outright elusive promise, in the possibilities of bioalgae. Dozens of companies all over the US and, in fact, the world, are attempting to find economical ways of making bioalgae an economical reality.

On the surface, it seems simple enough: Algae doesn't require traditional farming methods that include food stocks or even soil, and can use wastewater, and even seawater, in otherwise environmentally compromised locations, such as California's Salton Sea.

There are now dozens of bioalgae plant projects in North America alone, particularly around the hot, sunny southern states. Some are open-pond concepts while others are bioreactors that are challenged by the inefficiency of requiring artificial (read: energy-hungry) light. Yet, very quickly, technologies are being developed to grow algae in closed-loop tube systems that can operate even on the low ambient light of Canadian winters, such at the innovative W2 plant in Guelph, Ontario. The company is working on a patent for its ingenious method of solving the problem of algae clinging to the interior of the tube walls, choking off all light and killing the macrobiotic environment. In this case, bioalgae is actually not the company's main business—it concentrates on waste-to-energy technologies using high-efficiency plasma streams—but it is using algae growth as its method of carbon sequestration, with the happy offshoot of growing algae for biofuel production.

At the top of the algae-production chain, however, is the San Francisco-based Solazyme, founded in 2003. It has found a way to grow algae in standard fermentation facilities quickly, efficiently, and on a large scale. And Solazyme is not just producing fuel, but creating oils from algae to replace the oil in just about every traditionally petroleum-based product, from oleo chemicals, to cosmetics, to foods.

The same is true of Amyris, based in Emeryville, California, which started using its breakthrough science to develop an effective anti-malaria drug but has expanded its industrial synthetic biology platform to provide alternatives to a broad range of petroleum-sourced products.

Sapphire Energy, with facilities in San Diego, California; Orange Country, California; and Las Cruces, New Mexico, boldly states that it was "founded with one mission in mind: to change the world by developing a domestic, renewable source of energy that benefits the environment and hastens America's energy independence."

First- and second-generation biofuels have not necessarily met the same standards as conventional, petroleum-based gasoline, jet fuel and diesel. But Sapphire is developing what it calls "Green Crude," which is an algae-derived oil that is processed by the same industrial refining processes as current crude oil, yielding "drop-in" replacement transportation fuels.

"Green Crude," the company says on its website, "fits within the existing infrastructure—from refinement through distribution, including the retail supply chain for cars, trucks, and airplanes." It's projecting oil from algae before 2012.

The Missouri University of Science and Technology is also getting very innovative: With all the underground mines in the state, scientists such as Dr. David Summers are developing algae to grow in the carbon dioxide-rich mines, which maintain a stable temperature. "We can use artificial light in short intervals and fool the plants into thinking that days and nights are very short [for faster growth]," said Dr. Summers, professor of Mining Engineering at the university.

I am consistently amazed at the ingenuity of small companies and of researchers when it comes to bioalgae. For instance, a team of researchers from the University of Minnesota partnered with the Metropolitan Council for a project to identify and grow algae that thrives in wastewater. The subsequent pilot project for growing algae in a wastewater treatment plant in St. Paul, Minnesota, will serve two functions: removing nitrogen and phosphorus from the water and producing algae biomass for use in the manufacture of biofuels.

The town council of the smaller municipality of Reynolds, Indiana, approved a plan by Indianapolis-based Algaewheel to build a special system using algae to process the town's wastewater.

New Jersey-based Garden State Ethanol has selected a closed landfill site in Woodbine, Pennsylvania, for the location of a $200-million biofuel plant that would use more than 100 bioreactor tanks to convert algae into ethanol and biodiesel oil. This facility plans to produce 13 million gallons of biodiesel oil and 25 million gallons of ethanol each year.

There are even companies that are investigating growing what's called heterotrophic algae—that is, algae that can be grown without any sunlight, algae that can be turned into oil that can be converted into everything from biodiesel to jet fuel.

A two-acre test facility called Coyote Gulch near Durango on the Southern Ute Indian Reservation was expected to be producing 3,000 gallons per-acre per-year of biodiesel from algae by 2010. To be commercially viable, the facility will need to produce between 3,000 and 4,000 gallons of biofuel per-acre, per-year on 150 to 200 acres. Officials anticipate the Coyote Gulch facility could reach that point within the next three years. It's not there yet, but has, indeed, begun shipping biodiesel.

Despite all these amazing and clever advances, the technology behind mass-scale fuel production from bioalgae faces formidable challenges. At a National Biodiesel conference in February 2009, Colorado State University professor Bryan Willson reported that the bioalgae company he co-founded, Solix Biofuels, has the ability currently to produce algae biodiesel—at $32.81 a gallon. So for now, the energy cost of producing algae biodiesel remains far from economical.

If algae is grown in open ponds, it's susceptible to cross-contamination from unfavorable algae (all it takes is one bird flying from another pond to the bioalgae pond), requires vast quantities of water, and can only be cultivated in hot, sunny climates.

Indoor facilities are more protected from contamination but their photoelectric energy requirements are prohibitive.

However, there continues to be been some fascinating developments in biofuel research.

In February 2008, Richard Branson's Virgin Atlantic became the first airline to flight test a jet powered in part by biofuel. The Boeing 747-400 flew from London to Amsterdam, carrying in one of its four fuel tanks a 20 percent mix of biofuel derived from coconut and babassu oil. That followed Branson's 2006 announcement that he was pledging $3 billion over the following ten years into alternative fuel research.

In early 2009, a Boeing jet took off in Houston on a test flight with one of its two engines powered by a 50-50 blend of conventional aviation fuel and jet biofuel made in part from algae.

The aircraft manufacturer's managing director of environmental strategy told reporters "The properties of the fuel are fabulous, in fact, the bio part of the blend has a lower freeze point than Jet A. The fuels we're testing now have equal or better energy content than the Jet A requirements."

He said that the company producing the test fuel, UOP, a division of Honeywell, could turn most plant oils into the alternative jet fuel.

Similar tests have been conducted by JetBlue Airways, Air New Zealand, Continental Airlines, and Japan Airlines.

Since natural gas is not a renewable resource, I'm only going to mention in passing how encouraging it is that existing gas and diesel buses are increasingly being converted to natural gas. According to Natural Gas Vehicles for America, 125 transit agencies are now operating more than 10,000 natural gas transit buses on American highways, and 20 percent of new bus orders are for natural gas propulsion.

Until sustainable alternative fuels and energies become widespread, natural gas is the better choice, and has also been adapted by larger fleets of shuttles and such vehicles, most apparently at some of the busiest airports.

There has also been an increased private-sector embrace for cleaner-energy commercial vehicles. The city of San Francisco, for example, charges lower fees for hotels and parking companies that use only alternative fuel: $2.65 a trip vs. $7.95 for others (2007 numbers).

The burgeoning popularity of alternative-fuel and hybrid vehicles is encouraging and beginning to make economical sense for carmakers and car buyers alike. But the best and greenest solution for our general transportation needs is public transit, integrated into smart and sustainable urban planning, as I've said in previous chapters.

It has its controversies here in America, as it's seen by some as a "right" to own and operate a private vehicle. And, I certainly can't say that I don't enjoy driving myself. But given the choice between a multi-hour drive from my farm to catch a plane in Atlanta, and taking an economically friendly, high-speed rail train that takes a quarter of the time, lets me rest, relax, read or even nap, believe me, I'll take the train! For many of us, me included, this isn't yet an option. There have been plans for many years to build a high-speed rail that runs up through Middle Georgia, but it's not a reality yet.

According to the American Public Transportation Association, Center for Transportation Excellence, and the National Resources Defense Council, if one in ten Americans chose public transportation daily rather than use automobiles, we would reduce our reliance on foreign oil by 40 percent. The savings would be equivalent to enough oil to power a quarter of all homes for an entire year.

If one in five left their cars at home and took public transportation, our carbon monoxide (not dioxide) emissions would be 20 percent less, a greater savings than the combined emissions from all chemical manufacturing and metal industries.

The world's most efficient rail system is run by the Japanese. Their now-famous bullet trains went into operation, as did similar rails in Europe, back as far as in the 1960s and are the most popular way to travel. In fact, high-speed rail is more convenient and desirable that some air services are no longer viable, such as Paris to Brussels or Cologne to Frankfurt.

What's more is that it's the least environmentally damaging way of people to get from one place to another (in place of any distance beyond walking or bicycle, that is). The energy consumption per passenger per mile is lower by far, and there's a dramatically reduced land usage for passenger capacity as opposed to freeways.

Even in the more rural or mountainous areas of Japan not suitable for high-speed trains, the Japanese are converting their pollution-spewing diesel-electric locomotives with hydrogen-powered fuel cells, and they capture the energy used in breaking to charge batteries.

There has always been the argument that the continental United States is simply geographically too large to make rail economical, given, among other things, the infrastructure to construct a mass system passengers will find more convenient than their cars.

These days, Turkey, Taiwan, and South Korea are among countries with successful high-speed rail.

Sadly and surprisingly, as of this writing, America has none.

However, in June 2009, Quentin Koop, the chairman of the California High-Speed Rail Authority, announced that an 800-mile statewide system of trains, some of which will travel in excess of 200 miles an hour, had been approved.

"California is the only state in the country that already has in place $9-billion in voter-approved financing, environmental clearances and an adopted route for a true high-speed train," said Koop.

That announcement followed President Barack Obama's speech in April 2009, as part of his national recovery plan, to build high-speed rail all over America.

In part, what the president proposed was: "a vision for

Now recognized all over the world, the Japanese "bullet" trains such as this one speeding through the Ginza District in Tokyo, have become a favored method of travel for many Japanese. *Photo courtesy Wallpedia.com*

high-speed rail in America. Imagine boarding a train in the center of a city. No racing to an airport and across a terminal, no delays, no sitting on the tarmac, no lost luggage, no taking off your shoes (in a security check). Imagine whisking through towns at speeds over 100 miles an hour, walking only a few steps to public transportation, and ending up just blocks from your destination. Imagine what a great project that would be to rebuild America.

"In France, high-speed rail has pulled regions from isolation, ignited growth, re-made quiet towns into thriving tourist destinations. In Spain, a high-speed line between Madrid and Seville is so successful that more people travel between those cities by rail than by car and airplane combined. China, where service began just two years ago, may have more miles of high-speed rail service than any other country just five years from now. And Japan, the nation that unveiled the first high-speed rail system, is already at work building the next: a line that will connect Tokyo with Osaka at speeds of over 300 miles per hour.

"There's no reason why we can't do this," Obama said in his speech. "This is America. There's no reason why the future of travel should lie somewhere else beyond our borders. Building a new system of high-speed rail in America will be faster, cheaper and easier than building more freeways or adding to an already overburdened aviation system—and everybody stands to benefit."

As Obama pointed out in February 2009, China has realized that the era of cheap and easy oil is over; the Chinese have taken a good look at America and decided that we got it wrong: The automobile is NOT the way to go. In recent years they have experienced their own problems with traffic, and over the past year, the country has put itself well on its way to converting the entire country to sustainable, green transportation, building 5,000 miles of brand new high-speed rail comparable to the French TGV (200 + mph), plus 36 new, comprehensive urban, citywide systems. According to one co-operative of American designers, engineers and planners, the new Shanghai metro system will be the largest in the world when complete in just a few years.

"You go to Shanghai, China right now," Obama told reporters, "and they've got high-speed rail that puts our railroads to shame. America has always had the best infrastructure." Not anymore.

When I think of this in environmental terms, in terms of smart and sustainable growth of this country, it makes so much sense; the future of our transportation models cannot be the same as our past.

While there are all these varying proposals for alternative fuels and alternative vehicles and modes of transportation, some more immediate steps are possible. Among them, proposals to lock gasoline and diesel at $4 a gallon—no matter what OPEC's output and the oil companies dictate. Ray Anderson is among the most vocal proponents of increasing federal gasoline taxes to keep gas at $4 a gallon—which would, among many factors, let car buyers truly gauge the economy of buying hybrids.

Yet another proposal, which has been around for years but in 2009 took a leap forward, is the idea of taxing drivers based on the amount they drive: a by-the-mile road tax. The technology wasn't functionally available in years past, but some say now that with GPS, it would be much more realistic to enforce.

It is definitely controversial, and critics see such a plan as an infringement on freedom and privacy. But a number of transportation officials are looking further down the road: As alternative fuels and alternative vehicles such as hybrids and electric or hydrogen-powered cars become more popular and more widespread, the traditional by-the-gallon tax on fuel is not going to cover road building and maintenance.

The state of Missouri, like other states and the federal government, has seen gas tax revenue steadily decline, in part because of the failing economy but also, officials admit, because of rising mileage in newer vehicles and alternative-fuel vehicles.

At the end of a two-year study, the multi-jurisdictional National Surface Transportation Infrastructure Financing Commission voted unanimously to move forward with a field test of a road tax, now being conducted by the University of Iowa. The $16-million field test will eventually include 2,700 vehicles in six states. The vehicles, equipped with computers and GPS devices will track the miles traveled and send the data wirelessly to a billing center that will generate simulated bills.

While critics also complain that this high-tech approach might also allow authorities to track drivers' speeds and possible traffic-law infringements and send out tickets accordingly, the commission is also exploring the low-tech approach of simply recording each vehicle's annual odometer reading. However, the high-tech approach is favored, as proponents argue that the information gathered via satellite could allow officials to reduce traffic congestion, particularly by charging a different by-the-mile rate based on rush hour, for instance.

The commission set 2020 as the target year for phasing out the federal fuel tax, which is currently 18.5 cents a gallon. The road tax would, the commission estimates, be between one to two cents a mile for cars and light trucks.

So as we can see, we are coming to a cusp concerning transportation in our country. We are seeing many new technologies emerge and begin to play a role in how we get from point A to point B. We all need to keep our eyes and our minds open as to the ones that show the most promise, and that are the best and most practical for us to pursue. In the meantime, we should all play our part in being as energy efficient as possible when we look at how we get around. It is encouraging to see so many folks these days paying closer attention to this challenge, and I know that together, we'll be able to better our mobility methods.

When a House
Is More than a Home

Smart and Green Buildings

*"Besides being a super efficient and healthy home,
a green home can be aesthetically pleasing beyond your
imagination. Your home can also be affordable.
With the rising costs of fuel, a green home makes sense."*

Laura Turner Seydel

When we think of "smart" houses we generally think of homes that are sort of like big computers—as one home builder theorized.

As far back as 2006, at a conference in California of more than a hundred of the nation's top home builders, speakers were predicting "online" houses: Buildings that, through a secure website, you could turn lights on or off, adjust the heating or cooling, lock or unlock doors, from anywhere in the world.

As MSNBC reported at the time, such homes "can send you messages. Door sensors can tell you when (or if) the kids have arrived home; a motion sensor can tell you whether Grandma got out of bed this morning. One conference speaker claimed that the most commonly stolen item in homes is prescription drugs, often by cleaners, baby-sitters or even visiting friends or family. 'Your house can text you,' he said, 'that your medicine cabinet was opened at 10:45 this morning.'"

Basically, any device that uses electricity can be put on a home network that can then be controlled remotely, whether that's through the internet, by voice command, a hand-held device or motion detectors which can turn lights on and off when people enter or leave a room and also control the temperature as desired.

Microsoft co-founder Bill Gates famously spent a reported $100 million on his smart home, which not only changes lighting and ambient temperature and humidity but goes so far as to change the digital pictures hanging on the walls to suit the taste of the person entering the room (if the person is wearing a personalized electronic tag).

Think of trash cans that monitor what's tossed away and then instantly generate an online shopping list for replacements. How about washers and dryers that sent you a text message that their cycles are done? Or refrigerators that create dinner recipes based on ingredients that have been scanned in, just like at the checkout line, when you've put them away once you got home from the grocery store? No more standing there with the fridge door (and your mouth) open wondering what to make, while letting all that cool air escape!

This is an extreme example, of course—but as Boyce Thompson, editorial director of the BUILDER group of magazines published by Hanley Wood, which organized this 2006 conference of builders, says, there is more motivation to build "smart" homes than the embrace of new technology or gimmickry or even possible convenience. It's an economic bonus.

New-home builders need to compete against the used-home market. In 2005, 8.2 million houses were sold in the US—7 million of which were "existing homes with outmoded floor plans, obsolete home wiring, and no home office space."

What's more important is that "smart" homes can save a third or more on electrical and gas consumption (and cost), according to nearly a dozen prominent solar-energy installation companies.

So like the motivation for real change in just about everything in our lives, the economics of smart, strong and sustainable living is turning out to be the strongest catalyst.

I'd like to point out a couple of the most prominent of the commercial retrofits taking place (out of the hundreds, maybe thousands, currently going on in America and around the world).

The one that caught my attention right off is New York's Empire State Building. Famously constructed in little more than a year during the Great Depression—from 17 March 1930 to its 31 May 1931 ribbon cutting—many things have made the Empire State Building special, from its architecture, one-time record-holder as the world's highest skyscraper, its remarkable observation decks, even becoming a character, of sorts, of its own in the original 1933 King Kong film with Fay Ray. But like all buildings of its era, efficiency was not part of the design, construction, or maintenance agenda.

I personally found it fitting that what's regarded by many as the "world's most famous office building" would be among the most prominent to undergo a futuristic retrofit. The owners of the building were just as aggressive in assembling their retrofit consultancy team as they were with their intent on taking the Empire State Building into the next century and beyond.

It's a retrofit costing hundreds of millions of dollars, but $20 million of that is earmarked for energy efficiency specifically. Co-owner Anthony Malkin may be an environmentalist, but he's also a capitalist: He wants to see payback for his investment. As he told reporters, "There was no assurance that what we were going to do was going to be successful," he said. "We knew that if we could do this work at the Empire State

A team of experts from all over America advised on a $20-million retrofit of the famous Empire State Building which is expected to save nearly $4.5 million a year in operating costs—and serve as a high-profile model for what former president Bill Clinton (whose foundation is deeply involved in the retrofit) describes as proving the business value of environmentally economical retrofits.

Building, one of the largest tourist attractions in the world, the world was going to stand up and take notice."

He went to the best for advice: The famous environmental consulting firm Rocky Mountain Institute in Boulder, Colorado, engaged a team of experts from the Clinton Climate Initiative, a program of the New York-based William J. Clinton Foundation; Jones Lang LaSalle, a global real estate investment firm with headquarters in Chicago, and Johnson Controls, a Milwaukee-based firm that specializes in the building efficiency market and that he hired to oversee the retrofit. Ultimately, Malkin spent nine months investigating a reported sixty-seven ways to reduce energy use at the pre-World War II office tower.

All told, his $20-million investment will improve the skyscrapers 6,500-plus windows, each of which will be removed, a special film added, and the glass replaced with an inert gas inserted between the panes—all on site. The windows will reduce heat gain in the summer and heat loss in the winter. The cooling and heating systems are also being upgraded. Though it only makes sense, when the building was constructed and steam radiators were place under each of those 6,500 windows, half the heat went into the rooms as intended and the other half of the heat went out through the walls of the Empire State Building into the cold New York air.

Special insulating barriers are being placed behind the heaters now to keep all that expensive, CO_2-generating heat within the building, further reducing pollution and increasing efficiency.

Further, CO_2 sensors are being installed in every unit in the building, and tenants will have real-time access to exactly what their carbon footprint is and how much energy they are using.

High-efficiency lighting is being installed, as are sensors that will reduce artificial lighting when natural lighting reaches a pre-determined level in any given room.

Tenants save money and lower their environmental impact. All told, Malkin and his teams are expecting that the retrofit is going to save $4.4 million a YEAR in operating costs (paying for itself in less than five years) and raise the efficiency of the Empire State Building.

"The heck with making people 'do the right thing,'" Malkin said. "I would rather get them to do what makes economic sense. Everything here is about dollars. I'm improving my competitive position. I'm improving my ability to attract tenants and make more money.

"On the other hand, I'm also trying to change the world. We're creating jobs. And we will reduce the amount of money that is sent overseas for energy. That's a good security policy and economic policy."

Meanwhile, Malkin is out to prove by example that energy retrofits are a "commercially intelligent investment." He hopes the Empire State model will be replicated, and he's placed his team's findings online so that others don't have to reinvent the wheel.

According to New York Mayor Bloomberg, the project team is "showing the rest of the city that existing buildings, no matter how tall they are, no matter how old they are, can take steps to significantly reduce their energy consumption. If they lead the way, others will follow," he told a news conference.

As former President Bill Clinton has said, "We will never conquer climate change until we prove it's good business to do so."

When the project is completed in 2013, the building will be in the ninetieth percentile of energy-efficient properties in the United States, Jones Lang LaSalle said. Work has already started, and the building's energy use is expected to decrease by almost 20 percent during the next two years, when most of the measures will be implemented. Carbon dioxide emissions from the building are being slashed by 105,000 metric tons over a period of fifteen years, which is equivalent to CO_2 emissions from the use of approximately 11 million gallons of gasoline.

Buildings account for 80 percent of the carbon footprint of New York City, Mayor Bloomberg said, which is more metric tonnage than is emitted by the country of Portugal.

Malkin should be praised for his initiative, but he's following in some pretty solid footsteps: The Chrysler Building in New York, Wrigley Building in Chicago, Phoenix Tower in Houston, Prudential Tower in Boston, and Transamerica Pyramid in San Francisco, to name a few, are Energy Star-certified.

Energy Star, which surely by now you've seen on one or two (or more) of your household appliances, just marked its first decade as a voluntary ratings program administered by the US Environmental Protection Agency. According to the agency, out of 5 million commercial buildings in the US, slightly fewer than 10,000 have qualified for Energy Star rating—in 2009, a record 3,900 buildings measured up, as it were. Great news? Well, the sober fact is that at this rate, it will still take more than a thousand years for the US's commercial building stock to fully reach Energy Star certification.

A new group of international commercial leaders—CEOs of some of the top two hundred companies in the world, from the US to the European Union, Japan, Brazil, and India, call themselves the World Business Council for Sustainable Development.

They have proclaimed that the world is "sleepwalking into crises."

"Building professionals, owners, and users do not grasp the urgency and remain unmotivated to act," they said in one report said. "Business-as-usual inertia is a drag on progress. ... The sleepwalking path achieves occasional advances, but these are soon lost and total energy consumption is much higher by 2050. The number of low-energy buildings grows erratically and slowly.... The building sector must radically cut energy consumption—starting now—if countries are to achieve energy security and manage climate change."

With Malkin, that's preaching to the choir. "If we don't cut the energy consumption in cities, we cannot sustain life as we know it on Earth," he said.

Worldwide, commercial and residential buildings account for 40 percent of global energy consumption and the resulting carbon footprint, according to the World Business Council. That's more greenhouse gas being emitted from buildings than from cars, trucks, trains, and planes combined. In cities, where more than half the world lives, buildings account for up to 80 percent of the carbon footprint, and in that category, office buildings emit more greenhouse gas than any other commercial structure.

One of the Rocky Mountain Institute's consulting engineers, Caroline Fluhrer, who is working on the Empire State Building retrofit, says, "Everybody recognizes that over 70 to 80 percent of the buildings that exist today will exist in 2050. We can't just focus on new buildings. We need to retrofit our existing stock. It's a huge opportunity."

Politicians and various study groups go back and forth on how much of these kinds of measures should be mandated, how many should received tax credits—what the value and longevity of those tax credits should be, and so on.

But the point is, as most of these proponents agree—that "we're finally getting the message out," says Karen Penafiel, Vice President of Advocacy for the Building Owners and Managers Association International (BOMA), a Washington, D.C., trade group, "Finally getting the message out that this makes sense, not just from the tree-hugger mentality, but also making the financial case."

Maura Beard, an EPA spokeswoman, says there's nothing pie-in-the-sky about energy-efficient commercial buildings, "The effort to be environmentally sustainable is an important movement in the commercial building arena right now. These are real buildings operating and saving energy."

One of the benefits of retrofitting a building to Energy Star standards is the increase in the number of desirable tenants. "I'm attracting larger tenants with better credit, firms with their own mandates for sustainability," Empire State Building's Malkin says. "The point is, we're taking things in a whole new direction from where they have been. This is not theory. This isn't a neat slide show on the basis of what could be done. It's happening right now."

"The idea that the Empire State Building would undergo a green retrofit is immensely inspiring to building owners across the board, whether it's in New York or in any other city, because the Empire State has always been the signature building of New York," adds Carol Willis, founder, director, and curator of the Skyscraper Museum.

As Willis puts it, "The Empire State Building is the best place to go in order to see the city of New York and the lay of the land as you look out towards the continent or towards the ocean … The Empire State Building stands in this kind of exceptionalism that hopefully will never be compromised."

In Chicago, the former Sears (now Willis) Tower is undergoing an even more aggressive retrofit. On www.greenbuildingfocus.com, officials proclaimed that nearly 40 years after its construction, the Chicago tower—the world's third tallest building—is embarking on what could be its greatest adventure: a $350-million, top-to-bottom, environmental retrofit that would add wind turbines, solar panels, and roof gardens to its iconic profile and trim its electricity use to a fraction of current consumption.

The project was announced by the group that owns the 110-story building, American Landmark Properties, in partnership with New York-based investors Joseph Chetrit and Joseph Moinian. John M. Huston, who co-heads American Landmark Properties with Yisroel Gluck, said the retrofit would help maintain the building's competitive edge long into the future, although the decision was also personal.

"We baby boomers have done a lot of things to the planet that are not very admirable. We need to correct some of those things," Huston said. "When I leave this building, I want it to be in better shape than when I arrived five years ago."

Project officials are calling the retrofit the most significant of its kind ever attempted at an existing building. All of the building's 16,000 windows are being replaced (the Empire State Building has less than half that number), which alone could save up to 60 percent of heating energy. Energy-efficient mechanical and lighting systems are being installed, and the building's 104 elevators and 15 escalators, along with its plumbing systems, are being modernized.

Also planned is on-site renewable energy. Solar hot water panels would adorn the ninetieth-story roof, which is already carpeted with an experimental garden, and several varieties of roof-mounted wind turbines will be tested for their performance at those altitudes.

In all, the building's base energy consumption would be reduced by a whopping 80 percent, saving 68 million kilowatt hours annually or 150,000 barrels of oil every year—enough electricity to power a Chicago neighborhood of 2,500 homes for a year. Those achievements, along with green cleaning, recycling and bike-sharing programs already in place, should be enough to earn

LEED Platinum, the highest sustainability designation of the US Green Building Council's LEED rating system, Huston said. The cost of the retrofit is due mostly to the building's cavernous size. It has 3.8 million square feet of rentable space, which makes it about 30 percent larger than the Empire State Building.

The bulk of the work currently underway is expected to be complete in roughly five years. The project will create almost four thousand jobs, according to project officials.

According to Huston, ownership will make a "significant" equity investment in the project, and it is pursuing government and nonprofit funding. The retrofit cost does not include a proposed hotel adjacent to the tower that was recently announced.

"It's a lot of money, and we are pursuing a lot of different financing alternatives," Huston said.

All of the operational cost savings generated by the project will flow directly to tenants, he added. Yet, the impact of the project, like the one at the Empire State Building, will reach far beyond the walls of the building, those involved with the retrofit say.

A Sustainable Technology Learning Center is planned to educate the more than one million visitors to the tower each year on ways to save energy and money. Additionally, the tower hosts about a thousand people annually who come from all over the world to learn how to design, build and operate a building of that size. Now, they will also learn how to improve the energy efficiency and sustainability of existing commercial towers, Huston said.

Research has show LEED ratings have become the equivalent of a gold star for eco-friendly tenants, too. A recent analysis by real estate researcher CoStar Group found that green-certified buildings had fewer vacancies than other buildings with similar age, size, and location.

Again, from the www.greenbuildingfocus.com site:

"The CoStar study, which included about three thousand green-certified offices, found that buildings with the council's certification enjoyed higher occupancy rates (90.3 percent) than their peers (84.7 percent) in the first three months of 2009. Certified buildings have fetched higher lease rates for several years. The CoStar report said the buildings rented at an average of $38.86

per square foot in the first quarter of 2009 compared with $29.80 per square foot for their peers."

"This isn't just a 'We are doing the right thing' movement," said Marc Heisterkamp, US Green Building Council's director of commercial real estate. "In the end, the numbers pencil out."

LEED certification has become a desired hallmark, just as the Energy Star tag on appliances. As the EPA's Maura Beard likes to say, in reference to the blue Energy Star logo, "The first step to green is blue."

Which brings us down to the everyday level of you and me. No, we're not about to sink $20 million into retrofitting our homes to be more energy efficient. But I've used the Empire State Building as what I believe to be one of the extreme and exciting examples of "smart" or "green" retrofits; the theories are sound and can be distilled down.

Sure, Bill Gates spent a fortune on his "smart" home—again, in part as an example of what's possible in the extreme; motion-detection light sensors are not expensive to install in anyone's home yet can save a great deal over the course of a year in electricity use.

Atlanta-based Laura Turner Seydel and her husband Rutherford have long been environmental activists, co-founders of Upper Chattahoochee Riverkeeper, and are both active on the boards of many other local and national groups including: Earth Share Georgia; the Nature Conservancy of Georgia; the North Georgia Water Planning District Board, the League of Conservation Voters Education Fund, and other worthwhile and notable causes.

The founding of the US Green Building Council (USGBC) in 1993 and program introductions by the council—especially their Leadership in Energy and Environmental Design (LEED) Green Building Rating Systems for New Construction, one of the council's many programs—got the pair thinking about plans to build their own "ecomanor" in Atlanta.

They wanted to change the perception of a green home. "Everybody has in their head a picture of an environmental home—usually some space-age design," Laura told one CNN interviewer. "We wanted to prove that it doesn't have to look odd."

As they say publicly on their website, eco-awareness has been a way of life for Laura and Rutherford. Years of earth-friendly living and community involvement have fueled the inspiration for their EcoManor residence. Inspiration was not one specific item or event, but more a continuation of their current lifestyle and a promise to their family that they would always do their part to be green.

Growing up, Laura Turner Seydel was more aware of environmental issues than most children. As daughter of CNN founder and philanthropist Ted Turner, she was exposed at an early age to how very ecologically desperate some areas of the world are. Rutherford was awakened to alarming environmental issues within Atlanta when he joined the Ecology Club at Lovett High School, which backs up to the eastern bank of the struggling Chattahoochee River. Recognizing the potential for her efforts, Laura began her commitment toward working to improve the environment in every way she could.

Together, Laura and Rutherford have established themselves as ecological activists, committed to making a difference in their own back yard.

"The single biggest inspiration for EcoManor occurred during a 1994 vacation to Colorado and trip to the Rocky Mountain Institute," they say. As I've mentioned before, the Rocky Mountain Institute in Boulder is a nonprofit organization guided by core principles of energy, buildings and land, businesses, climate transportation and water.

"Amazed at the Institute's energy efficiencies and the documented impact green building could make to the environment, Laura and Rutherford began to research building options for their own eco-home," they report on their site www.ecomanor.com.

But living "green" and promoting the ecology through various programs was not enough for the Seydels. While they did what they could to "walk the talk" by using recycled or bio-degradable products and monitoring their energy and utility bills, the rising costs of fuel and various energy and water shortages kept them questioning, "What more can we do for our home?"

The formation of the US Green Building Council (USGBC) in 1993 and program introductions by the council have made the

Seydels' green residence vision a reality. The USGBC is the nation's leading nonprofit coalition for advancing buildings that are environmentally responsible, profitable and healthy places to live and work. It is the USGBC that runs the LEED certification program discussed earlier in this book. (www.usgbc-ngcc.com)

LEED for Homes program is a rating system established to define "green building" and ultimately transform mainstream residential building towards more eco-friendly practices. The program offers a much-needed tool for homebuilders, homeowners, vendors, and local governments for building environmentally sound, healthy, and resource-efficient places to live. The certification is based on a checklist of environmental factors in six categories including: sustainable sites; energy and atmosphere; water efficiency; materials and resources; indoor environmental quality; and innovation and design process.

"Besides being a super-efficient and healthy home, a green home can be aesthetically pleasing beyond your imagination," Laura says. "Your home can also be affordable. With the rising costs of fuel, a green home makes sense." Working in tandem with SouthFace Institute, DR Construction, DES-SYN, Ed Castro Landscaping, and Harrison Design Architects, plans were drawn for EcoManor. "Ultimately, our goal is a livable world for future generations," added Rutherford. "EcoManor is an example of how green living can be possible."

As they publicly say, "the Seydels hope that by building EcoManor, the home can be used as a tool to illustrate the opportunities and benefits of earth-friendly, energy-efficient homes. The home will serve as a showcase to demonstrate life in a green, eco-friendly way through the use of eco-friendly products, energy-efficient products, and environmental options. More importantly, EcoManor serves as an educational tool for builders, architects, designers, vendors, landscapers, educators, and homeowners in an effort to promote green living, conservation options, and improved residential building practices. EcoManor is the first house ever to be certified by three of the country's leading green initiatives: the LEED standard, Greater Atlanta HBA's EarthCraft House program, and National Wildlife Federation's Backyard Wildlife Habitat program."

Laura Turner Seydel and her husband Rutherford built a model of the possibilities of future home development with the construction of their Atlanta "EcoManor." *Photo by DSH*

According to the family—and remember that many of these tricks and tips can be applied to the most modest home or even apartment:

EcoManor is the first residence in the Southeast to achieve LEED status, combining advanced insulating and air sealing techniques, Energy Star appliances and lighting, a ground source heat pump system and photovoltaic solar panels that will virtually power all of the home's daily electrical needs.

EcoManor Demonstrates Healthier and Resource-efficient Living

Low VOC (volatile organic compound) or organic paints, stains, and sealants emit little or no off gassing of chemicals to provide a healthier indoor environment.

Natural fiber fabrics on furniture and rugs also keep the air healthier to breath in the EcoManor.

Special household cleaning products and natural laundry and bathroom soaps keep from contaminating the water and air.

Soy-based insulation and pressed hay straw cabinets and wheat straw doors are formaldehyde-free and made from natural materials.

Properly sized heating and air conditioning systems using HEPA filters along with controlled ventilation help ensure any pollutants in the house are filtered or exhausted to the outside.

Wood floors are locally grown and from an environmentally certified plantation-grown wood.

Many of the materials used to build and decorate the house can be recycled.

EcoManor uses several means to conserve energy and water.

Solar tubes and skylights provide natural lighting throughout helping to save energy.

Twenty-six solar panels convert the sun's rays into electric energy.

A solar window in the master bedroom collects the sun's afternoon energy.

Windows on the southern side use a concept called Passive Solar Energy to capture the winter sun's warming rays to naturally heat the house.

Ground source heat pumps efficiently heat and cool the house.

Tankless water heaters provide instant hot water that helps save energy.

A smart system in the home controls a central switch-board that is programmed to offer special economy settings when the Seydels are away.

Foam and cellulose insulation make the home extremely energy efficient and quiet.

New, dimmable, compact florescent lights are energy-efficient, radiate less heat and provide the highest quality of light.

Automated faucets are used to lower water consumption.

Rainwater is channeled into cisterns that supply water for the home's toilets.

Dual flush/ low flow toilets from TOTO require less water to operate.

Greywater collected from the sinks and showers is filtered then collected in a cistern for watering the landscape.

Drought-tolerant landscaping requires less water and maintenance.

The EcoManor is an example of a large, upscale home that can be incredibly energy efficient. While it possesses mansion-like dimensions, "EcoManor is 6,200 square feet, but … is so efficient that we still conserve more resources and have lower utility bill costs than our neighbors," Laura says. In a 2009 interview with Michael Eastman, Laura said:

"After adding a few extra bells and whistles, like a permanent doormat made from recycled materials to keep dirt and toxins from being tracked inside the house, we achieved the Gold status. For us, Gold was the highest level of certification we could be awarded. Because of the size of the house, being larger than 2,500 square feet, we were automatically deducted 10 points that kept us from Platinum contention. We made the decision to build larger than the maximum square footage set forth by the US Green Building Council (USGB) because we have a large family that used every square inch of our previous 6,000-square-foot home. There are always houseguests in and out and we are constantly entertaining.

"Originally we were going to build our new home to EarthCraft standards, but my husband Rutherford was working closely with Dennis Creech, co-founder and director of the Southface Energy Institute, who informed us of the pilot program for LEED for Homes. He was so in tune with the latest environmental building practices that with him on our side we knew what we had to do. When the opportunity came to us to be the first LEED-certified home in the country we knew we had to invest a lot of ourselves and convince the right people in Atlanta to do the same thing. We already had EarthCraft-certified builders in place, so it wasn't hard for Rutherford to convince them to become LEED-certified. From there, we aligned ourselves with the right industry subcontractors who were experts in their fields and the rest fell into place.

"LEED for Homes was in its pilot program when we started rebuilding and it only made sense for us to be part of it. Instead of doing a minor green renovation, we were awarded four environmental certifications for our efforts in building EcoManor. EcoManor is also Energy Star rated, which means all of our appliances and mechanics are Energy Star approved and use less energy and water than standard appliances. We focused a lot of our attention on the outdoor landscaping and received the National Wildlife Federation's Backyard Certification. A good portion of the backyard was left in its original state, but we added a water feature for birds and other creatures, planted all indigenous and drought resistant plants, as well as planted for pollinators."

I've begun here by illustrating the extremes, with the hope that by showing you what can be achieved on massive scales—whether retrofitting of the Empire State Building or building the Seydel "EcoManor"—it will make the building requirements and techniques of the average American seem all the more reasonable, economically feasible, and ecologically wise.

First of all, if you're in a position to be constructing a new home, check out what the www.nahbgreen.org/Resources/Homeowners site advises:

Key Components of a Green Home. Green homes incorporate environmental considerations and resource efficiency into every step of the building and development process to minimize environmental impact. The design, construction, and operation of a home must focus on energy and water efficiency, resource-efficient building design and materials, indoor environmental quality, and must take the home's overall impact on the environment into account.

Energy-Efficient Features. Many of the energy-efficient qualities of a green home are easy to spot. Appliances, windows, and water heating systems will likely have Energy Star ratings. The home should also include efficient lighting fixtures and bulbs, such as compact florescent lamps (CFLs). Renewable energy sources, such as photovoltaic electricity and water heating systems, further decrease the overall energy consumption within the home.

Water-Efficient Features. Fixtures and appliances such as low-flow showerheads, faucets, and toilets, and Energy Star dishwashers and washing machines all conserve water. Programmed, low-volume irrigation systems, rainwater collection systems, wastewater treatment systems, and hot-water recirculation systems also save water.

Resource-Efficient Features. These decisions—from home size, to orientation on the lot, to floor plan layout—are made in the design of your home and development of the lot. The house orientation and design should take advantage of natural daylight to reduce lighting needs, and should use strategies to reduce heat gain in the summer and heat loss in the winter. The home should contain renewable materials, including renewable wood species such as pine, fir, spruce, or perhaps even bamboo; and recycled-content materials in carpets, tiles, and concrete formulations.

Indoor Air Quality Features. The heating, air conditioning, and ventilation system (HVAC) should be appropriately sized for an efficient and properly ventilated home. Fans in the kitchen and bathrooms should cycle fresh air inside, and release stale air. Low-VOC paints and finishes and wallpapers should be considered as well. While an expensive option to install, geo-thermal (energy) can save money in the long term and is a very eco-friendly and energy efficient option.

Outside the Home. In a green home, care should be taken to preserve trees and other vegetation native to the area. Landscaping should contain plants that are appropriate for the climate, and grouped according to water needs. Drought resistant plants should be considered in the landscaping decisions. Driveways and other impervious surfaces should be reduced as much as possible, and may be composed of gravel, permeable block pavers, grids, or other permeable systems.

Look for the Mark of a Certified Green Home. If you are in the market for a green home, look for the Green Certified mark issued by the NAHB Research Center. It is the homeowner's guarantee that the home was built according to one of the levels of green outlined in either the ICC 700-2008 National Green Building Standard or the NAHB Model Green Home Building Guidelines.

The NAHB Research Center is the sole certifier recognized by NAHB's National Green Building Program.

If you are simply renovating your existing home (Rose Lane and I have done it—we know there's nothing "simple" about renovating!), you have the opportunity to make some of these positive changes. For instance, we used special foam insulation (called Isolene) in our walls, ceilings, and floors when we renovated our kitchen and what we call our "great room." We installed energy efficient windows in the areas as well. The results were amazing, not only for insulating for temperature purposes, but it also helps with sound insulation. Our heating/cooling bill went down considerably and our comfort level went way up. We also used Energy Star appliances when we replaced our old fridge, freezer, and stove. Ours is an old farmhouse built in the 1850s and has presented us with challenges, as any old house will do. But little by little we've made headway, and whenever the opportunity presents itself to make positive changes, we do our best to upgrade. We've certainly learned that proper planning and execution in a renovation project can make a tremendous difference, and the results are significant.

One of the world leaders in large-scale, corporate real estate, CB Richard Ellis, is—like many of the company's competitors, very aware of the benefits of "green" renovations.

John O'Brien, head of CB Richard Ellis's investment team, recently told Toronto's *Globe and Mail* newspaper that, "Newer green buildings are generally much more effective at dealing with it. And while most companies who opt for green retrofits pay a premium in the short run, it's going to pay off long term."

"Green buildings used to just be 'want-to-have' properties," he says, "but they're rapidly becoming 'need-to-have.'"

Washington, D.C.-based writer and consultant Leanne Tobias, in her book, *Retrofitting Office Building to be Green and Energy-Efficient*, shares some of what she describes as absolutely essential tips when it comes to retrofitting an existing office or home to meet new, economical and green standards.

Get an energy audit: "When you see how much energy your building is using and how much you stand to save, you may just become a convert. In many cases, the provincial (or state) government will even pay to have the work done."

Find a qualified consultant: "Green building consultants can help mitigate the risks of a renovation. They can guide clients through unfamiliar processes and collaborate with contractors." She suggests starting by searching green building councils in the country and state you live in.

Pinpoint the most cost-effective strategies: Heating and cooling—"Eliminate waste in HVAC systems by programming on and off times. Utilize natural ventilation, and evaluate systems that run longer than they need to."

Lighting: "Replace incandescent bulbs with long-lasting LEDs or compact fluorescents. Use dimmers and sensors that turn off lights when no one is in the room."

Windows: "Rather than replacing them, consider adding a storm window or third layer of glazing."

Landscaping: "Make the switch from spray irrigation to drip irrigation to save water."

According to Washington's National Building Museum in a 10-tip plan to cut energy consumption, here's a list you can pass on to your contractor (or adopt yourself if you're doing your own home renovations.

Ten Tips to Go Green

1. Turn down the thermostat. Lowering it by just one degree can reduce heating energy costs by about 4 percent.

2. Use ceiling fans in the summer AND winter. By reversing the direction of the blades, warm air is pushed down, helping to keep rooms warm in winter.

3. Conserve energy by purchasing major appliances with an Energy Star rating. Compared to a 1990 model, an Energy Star-qualified refrigerator would save enough electricity to light a home for more than four and a half months.

4. Repair leaky fixtures. One drop per second from a leaky faucet can waste as much as ten gallons of water each week.

5. Install low-flow showerheads, faucets, and toilets. Low-flow faucets reduce water consumption and the cost of heating water by as much as 50 percent; using a low-flow toilet can save Americans 2.1 trillion gallons of water and $11.3 million nationwide every day.

6. Choose untreated textiles. Install carpeting, rugs, window treatments, and other textiles made from natural fibers, such as cotton or wool, which are untreated and free of toxins, such as pesticides or chemical cleaners.

7. Ask for flooring products made from renewable wood resources. Southern yellow pine, fir, spruce and even some hardwood species qualify, as does bamboo. Bamboo is one of the fastest-growing plants in the world, requiring no replanting and little fertilization or pesticides. Wood floors and other wood building materials that come from certified and sustainable forest sources are certainly desirable, and if possible, it's good to purchase wood that comes from a local source. Exotic and rare hardwoods that are extremely slow growing or in the endangered category should be avoided.

8. Select solid woods harvested from sustainably managed forests, when possible, for furniture or cabinetry, rather than pressed woods or composites that may contain formaldehyde or other chemicals that may be toxic and hazardous to your health.

9. Eliminate waste by choosing products that are biodegradable or recyclable. Consider the "lifecycle" of furnishings and accessories before purchasing: Are they made of materials that can be reused or recycled when the item eventually wears out or is no longer needed?

10. Recycle packing and shipping materials from any newly purchased item. Safely dispose of paint cans and other containers with contents that could potentially contaminate the ground or water supply.

Increasingly throughout the country, and, indeed, the world, new housing manufacturers are going into business regularly, even in the recent economic crisis, as they're finding more and more people are seeking prefabricated homes that take every possible advantage of their environment, of remanufactured and recycled goods, and basic designs that exploit location and physical placement on property to take the best advantage of light and shade.

Things are changing so rapidly, in fact, that instead of assembling a list of resources here that will be out of date, I'd highly suggest starting with the National Green Building Program (www.nahbgreen.org) and working your way from their helpful database to builders, contractors, and consultants they recommend who are more central to where ever you may be located.

Fighting Against the Finite

The Role of Our Renewable Resources

*"We can personally choose ... we can choose
individually to use a completely renewable resource.
I believe it's not just a fad—it's a movement."*

Jim Bernau
(Outspoken founder of Oregon's Willamette Valley Vineyards)

According to the US government's Energy Information
Administration, (EIA), America produced enough of its own
oil to meet requirements until about 1970.

Since then we have had to import ever-increasing amounts
of oil. We consume roughly 25 percent of the world's oil yet
produce less than half of what we need. As technology has
allowed more advanced drilling techniques to reach previously
unreachable oil fields, the massive, environmentally
devastating BP oil spill off the coast of Louisiana in 2010 has
shown how fraught with danger that is.

Given the political and national-security ramifications,
especially since 9/11, there has been an effort from the very
top of the American administrations—even from former
President and one-time oil man George W. Bush—to invest in
alternative, renewable energies.

The first and easiest renewable resource to come out of
the gate was ethanol, which has been mandated to be added

Just about any biomass, such as field grasses, can be used in place of feedstocks such as corn or soy to create biodiesel and other fuels—and place much less stress on the land, demand less (or no) fertilizer or pesticides. *Photo courtesy FreePixels.com*

to our gasoline in varied percentages. We've discussed this earlier in this book, but it bears a closer look here.

The trouble with the way in which America has been making ethanol is that it's been coming largely from corn and soy. Which is food. Right or wrong, biofuel was then blamed for the surge in food prices. The diversion of American corn from flour to fuel put flat corn bread out of reach for Mexico's poorest and caused riots in that country in 2006.

In 2009, 139 US ethanol plants produced fuel equal to 5 percent of US gasoline consumption. As of July that year, however, just 33 cellulosic ethanol plants were in the pilot or demonstration phase.

Corn ethanol costs $1 a gallon to make, but cellulosic fuel from stalks, leaves and straw costs are considerably higher—as much as $5 to $6 per gallon. It requires the injection of enzymes to convert plant matter into sugars that are then fermented into ethanol.

Michigan State University's Mariam Sticklen is one scientist trying to reduce that cost, to about $2 a gallon, by genetically engineering crops to produce their own enzymes. "It's still early days," she said, "but the world needs a no-food-for-fuel policy."

There is good, progressive, sustainable news to be found in all this.

In San Francisco, for example, the city has mandated a composting law that is believed to be the strictest in the nation. Residents now have three colored bins, one for recycling, one for true land-fill-bound trash, and a new one for compost. (The city, incidentally, was one of the first to ban plastic bags at supermarkets.)

Lawn clippings and food scraps will be sent to landfills where they can decompose quickly and produce methane gas—which is not only one of the most potent greenhouse gases, but can be collected for conversion to energy. The resultant compost will be headed to area farmers and vineyards to be used as natural, organic fertilizer.

"The city has been progressive, and they've been leaders and it appears that they're stepping out of the pack again," says Chris Peck, the now-retired spokesman for the state's Integrated Waste Management Board.

"The city of Bay Minette, Alabama, has been awarded $195,000 to work with Auburn University in Auburn, Alabama, and Cello Energy in Bay Minette, Alabama, to explore the feasibility of converting the city's municipal solid waste into a synthetic fuel that is similar to No. 2 diesel fuel oil. The city currently spends between $12,000 and $14,000 per month in dumping fees to dispose of household garbage, said Mike Phillips, a member of the Bay Minette City Council. He said the city hopes to reduce its solid waste disposal costs by up to 80 percent by separating its solid waste before dumping. It will then provide its carbon-based feedstock to Cello Energy in exchange for a price break on its fuel oil," according to www.biodieselmagazine.com.

At least that was the plan. Sadly for the biomass and biofuel industries, it turned out Cello Energy, a biofuel startup run by Alabama's former ethics chairman, Jack Boykin, and backed by both Silicon Valley Cleantech investors Khosla Ventures and pulp maker Parsons & Whittemore Enterprises, was ordered by a jury to pay more than $10.4 million in a fraud case. According to the

Alabama Press-Register, in 2007, Cello promised P&W that it would make $16-a-barrel fuel from cellulose derived from biomass such as hay, switchgrass and wood.

The newspaper reported that Cello accepted a $2.5-million investment from P&W in 2007 to help finance its first plant. Several months later it received a $12.5-million investment and a pledge for up to $25 million for construction and operation of additional plants from Khosla. Cello agreed to use discounted wood waste from the company as feedstock, but "a string of witnesses testified that samples of the fuel allegedly produced at Cello's facility … were derived entirely from fossil and not renewable sources," the *Alabama Press-Register* reported.

A jury decided Boykin's claims were fraudulent.

It was a setback for the public legitimacy of biofuel from biomass—certainly in terms of the risk of investing in such ventures, but Cello was, well, a bad apple in a huge bushel, if you will.

As I've mentioned in previous chapters, energy from biomass such as bioalgae, switchgrass, miscanthus, and waste wood shows enormous promise, and there are many companies solely focusing on this prospect. Eco-friendly wood may not be all the rage, but some companies and individuals are beginning to take notice at the retail level. While the Forest Stewardship Council has been, for the most part, the go-to resource for many companies, such as Home Depot and IKEA, which now require their suppliers of tropical wood to be certified, aiming to ensure wood is harvested in a sustainable and responsible manner, let us not forget that there are other certification options such as SFI, ATFS and PEFC, all of which have been discussed earlier.

At present, much like biofuels from non-fuel sources, using wood from sustainable sources can result in a higher cost for consumers, since, by its very implication, sustainable management implies the maintenance of the asset base to ensure that forestry harvests meet the needs of the present without compromising the continuity of the ecosystem and the goods and services that it provides.

Under the FSC certification program, sustainable forest management carries substantial costs in planning, training, assessment, and inventory tracking. These are previously unencountered expenses, and in other certification programs the costs are much less.

One could possibly compare unsustainable forestry management to oil, at least in the sense that if the timber resource is not effectively replenished in a reasonable time frame, there is not a renewable cycle. (Unlike oil, however, forests can eventually come back on their own—but it can still hardly be called a renewable resource if it the trees are not managed in a sustainable manner.)

We are making great strides in America, Canada, and most European countries in sustainable forest management and in developing fuels from the forest resource, and some countries like China are coming around in their management practices. But unfortunately, in most developing countries, especially those in South America—sustainable forest management is particularly unattractive since it lowers, temporarily, the immediate revenue from the forest.

Aside from the developed world engaging in a long-term vision and agreeing to pay more in the short term for wood products and keeping the revenue back to forests stable, it's a difficult challenge, and I hope we find a way to meet and solve it.

As an example of how we are improving the possibilities here in the US, in a long interview with the director of Georgia's Center of Innovation for Energy, Jill Stuckey, she points out that there are considerable resources being applied to increasing the yield from Georgia's well-managed forests through genetic research—from a current five tons per acre per year to seven or more tons a year. There is also research underway to make the other species more adaptable to the hot southern summers.

Says Stuckey: "Identified as one of Georgia's strategic industries, the renewable energy sector is poised for significant growth in the state. Georgia's plentiful bioenergy feedstocks such as plantation pine and agricultural residues including peanut hulls, blemished peaches and Vidalia onions, and pecan shells provide valuable resources for companies in the renewable energy industry.

"This means an increased profit by yield without increasing the cost to manufacturers. This presents a range of opportunities for Georgia and its tree farmers. With increased yields per acre, farmers would be encouraged to plant more threes."

And that is good for the environment in terms of carbon sequestration alone.

Jill made my eyes light up in an interview when she explained that Georgia's Suniva solar cell company now has more than a billion dollars in orders for its current technology, which is about 15 percent efficient. "They are on their way to becoming 18 percent efficient and working toward 21-21 percent efficiency. Those will make solar energy viable for the state of Georgia, even though its not one of the so-called sunshine states. If it works in Germany, it will work in Georgia."

Jill says that, in her opinion, "hopefully we've learned our lesson. Georgia Tech (Georgia Institute of Technology) and Georgia Power have been studying the possibilities of wind in the north Georgia mountains, and when the technology improves there may be some wind projects here. Right now we're sitting on the fence. In terms of tidal energy, that's something that Georgia Power and other southern energy companies are interested in, although the technology is very young. They're doing a bit of it in Europe and we're watching it very closely to see if it's feasible for us to pursue in the future."

I'm proud of how progressive Georgia is—in no small thanks to Jill Stuckey. As Jill explains, the state has set things up in order for alternative fuel companies to come to her department only, and not have to deal with multi levels of permits and various conflicting agencies. "What we've done is set up a one-stop shop," she says. "We're all the government you'd have to deal with ... you'd save six months or a year and millions of dollars and get a shovel in the ground to build an alternative-energy plant with all your necessary permits. We will give you far more than any other state could or would."

In an April 5th article she wrote "The Georgia Institute of Technology is home to the Strategic Energy Institute, which conducts research on biomass gasification and biochemistry, and is a leader in industrial process engineering. The state is also home to the Herty Advanced Materials Development Center, a $150-million-dollar non-profit research center, formerly dedicated to the pulp and paper industry and now focused on biomass commercialization."

And it all makes sense. As Jill points out, Georgia boasts "everything from traditional feedstocks, such as corn and soy beans, to non-traditional feedstocks, such as switch grass, miscanthus, and pine trees. Let's not forget that Georgia has some 24 million acres of forest land," she says. "*Forbes* magazine ranked Georgia third in the nation for potential biomass energy as measured by the amount of biomass available in the state. In addition, Georgia ranks number one in the nation for commercial timberland and boasts 10 million acres of agricultural land."

Jill says Georgia is looking as far into the future as possible—to a future, possibly, without any landfills. "We have to go that route. There's not going to be any waste in the future, we believe. There can't be; it all needs to be utilized one way or another. We have the technology to take polymers in scrap tires—any polymer for that matter—and convert it back into petroleum. Just undo it."

Jill's not just theorizing: The Global Resource Corporation is an American company that is doing exactly this, taking the recycling of plastics to a whole new level by turning them back into the oil and gas from which they were made.

All that is needed, claims the company, is a finely tuned microwave, and any mix of materials that were made from oil can be reduced back to oil and combustible gas, with a few, benign leftovers.

Jerry Meddick, director of product development at the New Jersey-based company, says that the key to their process is a machine that uses 1,200 different frequencies within the microwave range, which act on specific hydrocarbon materials. As the material is zapped at the appropriate wavelength, part of the hydrocarbons that make up the plastic and rubber in the material are broken down into diesel oil and combustible gas.

On a list of bullet points on the www.engineeringservicesout sourcing.com website, Meddick claims that, "Anything that has a hydrocarbon base will be affected by our process. We release those hydrocarbon molecules from the material and it then becomes gas and oil. Whatever does not have a hydrocarbon base is left behind, minus any water it contained as this gets evaporated in the microwave. Take a piece of copper wiring," says Meddick. "It is encased in plastic—a kind of hydrocarbon material. We release all the hydrocarbons, which strips the casing off the wire."

Not only does the process produce fuel in the form of oil and gas, it also makes it easier to extract the copper wire for recycling.

"See," says Jill, "these technologies are a reality—it just takes the political and corporate will to embrace them. Here in Georgia it's not that we've lessened the rules or standards, it's that Georgia has made alternative energy a priority. It's one of the reasons Range Fuels decided to locate here (I discussed Range and similarly minded companies, in a previous chapter.) Georgia has an enormous resource in its trees for use as a renewable biomass energy source.

And, as Jill says, "there is certainly enough biomass! We've been making paper in the state of Georgia for the past seventy years or so. We've been doing this a long time and haven't run out of trees. We've got 24.4 million acres of forest, more than anybody else except Oregon—but more of ours are accessible."

Jill also addressed the question if paper manufacturers were worried that the cost of pulp to make paper would jump—as the cost of corn as a food source jumped when it became a fuel source. She explained that with sustainable forestry and heightened technologies, there would be an increase in yields per acre, and tree farmers such as myself would be encouraged to plant more trees. So farmers like me would see an increase in profit through yield, not through pulp prices—so that paper manufacturers should be unaffected.

Of course, Georgia isn't the only state that is promoting these technologies, many others are embracing the possibilities of renewable energy sources, and each state has its own unique sources to tap. States like Arizona, New Mexico, Nevada, California, and the like have more sun than a state like Georgia and can focus on that resource. North and South Dakota, Texas, Kansas, Montana, Nebraska, and others are prime areas for wind farms. Most southern states and Pacific northwestern states are flush with biomass, and, of course, there is crossover technology in many states, such as Georgia. Any way you look at it, America has a variety of renewable resources that we can use for our energy.

No matter what clever advertising campaigns the coal industry tosses out about new technologies for low-emission mining and electricity generation from coal, coal is definitely not a renewable resource. Look back thirty or forty years to when there was consensus that we'd never run out of oil, at least for generations to come; it doesn't matter how much coal America (and China, and other countries) has under its mountains. Eventually we will run out.

It is no secret that here in America and in places like the former USSR, China, and other Asian countries, we depend heavily on coal for energy needs; it is also no secret that it is neither renewable nor clean. Many would say that "clean coal" is an oxymoron, no matter how that concept is touted or marketed, not to mention the environmental devastation that can be done in the mining process. If you've never seen a "mountain-top removal" operation, then you should. It's heartbreaking to see the top of a proud and beautiful mountain completely blown away to get to a coal reserve. We've all seen reports of coal mine explosions that have killed or severely injured workers and reports of companies that skirt safety regulations and the agencies that are supposed to police them turning a blind eye to their practices. But for now, it is a hard and simple fact that, like oil, we do have to depend on coal, at least in part. I hope we will do all we can, however, to move away from these resources—and in the meantime step up our efforts to police the companies that provide them.

I may be going out on a limb here, but I believe that the answers to our energy problems are simple. Simple—but not easy.

The most abundant source of energy in our solar system is the sun. Huge scientific resources are being dedicated to improving the efficiency of solar cells—even as of this writing, countries not known for their sunny climates, such as Germany, are harvesting ever-increasing amounts of solar energy.

I was always under the impression that my own state of Georgia had too many cloudy days to make solar power a significant option; that has changed, thanks to what Jill explained about advanced solar-cell technology right here at home.

It comes as no surprise that California is leading the way in the application of solar energy. In a November 2008 *L.A. Times* article,

"Los Angeles mayor Antonio Villaraigosa unveiled a long-range plan for the metropolis to meet one-tenth of the city's electrical needs by 2020 by adding 1,280 megawatts of energy from solar panels. Currently, 44 percent of the city's energy needs are met by burning coal. 'L.A. has everything it takes to make this work,' he said. 'We have the sun in abundance. We have the space. We have the largest municipal utility in the country.'"

The newspaper reported that "Under the mayor's solar plan, the largest share of solar power, or 500 megawatts, would come from generating facilities built by private sector companies in the Mojave Desert. Another 380 megawatts would be achieved through smaller programs, including one that would help low-income residents add solar panels to their homes and another that would allow customers to purchase shares of city-owned solar plants."

The mayor is also hoping that coal simply becomes uneconomical as Congress moves to impose ever-punitive carbon taxes in the coming years.

I mentioned in an earlier chapter that increasing number of people and companies are reclaiming used deep-fryer vegetable oil and creating biodiesel from it. Well, I discovered a husband-and-wife team in Wisconsin who are really bringing home the bacon, so to speak with alternative biofuel: they're using pork fat in their three-acre processing plant. It's the biofuel of choice for a pair of entrepreneurs building their business on pig fat.

"The pork gets run through microwaves to make precooked bacon, the grease falls off and that's what we use," Dan Kaderabek told the *Manitowoc Herald Reporter* of what he and wife Traci have been doing with their company, Bio Blend Fuels, since 2005. "Americans' bad eating habits ensure our supply."

Innovation is clearly the driving force in the world's quest for alternative, renewable energy. Check this out: Santa Coloma de Gramenet, a gritty, working-class town outside Barcelona, Spain, has placed a sea of solar panels atop mausoleums at its cemetery.

"The best tribute we can pay to our ancestors, whatever your religion may be, is to generate clean energy for new generations. That is our leitmotif," Esteve Serret, director Conste-Live Energy, a Spanish company that runs the cemetery in Santa Coloma and also works in renewable energy in an area where flat and open land is scarce in the sun-drenched area, told reporters and was quoted on MSNBC.

The 462 panels provide enough power into the local energy grid to power the equivalent of the needs for about sixty homes for a year.

Antoni Fogue, a city council member who was a driving force behind the plan, admits that the maverick plan was not well received at first.

"Let's say we heard things like, 'they're crazy. Who do they think they are? What a lack of respect!'" Fogue told the Associated Press.

But the placement of the panels has been done in as unobtrusive a manner as possible.

More than 450 solar panels installed on graves in a cemetery in Santa Coloma, Spain, are expected to add enough power to the local electrical grid to serve the needs of the equivalent of 60 homes a year.

Photo courtesy fractalenlightenment.com

"There has not been any problem whatsoever because people who go to the cemetery see that nothing has changed," Fogue said.

"This installation is compatible with respect for the deceased and for the families of the deceased."

While this is a little less palatable, there is a Canadian company Dynamotive working on an alternative green fuel made from human sewage. Scientists at the company's biofuel lab said the oil produced from human waste could be used instead of fossil fuels to generate heat and power in diesel engines and boilers.

OK, that's weird, I'll admit, but it's proof, at least, that people out there are thinking!

More realistically, as proponents of oil and coal keep reminding us, the practical application of harnessing the Earth's most abundant—and free—energy source is considerably challenging from a scientific aspect, with the multiple issues of harnessing it, converting it, and, especially, storing it. This is just one reason that, currently, solar energy contributes to only about .01 percent of the energy consumed in the United States (2008 figure).

True, solar power is increasingly used to power everything from the International Space Station, to orbiting satellites, to cell phones and other handheld devices. But as of 2010, even the best commercial solar systems produce electricity at five to six times the cost of other generation methods, according to the private National Academy of Sciences, which is a sister organization of the National Research Council.

Part of the challenge with solar energy, explains the academy, is that unless photovoltaic (PV) energy is consumed immediately, it must be stored—and we do not yet have the efficient and inexpensive technology to do so.

I have high hope that at least our future generations will engineer methods of harnessing what is the greatest, endless (well, for a few billion years!) supply of clean, free energy.

Another source of endless, renewable, and non-polluting energy is a little closer to home: our oceans.

It may not take a rocket scientist to recognize the power of the sea and tidal currents, but it is taking rocket scientists to attempt to harness it! Aerospace giant Lockheed Martin has dedicated a team of researchers to develop a pipe, which is an integral part of the technology behind Ocean Thermal Energy Conversion (OTEC)—a clean, renewable energy source that has the potential to free every non-land-locked country from its dependence on oil and coal.

"This has the potential to become the biggest source of renewable energy in the world," says Robert Cohen, who headed the US federal ocean thermal energy conversion program (OTEC) in the early 1970s.

Hans Krock, who has worked on OTEC designs for the University of Hawaii, the US Department of Energy, and others since 1980, says the problems now are less to do with the technology and more with scale. "Pilot tests have been done," Krock says. "It's not a matter of design, it's a matter of getting the economics right."

Krock, who founded OCEES in 1988, has started Energy Harvesting Systems, a firm with ambitious plans to build a 100-megawatt OTEC plant off the coast of Indonesia. The electricity it generates will be used to produce hydrogen, a green fuel that could be used to power zero-emission vehicles. Krock says he has funding for the $800-million plant, and it could be up and running within several years.

For Cohen, who has also waited decades for ocean thermal technology to come into its own, such a large plant seems overambitious, especially as it is coupled with the production of hydrogen, whose distribution structure is still largely undeveloped.

"Scaling up so quickly could be risky," warns Cohen to the Associated Press. "I'd like to see us move fast on ocean thermal but I think we have to be careful."

In an innovative move, the city of Toronto in Ontario, Canada, is harnessing the depths of Lake Ontario—but not to help heat the city. Toronto is using the cold water from the lake bottom to cool its government buildings.

According to *New Scientist Magazine*, "Makai Ocean Engineering of Waimanalo, Hawaii, helped construct the city's cold-water air-conditioning system that will save 60 megawatts of electricity when it is fully connected to buildings in the city's centre." The system works by pumping water at a temperature of 39 degrees Fahrenheit from a depth of more than two hundred feet and then sending it to buildings within the city via three pipes, each roughly three miles long. The cold water is then used to cool air. "Ocean thermal energy is the big prize, but cold-water air conditioning can play a major role in cutting energy needs, and it can do it today," says Reb Bellinger of Makai.

Of course, there is traditionally far more energy to be created from hydro sources such as dams than will ever be used for cooling down buildings. Once again, I turn to the National Academy of Sciences for the most up-to-date information on where we stand with hydroelectric power.

The Academy says that in 2008, roughly 6 percent of the nation's electricity came from hydro sources, but conventional hydroelectric sources have been pretty much exploited as far as they can be and still be considered ecologically sustainable. Oregon, Washington state, and California are the top-producing hydroelectric areas of the United States. It's an attractive alternative, renewable energy source, since it's inexpensive and does not emit greenhouse gases. And unlike wind (which I'll get to in a minute) and solar, it's a source of energy that is not intermittent. That is, the sun doesn't set on fast-flowing rivers and dammed-up lakes, and never stops blowing like the breeze.

However, traditional and current hydroelectric generation has the significant drawback of the concern that damming rivers and streams can disrupt or destroy local ecosystems and threaten the habitats of plants, fish, and animals. For example, salmon must swim upstream to spawning grounds in order to reproduce, but dams from hydroelectric plants block their path. In some cases, efforts have been made to build "fish ladders" that allow salmon to leap up a series of small steps past hydroelectric plants. Other negative ecosystem effects remain more difficult to address.

"For this reason, it is unlikely that conventional hydropower resources can be significantly expanded in the future," says the National Academy of Sciences in a statement.

Where future hydropower may succeed, it is indeed being tested by Scottish wave power company, OPD, which has leapt ahead of its rivals in attempts to bring its devices to market. Three of its Polaris devices, which use the motion of the waves to drive hydraulic rams and produce energy, are being deployed in the world's first commercial marine-energy project in Portugal, and four machines are set to be installed in Orkney in a Scottish Power-funded project that will be the world's biggest commercial wave project.

There are also plans for seven Pelamis machines for a project called Wave Hub, off the coast of Cornwall, that should be up and running by next year.

It's unlikely, given the limited scientific resources focusing on solar, wind, and biomass technology, however, to think that energy from the ebb and flow of our oceans is going to be a significant source of energy in the foreseeable future.

One of mankind's first sources of energy is also one of the sources that can help save the planet while providing us with an endless, if irregular, supply of electricity: wind.

We've used it to propel boats, grind grain into flour, and pump water from the ground (and fly kites with the kids on weekends!).

Now seen in the majority of states, huge wind turbines have doubled in number across the country between 2002 and 2006,

Wind turbines have, for many years, been an increasing part of the landscape in the desert around Palm Springs, California. The Dillon Wind Power Project alone, seen here, harnesses enough wind power to generate enough electricity to meet the needs of roughly 45,000 homes a year. *Photo courtesy National Renewable Energy Laboratory*

according to the National Research Council. Now, the US generates more electricity from wind than any other country in the world. While that's laudable, we use so much energy that wind still accounts for only 1 percent of our total requirements, according to the council.

A Wikipedia entry on wind energy reports that world wind generation capacity more than quadrupled between 2000 and 2006, doubling about every three years. At this writing, 81 percent of wind power installations are in the US and Europe. The share of the top five countries in terms of new installations fell from 71 percent in 2004 to 62 percent in 2006, but climbed to 73 percent by 2008 as those countries—the United States, Germany, Spain, China, and India—have seen substantial capacity growth from 2008 to 2010.

By 2010, the World Wind Energy Association expected more than 200 gigawatts of capacity to be installed worldwide, up from 73.9 gigawatts at the end of 2006—implying an anticipated net growth rate of more than 28 percent per year.

The federal government's Energy Information Administration predicts that by 2030, our wind-energy generation could account for 4.5 percent of our total needs. Conflictingly, the government's Department of Energy estimates that with high fossil fuel prices, federal tax credits, individual state programs, improvements to technology, and an accepting public, wind-energy generation could be as high as 20 percent by the same time.

One of the obvious and biggest drawbacks to wind energy is, like solar energy, it's not constant. Just as the sun goes down, wind is intermittent and unreliable. Also, the technology to inexpensively and efficiently store energy created by either solar or wind sources is not yet sophisticated enough to be practical.

Next spring Xcel Energy, the state of Minnesota, and a Virginia-based technology firm will test the first battery in the country capable of storing wind energy.

The breakthrough technology, which is the size of two semi-trailer trucks stacked atop each other, was built in Japan and shipped to Luverne, Minnestoa, where it will store electricity generated by the nearby Minwind Energy wind turbines. S&C Electric Company expects the equipment will be completely installed by April 2011.

The battery consists of a score of 50-kilowatt modules. When it is fully charged, the massive sodium-sulfur battery—which weighs about 80 tons—can store 7.2 megawatt-hours of electricity. That's enough to power five hundred homes for about seven hours. It will cost more than $5.4 million to buy and install the battery and analyze its performance.

The technology could help allay critics of wind energy who lament that no electricity is produced when there's no wind. If successful, the battery will store wind energy and release its power onto the electrical grid when the air is still.

"Energy storage is key to expanding the use of renewable energy," Xcel chairman and CEO Dick Kelly said. "This technology has the potential to reduce the impact caused by the variability and limited predictability of wind-energy generation."

Xcel, which invested $3.6 million in the project, expects the battery "to become very important to both us and our customers," Kelly said.

If it works, it will be a boon to the wind-energy option. But as of today it's unproven.

One of wind's other drawbacks is, unlike otherwise unobtrusive roof solar panels, massive, 200-foot wind turbines are a concern to landowners who believe they are an eyesore—or worse, a health hazard via electromagnetic fields that some claim can cause everything from headaches to cancer—none of which has been proven. It can not be denied that the turbines do make a certain amount of noise, which is one reason the master plan for the bank of turbines up and down the eastern seaboard won't run into resistance on that level—but it's certain to be fought by local residents who believe the windmills taint the ocean vista.

Furthermore, the "wind farms" of hundreds of turbines, such as that on the western end of the valley that contains Palm Springs, have proven deadly to birds and bats.

Despite these drawbacks, the advantages of garnering energy from the wind are arguably overwhelming: Wind is free. Wind energy does not contribute to greenhouse gases or other pollutants; it's domestic and lessens our reliance on foreign oil and domestic coal. And, as the National Research Council points out, wind turbines can be a boon to the economies of rural areas where farmers and other landowners can lease land to wind turbine companies and still have enough space to grow crops and raise cattle.

Wind energy's potential contribution is large, and with developments in storage technologies and an expanded and upgraded electrical grid, it could provide a substantial portion of our electricity.

The bottom line: According to the US Department of Energy's National Renewable Energy Laboratory, wind energy could generate 20 percent of the electricity needed by the eastern half of the country by the year 2024. It's going to cost $90 billion to build the windmills to accomplish this, however.

"Twenty percent wind is an ambitious goal," said David Corbus, the project manager for the study, told media. "We can bring more wind power online, but if we don't have the proper infrastructure to move that power around, it's like buying a hybrid car and leaving it in the garage.

Most of the windmills would be constructed off the eastern seaboard coast, the official said—which is why I predict it will be a public relations hurdle with residents in those areas.

While many state governments already require their utilities to provide a portion of "green" power from renewable energy sources, Corbus told the press that he believed it would take a nationwide, federal directive to achieve the 20 percent wind scenario.

As of fall 2010, there is federal climate change legislation on the table that would require US utilities to generate 15 percent of their energy from renewable resources by 2021—but many senators believe it won't be passed in a year in which health care and an uncertain economy have dominated lawmakers' time and attention.

Ultimately, the success of wind as a significant contributor to green power will come down to a careful balance of legislative and public acceptance.

What is currently the most significant form of alternative energy is biomass. In the latest figures from the National Academy of Sciences (2008), 7 percent of our energy came from all renewable resources combined, and nearly 4 percent of that was from biomass.

"Experts predict the contribution from biomass will likely increase more than 55 percent by 2030," the Academy reported recently.

Wood is the most common source of biomass, but grasses, crops such as soy and sugar cane and corn are also currently widely used as well. Landfill and manure are also lesser used, but just as effective.

Biomass is an alternative, renewable energy source with the broadest applications, able to provide energy to produce electricity, heat, chemicals, and biofuels for vehicles and even jet airplanes.

While it's increasingly being used in varying ways, the majority of biomass energy goes toward the industrial sector.

It differs from solar, wind, and hydroelectric generation in that while burning biomass releases greenhouse gases just as burning fossil fuels such as oil and coal does, there is a very significant difference: As a renewable resource, the trees and grasses planted and grown to replace bio harvests are carbon sequestrating, and compensate. As the National Research Council points out, were biomass power plants equipped to sequester 100 percent of the carbon released, biomass burning would ultimately be a net-zero carbon contributor to our atmosphere.

Council experts say more study is needed on what ultimate "carbon debt" might be incurred by increased use of biomass as our primary energy source—predicted to reach 55 percent by 2030—but recognizes that, regardless, it can be a job creator and will reduce some of the other greenhouse gases associated with burning fossil fuels and, perhaps most importantly, socially and politically, reduce our reliance on foreign oil.

Lastly is what's regarded as one of the more unlikely sources of renewable energy: the Earth itself. Geothermal energy—the heat found miles under the planet's crust—is clean, sustainable and endlessly renewable.

The temperature of lava spewing from volcanoes has been measured at, varyingly, between 1,300 and 2,400 degrees Fahrenheit. Temperatures of water or ambient rock not too far below the surface—within the easy reach of current technologies, easily pass 100 degrees.

One of the leaders in this technology is Nevada Geothermal Power, an emerging renewable-energy developer focused on producing clean, sustainable geothermal electric power from high temperature geothermal resources. The company has four properties: Blue Mountain, Pumpernickel, and Black Warrior—in Nevada—and Crump Geyser—in Oregon.

Currently, Nevada is operating sixteen geothermal power plants, generating about 333 megawatts of energy. While it's relatively inexpensive to exploit and has none of the negatives such as emissions, even geothermal has its drawbacks.

In 2006, Swedish scientist Markus O. Häring's geothermal project in Basel, Switzerland, while drilling for heat simmering within the deep underlying rock, hit more than a snag: The drilling set off an earthquake on December 8, 2006, severe enough to damage buildings and terrify residents. Thousands of aftershocks induced by the Basel project quake continued for months after it shut down. After litigation cleared Häring and his company of any wrongdoing, he stated publicly: "As a geologist I have a deep respect of nature and its complexity. The tremors that we triggered during our reservoir stimulation are a setback for the development of enhanced geothermal systems. As scientist and developer I do not try to find culprits but try to find answers and solutions for future developments. Innovation has a price, innovation is based on hard work and reflection."

While that put an end to geothermal exploration in Switzerland, it's done nothing to stop similar research in North America. In fact, in July 2010, a similar project using the same method began drilling deep into the ground—ground laced with fault lines, just two hours north of San Francisco.

The region, which straddles Lake and Sonoma counties, has already experienced swarms of small quakes set off by other, less-invasive geological scientific studies. But the company, AltaRock, says it picked an area that has suffered only small quakes and that it regards as stable enough to withstand a two-mile-deep tap to extract the heat of the Earth in the hopes of ultimately creating electricity.

According to a *New York Times* article in June of 2009, "The California project is the first of dozens that could be operating in the United States in the next several years, driven by a push to cut emissions of heat-trapping gases and the Obama administration's support for renewable energy.

"Geothermal's potential as a clean energy source has raised huge hopes, and its advocates believe it could put a significant dent in American dependence on fossil fuels—potentially supplying roughly 15 percent of the nation's electricity by 2030, according to one estimate by Google. The earth's heat is always there waiting to be tapped, unlike wind and solar power, which are intermittent and, thus, more fickle. According to a 2007 geothermal report financed by the Department of Energy, advanced geothermal power could, in theory, produce as much as 60,000 times the nation's annual energy usage. President Obama, in a news conference in July 2009, cited geothermal power as part of the "clean-energy transformation" that a climate bill now before Congress could bring about.

"Dan W. Reicher, an assistant energy secretary in the Clinton administration who is now director of climate change and energy at Google's investment and philanthropic arm, said geothermal energy had "the potential to deliver vast amounts of power almost anywhere in the world, 24/7."

"Power companies have long produced limited amounts of geothermal energy by tapping shallow steam beds, often beneath geysers or vents, called fumaroles. Even those projects can induce earthquakes, although most are small. But for geothermal energy to be used more widely, engineers need to find a way to draw on the heat at deeper levels percolating in the earth's core.

'Some geothermal advocates believe the method used in Basel, and to be tried in California, could be that breakthrough. But because large earthquakes tend to originate at great depths, breaking rock that far down carries more serious risk, seismologists say. Seismologists have long known that human activities can trigger quakes, but they say the science is not developed enough to say for certain what will or will not set off a major temblor.

"Steven E. Koonin, the under secretary for science at the Department of Energy, said the earthquake issue was new to him, but added, "We're committed to doing things in a factual and rigorous way, and if there is a problem, we will attend to it."

In the next chapter I'm going to describe to you one of the things about next-generation research that can only be described as having a "wow" factor. Before we get there, I have to say that I rather got a "wow" reaction when I discovered Bloom Energy.

The California company, which was enormously secretive for a number of years, first went public with a piece on *60 Minutes* and then made a public announcement in late July 2010, unveiling its much-whispered about "Bloom Box."

K. R. Sridhar, the founder of the company, says the underlying technology came from an oxygen generator that had been developed for a scrapped NASA Mars program. Backed by an estimated $400 million in private investors, Bloom converted the device into a simple fuel cell that takes oxygen in one side, a gas (natural gas or biogas from a landfill or even a solar source) in the other side and: Presto! Electricity. They call this an "electro-chemical process" and claim it's green energy, and that it does not produce greenhouse gases—though a scientist interviewed by the *Christian Science Monitor* disagrees, claiming the device is bound to "exhale" some small quantity of carbon dioxide.

The units are the size of refrigerators and, according to Sridhar, two of them can power an average, high-consumption American home. A single block can power an average European home (Americans use far more electricity than any other culture), and one could power up from four to six homes in, say, India.

He says a stack of sixty-four can power a small business like Starbucks.

Currently, the corporate-sized cells cost up to $800,000. But it is a reality, and for nearly eighteen months Google has been running its data center on a bank of Bloom Boxes, just as FedEx and Walmart and eBay have been deriving up to 15 percent of their energy needs from the units.

Bloom makes about one box a day at the moment and believes that within five to ten years it can drive down the cost to about $3,000 to make it suitable for home use. As Sridhar declares, "You'll generate your own electricity with the box, and it'll be wireless. The idea is to one day replace the big power plants and transmission line grid, the way the laptop moved in on the desktop and cell phones supplanted landlines. This invention, working on Mars, would have allowed the NASA administrator to pick up a phone and say, 'Mr. President, we know how to produce oxygen on Mars,'" Sridhar told *60 Minutes*.

"All those modules that we saw go into this big box. Fuel goes in, air goes in, out comes electricity," he explained.

When asked if Bloom Box was intended to supplant the grid, the company's John Doerr told *60 Minutes*, "The Bloom Box is intended to replace the grid ... for its customers. It's cheaper than the grid; it's cleaner than the grid."

"Now, won't the utility companies see this as a threat and try to crush Bloom?" interviewer Leslie Stahl asked.

"No, I think the utility companies will see this as a solution," Doerr said. "All they need to do is buy Bloom Boxes, put them in the substation for the neighborhood and sell that electricity and operate."

"They'll buy these boxes?" Stahl asked.

"They buy nuclear power plants. They buy gas turbines from General Electric," he pointed out.

To make power, you'd still need fuel. Many previous fuel cells failed because they needed expensive pure hydrogen. Not this box.

"Our system can use fossil fuels like natural gas. Our system can use renewable fuels like landfill gas, bio-gas," Sridhar told *60 Minutes*. "We can use solar."

Only time will tell whether this "holy grail" of energy production becomes a widespread reality.

But no matter what, it's a clear indication that many of the world's top scientists are searching for a way to find mankind a clean, renewable source of energy that is sustainable and poses no threat to the environment. If we encourage this kind of innovation and if we press our lawmakers to find ways to support and incentivize these various paths to better, cleaner, and renewable energy, then certainly we are on the road to a better future for ourselves and for future generations. Surely that's what we all would like to see.

Biomimicry

Nature Knows Best

"(This) introduces an era based not on what
we can extract from the natural world,
but on what we can learn from it."

Janine Benyus

I met a wonderful person named Janine Benyus in 2008 at a fantastic conference in California called "Fortune Brainstorm Green." I was asked by my friend Andy Serwer, managing editor of *Fortune* magazine and by some of the other good folks at *Fortune* to attend and to take part in a panel discussion on forestry issues (and of course to play a few tunes!). I was fascinated with Benyus's presentation at the conference on something I had never heard about before called biomimicry. I just love the "wow!" factor, when I discover something new, hopeful, and encouraging. Benyus certainly wowed me with this concept. She is one of the pioneering scientists dedicating their careers and lives to the future of our species, and our planet.

While the US National Biological Service, a part of the US Geological Survey, warns that one half of all native ecosystems in the country are degraded to the point of being endangered, biomimicry is a growing, encouraging trend: (from bios, meaning life, and mimesis, meaning to imitate).

Dr. Janine Benyus, the world's leader in biomimicry. *Photo courtesy Jane Benyus.*

It's been around forever, in practice. Basically, it's watching Mother Nature at work and taking inspiration or finding innovation from her. It's the original technology, so to speak. Like chimps who use grass or sticks to probe and "fish" for termites and ants, which, it's been said, they learned from the behavior of long-beaked birds and anteaters.

One of the leading proponents of the movement, biologist Benyus has brought the science to the forefront in recent years: "Biomimicry is a design discipline that seeks sustainable solutions by emulating nature's time-tested patterns and strategies, e.g., a solar cell inspired by a leaf," she says. "The core idea is that Nature, imaginative by necessity, has already solved many of the problems we are grappling with: energy, food production, climate control, non-toxic chemistry, transportation, packaging, and a whole lot more.

Indigenous peoples relied heavily on the lessons and examples of the organisms around them. Alaskan hunters still stalk seals in exactly the same way that polar bears do, for instance. Many early Western inventions, such as the airplane and the telephone, also took their inspiration directly from nature."

While her book, *Biomimicry: Innovation Inspired by Nature*, was first published more than ten years ago, it has an ever-widening sphere of influence. Now, Benyus lectures widely and consults; she is also a co-founder of the nonprofit research Biomimicry Institute (biomimicry.org) and its new information site AskNature.org. She co-founded the Biomimicry Guild—a for-profit consultancy with a "dial-a-biologist" service to companies and government agencies (a list of which includes General Electric, Hewlett-Packard and NASA) trying to embrace or even invent new technologies, or adopt sustainability focused business practices. She contends that every business should have a biologist on staff and on its board of directors.

"Often we find ourselves being asked not just how to green a product but how to begin greening a whole company," Benyus says.

In a sense, we can look back as far as Leonardo da Vinci's keen observation of birds in his detailed sketches of "flying machines" to recognize that some scientists have looked to nature to solve our riddles. And, indeed, when the Wright brothers did finally succeed in building the first airplane in 1903, their design derived inspiration from watching pigeons in flight.

One of the most famous, early, examples of "modern" biomimicry happened in 1948 when a Swiss inventor named George de Mestral returned from a nature hike with his dog, each of them covered with annoying burrs from a plant. (It's by sticking to animal fur, and, well, your jeans, that certain seed sacs catch a ride to fertile new ground to grow.) Mestral put one of the burrs under a microscope and discovered it had many tiny little hooks, which had become looped through strands in the fabric of his pants. Because Mestral was listening to the lesson Mother Nature was trying to teach him, the world had Velcro just a few years later.

Engineer Jack Steele coined the term "bionics" back in 1960, explaining it as "the science of systems which have some function copied from nature."

Author Martin Caidin brought the whole underlying concept of "bionics" to the public eye with his science fiction novel *Cyborg* in 1972—which went on to spark the TV series *The Six Million Dollar Man* and its spinoffs.

Currently, a team of researchers under the global scientific collective ZERI Foundation (Zero Emissions Research & Initiatives) umbrella and its Japanese partners are assembling a list of the top 100 of "nature's best" inventions as inspiration for new technologies which are not just Earth-friendly but have the potential to generate hundreds of thousands of jobs (or more) and help spark a new "green economy."

Although it counts scientists from all over the world as part of its collective, the ZERI project is headed by Gunter Pauli out of the Politecnico di Torino in Italy. So far, the group has identified potential inventions such as bacterial control inspired by red algae; building material made from CO_2 inspired by mollusks; fog (clean water) harvesting inspired by a desert beetle; pacemaker replacement inspired by humpback whales; fire retardant inspired by animal cells; self-assembling glass inspired by sea sponges; wound healing inspired by flies; adhesion without glue inspired by geckos, and dozens of other possibilities, in its quest to chronicle its "Top 100 List" of biomimicry models.

So, biomimicry has come into being as a science of it own—and its scientists are now being referred to as "bioneers," on a quest to see what we can learn from nature rather than extract from nature. The word was coined by entrepreneur, author, journalist, and filmmaker Kenny Ausubel, co-CEO and founder of Bioneers, a Santa Fe, New Mexico-based nonprofit "dedicated to disseminating practical and visionary solutions for restoring Earth's imperiled ecosystems and healing our human communities." In 1990, Ausubel launched the annual Bioneers Conference with his producing partner, wife, and Bioneers co-founder, Nina Simons.

According to www.bioneers.org, "The Bioneers Conference attracts more than three thousand people each year to the national conference in San Rafael, California, and is beamed by satellite simulcast to close to twenty localized Bioneers conferences across the US and Canada to another ten thousand attendees."

The Bioneers organization's founding perspectives are natural medicine. "Nature has a profound and profoundly mysterious ability for self-repair. The primary source of healing lies in nature. In environmental restoration as in medicine, the role of the practitioner is to support nature to heal itself. This principle became foundational to Bioneers," the Bionneers.org site proclaims.

Nature's solution is the second of the organization's three founding principles: "Nature has solved all the ecological challenges we're trying to address. Practitioners such as John Todd, Amory Lovins, Wes Jackson, and Donald Hammer, as well as traditional indigenous practices, were a primary inspiration. Biomimicry has been a core focus since Bioneers' inception," the organizers say. Finally, biocultural diversity rounds out the group's perspectives: "In nature, diversity is the very fabric of life. Because change is the only constant in nature, diversity is the source of resilience to adapt to change in both natural and human systems. Successful adaptation requires keeping open the greatest range of biologically and culturally diverse options," they say.

There is a long list of recent biomimicry success stories and, in fact, Benyus's upcoming book will, like the ZERI foundation, concentrate on the top 100 solutions to many of our problems that have been found in nature already.

Benyus is widely seen at the forefront of the maverick scientific movement, and at conferences and in her book she cites just a few of the breakthroughs in promising new technologies, such as the ongoing development of surgical glues based, not on scientists having built new chemicals from the ground up but, rather, from studying certain sea worms and the methods by which mussels attach themselves to shoals and boats. Man has yet to "invent" better glue that works underwater. By being inspired by these natural examples, eventually surgical pins and similar invasive devices will be replaced by a natural glue that adheres better, is safer, and is generally more effective.

For scientists at the University of Bath in England, it was a challenge when the Ministry of Defence asked for the creation of an adaptive fabric that could "breath" much more efficiently. The researchers looked to pine cones, which open and close as humidity changes. Now, the university's biometrics lab is developing a woven textile that has tiny flaps that will open and close to suit the environment.

Another example of biomimicry is the evolution of the famous Japanese "bullet" train that travels at speeds of up to 300 miles an hour. When it was first put into service, it created a bit of a public noise nuisance since at such speeds it would create a sonic boom every time it emerged from a tunnel (like planes do when they exceed the speed of sound, though with the train it was due to the immediate change in pressure at the mouth of the tunnel).

In order to fix the problem, Japanese scientists considered the kingfisher bird, which dives steeply and very quickly from high in the air into water to catch fish, yet creates very little splash when doing so. When the front of the train was redesigned to resemble the bird's beak, the sound problem largely disappeared. Doubly beneficial was that the train was also able to go faster and use less energy when it was operating.

In the early 1990s, the lead architect of the Zimbabwean capital Harare's Eastgate Centre, a large commercial and business plaza—a man named Mick Pearce—found huge inspiration in the amazing, sometimes huge, termite mounds that dot the countryside. Despite massive changes in outside temperatures during the day and night, the way in which the insects construct their mounds keeps the interiors at a near-constant temperature.

Since nearly 90 percent of the cost of operating commercial buildings comes from heating and cooling them, Pearce clearly had a great idea to copy Mother Nature and, with the help of an engineering team, designed what's probably the largest, passively heated and cooled building: It has no conventional heating or cooling systems yet remains a constant temperature comfortable for its inhabitants.

Pearce's Eastgate building uses the mass of the building itself as insulation and the diurnal temperature swings outside to keep its interior uniformly cool. With the firm Ove Arup & Partners, Pearce devised an air-change schedule that is significantly more efficient than other climate-controlled buildings in the area. Fans suck in fresh air from the atrium, blow it upstairs through hollow spaces under the floors and from there into each office through baseboard vents. As the air rises and warms, it is drawn out through forty-eight round, brick funnels. During cool summer nights, big fans send air through the building seven times an hour to chill the hollow floors. By day, smaller fans blow two changes of air an hour through the building. As a result, the air is fresh, much

Termites live in extremes: extreme heat during the day and extreme cool at night. Their mounds are ventilation structures that maintain temperatures, CO_2 levels, and humidity levels in the nests below the ground. *Photo by J Brew, Courtesy of The Biomimicry Institute.*

The Eastgate Centre: A huge shopping and residential and business complex in Africa without conventional heating or cooling—instead, influenced by the passive heating and cooling of termite mounds. *Photo by Mandy Paterson, Courtesy of The Biomimicry Institute.*

more so than from an air conditioner, which recycles thirty percent of the air that passes through it.

Fairly recently, a team of scientists and engineering students in England announced a radical plan to make airplane wings simulate "flapping."

The idea came from ... sharks.

Despite what you might imagine, sharks do not have smooth skin; their skin is covered with little ridges that actually allows them to swim more efficiently with less drag, than they would otherwise. Researchers have taken this concept and applied it to airplane wings. By applying tiny jets to redirect the air over wings, the engineers are simulating the effect of a plane's wings flapping, much like an insect or bird's; the result is such that an equipped plane would fly with lower resistance and use less fuel—perhaps as much as 20 percent less, according to the Engineering and Physical Sciences Research Council and the Airbus aircraft manufacturer. Still a concept, they say wings for testing could be a reality by 2012.

A great example of a company being forward thinking, not just in terms of creating or enhancing business for itself, but also by looking toward nature to make the best economic use of what otherwise might be waste material, is Ray Anderson's Interface. A billion-dollar Georgia company, Interface is the leading manufacturer of commercial floor coverings, and it was a leading example of an environmentally harmful textile manufacturer until Anderson had an epiphany about the 1.224 billion pounds of raw material his company consumed in 1995 alone.

On its quest to make Interface carbon-neutral, Interface's "Eco-Dream Team" brought Benyus aboard. The first remarkable innovation to come from the team is a line of office carpeting that mimics the "ordered chaos" of a forest floor. A standard, or single-colored carpet needs to be entirely replaced when part of it becomes worn or damaged. Interface designed a patchwork carpet of 18-inch tiles that imitate the never-the-same-in-two-places look of a forest floor; when an area of carpet is damaged or worn, a few abstract-looking tiles can be replaced, instead of the whole carpet. "No matter how you rearrange the elements of a forest floor—the leaves, twigs, etc.—the forest floor still looks seamless and natural," Benyus says.

And, just like a forest floor, the worn tiles are recycled.

One of the most tangible examples of biomimicry is the current research into exactly how plant leaves photosynthesize so we can use this knowledge to make the next-generation of photovoltaic cells. By understanding how leaves work, scientists say they will be able to, in theory, double the efficiency of new photovoltaic cells by roughly 40 percent. There is also some thought that we'll have the ability to capture the majority of solar energy hitting a surface—beyond the visible spectrum—and not only that, but instead of having what we think of right now as solar panels, we will have the ability to mix photovoltaic materials into paints or other liquids and cover the roofs of all our buildings—or cover the surfaces of our cell phones and portable computers. We already have computer bags with pliable solar collectors and other items, though their efficiency is lacking, and scientists have adapted the idea of lily pads, using their basic, natural design to create next-generation solar energy collectors.

Thomas and Ana Moore and Devins Gust at the University of Arizona are at the forefront of leaf-energy studies. Their work into determining exactly how leaves capture energy so efficiently, and without pollutants such as silicone and petrochemical compounds, hopes to lead to a molecular-sized solar cell that mimics photosynthesis.

Insect scientist Thomas Eisner at Cornell University is one of the founders of a relatively new field of science, dubbed "chemical ecology." Among the studies he and his professor wife and collaborator Maria are conducting is a behavioral examination of insects' relationships with plants. Broadly described, it's letting insects tell us which plants might yield beneficial new drugs; if an insect avoids a certain leaf, they believe the plant must contain secondary compounds that it uses for defense—strong compounds that may help humans. As he describes in his terrific book *For Love of Insects*, Eisner writes, "to understand the success of insects is to appreciate our own shortcomings."

Similarly, scientists have begun serious study of animals that self-medicate—a clear indication that sometimes they know more than we do, and something we need to pay close heed to.

Ugandan and French scientists are looking for new drugs for humans by studying the behavior of chimpanzees. Dr. Sabrina Krief, a French veterinarian and professor at the National History Museum in Paris, discovered chimps in Uganda's Kibale forest that ingest Aneilema aequinoctiale leaves in the morning and Albiza grandibractcata bark in the evenings to rid themselves of intestinal parasites. Another chimp, which was ailing from a fever, was observed chewing only Trichilia rubescens leaves for a day. The scientists later discovered that the plant is effective against malaria.

"These findings have allowed us to discover new plant molecules with significant properties against malaria, worms, or tumors," Krief said. "It's quite rare to find active molecules but especially new molecules which might put us on the path to developing new pharmaceuticals, which is the ultimate goal of the project."

Capuchin monkeys in Costa Rica use the Piper plant, a member of the chili family, as a painkiller and insect repellent. They also rub their fur with millipedes, which excrete a toxin that kills insects and bacteria.

European starlings use wild carrots in their nests because they have a substance in them that repels mites. The same substance has been found in Neem leaves, which are now used as a human insect repellent.

Other scientists have observed brown lemurs rubbing their bodies with dill weed, which, they've discovered, repels insects.

And this behavior is not limited to primates: Open University's Cindy Engel, a lecturer in environmental science, discovered a species of caterpillars that, when infected with parasites, eats plants that are toxic to those parasites.

Benyus says, "As we learned to synthesize what we needed from petrochemicals, we began to believe we didn't need nature, and that our ways were superior. Now, with the advent of genetic engineering, some of us have come to fancy ourselves as gods, riding a juggernaut of technology that will grant us independence from the natural world.

"Biological knowledge is doubling every five years, growing like a pointillist painting toward a recognizable whole. For the first time in history, we have the instruments—the scopes and satellites—to feel the shiver of a neuron in thought or watch in color as a star is born. When we combine this intensified gaze with the sheer amount of scientific knowledge coming into focus, we suddenly have the capacity to mimic nature like never before."

Benyus points to the manufacturing sector as example of mankind inventing something that didn't need to be invented:

"Right now, we use what's called 'heat, beat, and treat' to make materials. Kevlar ... the stuff in flak jackets ... is our premier, high-tech material. Nothing stronger or tougher. But how do we make it? We pour petroleum-derived molecules into a pressurized vat of concentrated sulfuric acid, and boil it at several hundred degrees Fahrenheit. We then subject it to high pressures to force the fibers into alignment as we draw them out. The energy input is extreme and the toxic byproducts are odious.

"Nature takes a different approach. Because an organism makes materials like bone or collagen or silk right in its own body, it doesn't make sense to "heat, beat, and treat." A spider, for instance, produces a waterproof silk that beats the pants off Kevlar for toughness and elasticity. Ounce for ounce, it's five times stronger than steel! But the spider manufactures it in water, at room temperature, using no high heats, chemicals, or pressures. Best of all, it doesn't need to drill offshore for petroleum; it takes flies and crickets at one end and produces this miracle material at the other. In a pinch, the spider can even eat part of its old web to make a new one.

"Imagine what this kind of a processing strategy would do for our fiber industry! Renewable raw materials, great fibers, and negligible energy and waste. We obviously have a lot to learn from an organism that has been making silk for some 380 million years.

"The truth is, organisms have managed to do everything we want to do, without guzzling fossil fuels, polluting the planet, or mortgaging their future. What better models could there be?"

In Oxford University's zoology department, David Knight and Fritz Vollrath have been working on a sustainable fiber manufacturing process that mimics spiders—without heat or toxins.

Benyus declares that biomimicry is "innovation inspired by nature. The core idea is that nature, imaginative by necessity, has already solved many of the problems we are grappling with. Animals, plants, and microbes are the consummate engineers. They have found what works, what is appropriate, and most important, what lasts here on Earth. This is the real news of biomimicry: After 3.8 billion years of research and development, failures are fossils, and what surrounds us is the secret to survival."

Biomimicry is not without its dangers, however. Benyus and others caution: "... any technology, even if it's a technology inspired by nature, can be used for good or bad. The airplane, for instance, was inspired by bird flight; a mere 11 years after we invented it, we were bombing people with it."

But the fact is, we can learn so much from nature that we should be looking closer at the benefits biomimicry can offer. Using the ancient systems that nature has developed with our own intellect and the incredible technologies available, we can solve many of the problems that face us in harmony with the natural world.

Green Spaces

Bringing the Country to the City

*"Nature is the true revelation of the Deity to man.
The nearest green field is the inspired page from which
you may read all that it is needful for you to know."*

Arthur Conan Doyle

Are you getting enough Vitamin G? That would be Vitamin G as in green space. According to 2009 statistics from the US Census Bureau, 81 percent of Americans live in cities or their surrounding suburbs, and studies everywhere from Ohio State University's Environment and Natural Resources School to universities and research centers all over the world, including the UK-based Faculty of Health, established by the three Royal Colleges of Physicians of the United Kingdom (London, Edinburgh, and Glasgow), human activity in the natural environment has many benefits for our health.

"Programs which encourage physical activity in green spaces and natural environments should continue to be fully supported," the scientists from the Royal Colleges of Physicians said. "Access to nature can significantly contribute to our mental capital and wellbeing. Safe, green spaces may be as, or perhaps more, effective as prescription drugs in treating some forms of mental illnesses. Until recently there has been little policy in place encouraging mental health practitioners to be innovative in including green space in their therapy options."

And it's not just for the benefit of humans.

Even the smallest urban green spaces are helpful for migrating birds, according to researchers at Ohio State University. Stephen Matthews, from the school of Environment and Natural Resources at Ohio, and co-author of a study on the importance of maintaining green spaces in high-density towns and cities as migrating birds look to stop to rest and look for food, said even the smallest urban green spaces are helpful for migrating birds like thrushes.

He says: "Migratory birds are finding it increasingly difficult to find adequate food and shelter in urban areas as they fly from their winter refuges towards summer breeding grounds."

He warned that the conservation value of preserving even small, fragmented woodland sites within urban areas is a "lifeline for any type of birds, especially for migratory birds such as swifts and swallows, which generally migrate on a broad front," he said in his study.

So not only do we need to protect the green spaces we have currently in our urban areas, we need to create more where and when we can.

New York's Central Park: One of the greatest green spaces in any of the world's urban settings. *Photo by Scott Cunningham*

When I think of urban parks and green spaces, I think of New York's remarkable Central Park, which is Manhattan's true oasis in one of the densest urban centers in the world.

It's a polarizing example of how crucial green space is for urban development of any size, for important reasons beyond the obvious aesthetics. Accelerated tree growth in cities offsets carbon, creates oxygen, offers shade and, from a human-health aspect, offers important opportunities for exercise and recreation. This is increasingly important as the younger generation of plugged-in kids has a disaffection and disconnection from nature—nature deficit disorder, as author Richard Louv coined in his book, *Last Child in the Woods*.

Research in environmental psychology by universities in the US, England and Scotland, and yet another in the Netherlands, has shown that a natural environment has a positive effect on well being through restoration of stress and fatigue. Research has shown a positive relationship between the amount of green space in the living environment and physical and mental health and longevity.

The London Wildlife Trust said while there was more pressure than ever on green spaces from development, there was a "greater recognition of their importance." The trust cited new London schemes such as the Heritage Lottery-funded Capital Woodlands, which is rejuvenating six flagship sites across London, as a step in the right direction.

Vancouver, Canada, is famous for its own Stanley Park, which is more than 10 percent larger than New York City's Central Park and almost half the size of London's Richmond Park. It boasts "A five-and-a-half-mile seawall path circles the park, which is used by 2.5 million pedestrians, cyclists, and inline skaters every year. Much of the park remains forested with an estimated half million trees as tall as 249 feet and hundreds of years old." With roughly 120 miles of trails and roads in the downtown park, the Project for Public Spaces has ranked Stanley Park as the sixteenth best park in the world and sixth best in North America.

A terrific New York-based non-profit organization, the Project for Public spaces works around the world to improve cities. "Our urban parks program focuses on improving parks as community and economic assets that help revitalize neighborhoods and downtowns. We work with communities interested in creating park destinations that foster healthy activities within the park and the surrounding community," the project's mission statement says.

It's worth mentioning, briefly, that aside from green spaces, the project's mandate is to improve downtown cores with the creation or restoration of public institutions such as museums, government buildings, and libraries, making cities become more livable, sustainable, and authentic.

The project has also played a public role in fostering the establishment and enhancement of local economies and communities by supporting the pivotal role markets play in supporting public health and local food systems.

"When people think about great cities, it's often the intangible qualities—vitality, sense of place, and positive experiences—that they remember most," the program says. It continues:

"PPS works with developers and communities to create these kinds of neighborhoods, where a broad array of activities and destinations create the conditions that attract people, and where residents and visitors alike feel comfortable, welcome and safe.

"PPS's program to facilitate the "return of the public square" focuses on reinvigorating existing squares and working with cities to create new ones. The goal is to create squares that become important gathering places for the local community. Success depends upon both physical improvements to the space and a strong management program.

"Waterfronts around the world are undergoing major transformations. While shifts in industry have left some rusty and dilapidated, many others are being re-imagined as thriving public spaces the whole community can enjoy."

The late American urbanist, analyst, and journalist William H. Whyte once said, "It is difficult to design (open) space that will not attract people—what is remarkable is how often this has been accomplished."

Today, many public spaces appear intentionally designed to be looked at but not touched. They are neat, clean, and empty—as if to say, "no people, no problem!" But to us, when a public space is empty, vandalized, or used chiefly by undesirables, this is generally an indication that something is very wrong with its design, or its management, or both.

The trouble, traditionally—and I don't think it takes a scientist, expert, or even a huge university study to tell you—is that urban green space is under strong pressure due to increasing urban development, especially for lower-income families without resources to move to greener areas outside the cities.

I have heard this described by many researchers and in various publications as "environmental injustice," as elected civic officials and city planners historically have viewed green space as more of a luxury (an expensive one where urban land is at a premium both in quantity and value) rather than a basic necessity, and are completely blind to the scientifically proven and potent effects of green space in our living environments on health, general psychological well-being, and even social safety.

"Vitamin G" is very real!

The late Judith Zuk, who was the chief executive officer of Brooklyn Botanic Garden, was a fierce supporter of urban green space as a natural and necessary coexistence:

"I remember as a kid growing up in New Jersey that I always loved being out in the garden. My grandmothers were both great gardeners and our landlady was a frustrated gardener whose husband had paved over most of the gardening space. She spent the subsequent years reclaiming the asphalt," Zuk said on the www.udel.edu site. Zuk, who passed away in 2007, celebrated the Brooklyn Botanic Garden as one of the densest urban centers in America, if not the world, lurks just beyond its gates. "I think we are the finest urban, botanic garden in the country. There are many gardens that are equally good, some more beautiful, but we are the one that is most centrally, smack-dab in the middle of the city," she said.

In an interview on the website, Zuk continued that, "we provide for the people around us is an extraordinary combination of things. Brooklyn is the largest of the five boroughs in New York City. We have two and a half million people in Brooklyn alone, which means that one of every hundred people in the US is a neighbor of ours. Of the 80 square miles in Brooklyn, 52 acres comprise the garden.

"There are just thousands of people hungry for some green space; they crave beauty, just as they crave the natural environment. They really treasure the garden. There are 93 ethnic groups in the borough, and people don't always live peacefully among each other out there in the street. But, when they come into the garden, it is as if the surroundings transform them. It is a very civilizing, very inspiring environment."

And Zuk was well aware of the effect of educating children on the beauty, the importance, and the fragility of nature—exactly the reason Rose Lane and I like entertaining school trips to our own Charlane Plantation. Rosie and I built our nature trail many years ago and have made it available for our guests to use, as well as for ourselves and our family to enjoy. But the most pleasure we get is from the young kids and their teachers from area schools that come out from time to time and walk the trail. Young folks get so excited when they encounter nature, and they are getting good exercise when they walk the trail while at the same time learning about the natural world.

"I know what you can do if you take a small child and you feed positive ideas into his head. He will carry them with him his whole life," Zuk was quoted as saying.

My friend Bette Midler founded a wonderful organization in the New York City area called the New York Restoration Project (see: www.nyrp.org/). Founded in 1995 and going strong ever since, NYRP identifies under-resourced parks and gardens and otherwise derelict and neglected properties throughout the city's five boroughs and renovates them into beautiful and useful green spaces. I had the honor and pleasure of helping with one of these projects in the early 2000s when former New York Giants' wide receiver Amani Toomer and I worked on the High Bridge Park in South Bronx for NYRP. It was great fun to join in, and today the park is clean, green, and used by hundreds of visitors a day. Bette and NYRP have renovated countless parks and gardens, and the organization stands as a shining example of how cities and metropolitan areas can revive these properties into useful and attractive areas that people can enjoy and appreciate.

While our own capital city of Atlanta, Georgia, has been challenged by rapid growth and sprawl, the city has done its best

Chuck with a group of kids exploring nature in New York's Central Park.

to build and maintain its city parks and green spaces dotted around the area. While not at the top of the list of the nation's most parks (as we will discuss later in this chapter), it still has some great green spaces.

The famous Piedmont Park is a great example, right in the downtown core. It is one of the city's best places to visit, and is extremely well run by the Piedmont Park Conservancy. The 185 acre park has a public swimming pool and tennis courts, and lots of places to bike, roller blade, and skateboard. The gocitykids. parentsconnect.com/attraction site boasts that 'in 2006, the park re-opened the historic Active Oval and ball fields. The $1.8-million restoration project included adding two softball fields, two soccer fields, regulation size sand volley ball courts, a running track, new drinking fountains, benches, and a shade pergola for viewing the games. In 2007, the Mayor's Grove Boundless Playground opened. Both play areas are very popular and well designed. Yet another improvement was made in 2010, with an additional fifty or so acres being renovated. The Piedmont Park Conservancy, the nonprofit member- and donor-funded organization that manages the park, hosts Saturday Safari events May through September, and the science and nature workshops are very popular."

During summer, the park offers a terrific day camp, and on Saturdays during vegetable high seasons, the Piedmont Park Conservancy and the city's Department of Parks, Recreation, and Cultural Affairs runs a market.

A decade ago, local governments and the state recognized the importance of green space in the light of the runaway development of Atlanta in particular. In 2000, under the governorship of Roy Barnes, the Georgia legislature passed a bill establishing the Georgia Greenspace Program, which encouraged counties to voluntarily set aside 20 percent of their land as green space and enact local laws that permanently protect land and water, including agricultural and forestry land, protecting river, stream, and lake water quality, reduction of soil erosion, and flood dangers. The act also offered protection of native plant and animal habitats.

The allocation of $30 million a year for three years for the acquisition of county green space ran out quickly and has not been refunded, but unless the act is rescinded or amended, at no time in the future may development occur on the preserved land if the construction is incompatible with green space functions.

I've mentioned the Atlanta BeltLine in terms of its impact on transportation, but it's also one of the biggest and most ambitious undertaking to increase green space anywhere in America. It will increase the city's total green space by nearly 40 percent, adding nearly 1,300 acres of parks linked by a 22-mile loop around the city through the conversion of a railroad right-of-way, according to plans.

Along with the green space and transit routes, the BeltLine project is also proposed to include nearly 28,000 housing units and create more than 30,000 jobs in over a twenty-five-year span. The BeltLine concept was approved by the city in 2005, and two years later the city began purchasing land for what lawmakers call the "Emerald Necklace" that will encircle the metropolis. The first groundbreaking ceremony on the ambitious project was held in 2008, and the first section of the BeltLine was completed just one year later.

In June 2010, John Somerhalder, chairman of the board of the BeltLine Partnership, announced that "a year from now, Atlantans will walk, jog and bike from Piedmont Park to Freedom Park, connecting to what will be the first new Atlanta BeltLine park to open—Historic Fourth Ward Park."

The BeltLine is one of many greenbelts, which have been established in America (and, indeed, in cities all over the world). Notable examples include Portland, Oregon; Twin Cities, Minnesota; Virginia Beach, Virginia; Lexington, Kentucky; Miami-Dade County, Florida; nearly two dozen communities in the San Francisco Bay area; Staten Island, New York; Austin, Texas; and Boise, Idaho. New York is also in the game with their High Line project.

Ann Arbor, Michigan, meanwhile, is acquiring conservation easements on agricultural land around the city without the establishment of an urban growth boundary.

Womens' rights and environmental activist Wangari Maathai launched the Green Belt Movement in Kenya in 1977 as a small tree-planting program to address the challenges of deforestation, soil erosion, and lack of water in her home country. Her organization has overseen the planting of more than 40 million trees across Africa and in 2004 Maathai became the first environmentalist to be awarded the Nobel Peace Prize. Why peace? "There can be no peace without equitable development, and there can be no development without sustainable management of the environment in a democratic and peaceful space," said Maathai in her Nobel acceptance speech.

According to the site environment.about.com/od/biodiversity conservation/a/greenbelts.htm, "Greenbelts in and around other urban areas have probably not saved any lives, but they are important nonetheless to the ecological health of any given region. The various plants and trees in greenbelts serve as organic sponges for various forms of pollution, and as storehouses of carbon dioxide to help offset global warming.

"Trees are an important part of the city infrastructure," says Gary Moll of American Forests. Because of the many benefits trees provide to cities, Moll likes to refer to them as the "ultimate urban multi-taskers."

"Greenbelts are also important to help urban dwellers feel more connected to nature. Dr. S. C. Sharma of the Council of Scientific and Industrial Research in India believes that all cities should "earmark certain areas for the development of greenbelts [to] bring life and color to the concrete jungle and [a] healthy environment to the urbanities."

"Greenbelts are also important in efforts to limit sprawl, which is the tendency for cities to spread out and encroach on rural lands and wildlife habitat. Three US states—Oregon, Washington, and Tennessee—require their largest cities to establish so-called "urban growth boundaries" to limit sprawl through the establishment of planned greenbelts. Meanwhile, the cities of Minneapolis, Minnesota; Virginia Beach, Virginia; Miami, Florida; and Anchorage, Alaska, have created urban growth boundaries on their own. In California's Bay Area, the nonprofit Greenbelt Alliance has successfully lobbied for the establishment of twenty-one urban growth boundaries across four counties surrounding the city of San Francisco.

"The concept has also caught on in Canada, with the cities of Ottawa, Toronto, and Vancouver adopting similar mandates for the creation of greenbelts to combat sprawl. Urban greenbelts can also be found in and around larger cities in Australia, New Zealand, Sweden, and the United Kingdom.

Just as Atlanta—and Georgia as a whole—is stepping up to the plate and embracing green space as a necessity rather than a luxury, our most significant major urban centers should be celebrated for the green spaces they have managed to preserve over the past hundred years or more.

For instance, Philadelphia's Fairmount Park is the largest city-owned park in the world—not just one, single park but sixty-three neighborhood parks comprising more than 9,200 acres and more than 10 percent of the land within the city and county of Philadelphia.

Seattle's Freeway Park is remarkable, just as the city-wide park system of the Twin Cities of Minneapolis/St. Paul is unmatched in its size. Minneapolis contains scores of parks, lakes, ponds, and greenbelts all the way into its urban core—where more than 60 percent of workers use public or alternative transportation.

Despite having a population of less than 150,000 residents, the city of Salem, Oregon, has a green space network spanning more than forty parks.

The Pittsburgh Parks Conservancy has completed extensive ecological restoration work in Frick Park, relatively recently adding 106 acres and restoring the Nine Mile Run stream valley.

Chicago has its famous Lincoln Park—which began as a small public cemetery on what was then the city's northern fringes, and is now the front yard for most of the north edge of the city and sports a bird sanctuary, a paddleboat lagoon, a pond with prairie plants and wildlife, and statues of historical figures from Abraham Lincoln to Johann Friedrich von Goethe.

New Orleans boasts a 1,300-acre park right in its heart, called City Park, with one of the largest stands of live oak trees in the world.

Dallas has its famous Versailles Park, Houston its Hermann Park with its remarkable Japanese Garden, and Denver has Washington Park.

Los Angeles, one of the vastest cities in terms of acreage, boasts a very sustainable park system, which includes the Mildred E. Mathias Botanical Garden—the most extensive in the country. The city, with its temperate southern California weather, boasts Descanso Gardens, Beverly Gardens, and probably the most famous, Griffith Park in the Santa Monica Mountains, which can make you feel as if you're in the country when in fact you're right smack in the middle of Hollywood!

I can't, of course, list through all the famous parks in every American city, but it bears noting—and is a remarkable story in itself—that one man alone is largely responsible for many of our country's greatest green space landmarks. Nineteenth century landscape architect Frederick Law Olmsted (26 April 1822–28 August 1903) was one of our country's first and most vocal proponents of green spaces. And he was certainly a man of action as well as words: Not only did he design Central Park and Prospect Park in New York, but was the man behind park systems in Buffalo, New York; Riverside, Illinois; Mount Royal Park in Montreal, Canada; and the Emerald Necklace in Boston, Massachusetts—which was the beginning of that city's moniker as the "Emerald City." Olmsted also designed Deering Oaks Park in Portland, Maine; the Belle Isle Park in the Detroit River for Detroit, Michigan; the Presque Isle Park in Marquette, Michigan; the Grand

Necklace of Parks in Milwaukee, Wisconsin; the Cherokee Park and entire parks and parkway system in Louisville, Kentucky; and also worked on the landscape surrounding the United States Capitol building. He was on the team that worked on the Biltmore Estate in Asheville, North Carolina. Along with America's first true forester Gifford Pinchot and the Biltmore's owner, George Vanderbilt II, Olmstead helped to design one of the most stunning and historic properties in the US.

Truly a remarkable man, Olmstead was described by his friend and colleague Daniel Burnham as "An artist, he paints with lakes and wooded slopes; with lawns and banks and forest covered hills; with mountain sides and ocean views."

In the summer of 2000, a federal green space bill was being considered and sparked a heated debate about buying more land for soccer fields, open space, and hiking trails all over the nation. The Conservation and Reinvestment Act proposed taking taxes from offshore drilling and putting the money into buying public lands to restore eroded beaches, create new urban parks, and protect wildlife. It was supported by conservation groups, along with sporting goods companies, but opposed by property rights groups and western Republicans, who are wary of federal ownership of land.

Unfortunately, the bill died on the vine.

I think the lawmakers missed the big picture, which I began talking about at the beginning of this chapter: More green space, especially urban forests, provide fresh air and clean water for people, animals, and plants, preserves good agricultural land, provides residents of the region with access to parks, hiking trails, rivers, lakes, and other recreational lands, and in some cases, greenbelts preserve historic communities, villages, towns, and hamlets.

Collectively, urban trees in the United States account for nearly one-quarter of the nation's total tree canopy cover. I think of trees as nature's own solar-powered technology, helping mitigate urban ecosystems, and while obviously urban forests aren't an all-in-one answer to urban America's problems, they certainly make towns and cities more livable and healthier.

In fact, green spaces of all sorts are a proven benefit to public health and should be a priority.

As Amy Zlot, an epidemiologist with the Oregon Department of Human Services, wrote in the *American Journal of Health Promotion*, the degree to which city people walk or ride bicycles as a primary mode of transportation depends largely on how much green space is available.

"Because engaging in moderate physical activity such as walking or bicycling can improve health outcomes, understanding strategies that increase these behaviors has become a public health priority," she wrote.

In a survey of more than half a million people in thirty-four urban areas, Zlot and fellow researchers discovered that San Francisco had the highest percentage of people who walked or bicycled for recreation and the highest percentage of parkland. New York City had the highest percentage that walked or bicycled for basic transportation, and the third highest amount of parkland.

Atlanta had the lowest percentage for recreational walking or bicycling and the second lowest percentage of parkland, while Memphis, Tennessee, had the lowest proportion of people who walked or rode for transportation purposes and the sixth lowest percentage of open space. San Jose, California, actually had the lowest percentage of parkland; however, when Atlanta's BeltLine (discussed earlier in this chapter) is completed, it should take it out of the cellar.

"In this set of observations, walking and bicycling for transportation was positively associated with parkland acreage," wrote Zlot.

From varying sources, including the American Podiatric Medical Association, and various news reports, as well as Zlot's study, top 10 cities for recreational walking and bicycling are: San Francisco, Milwaukee, Oakland, San Diego, San Jose, Pittsburgh, Sacramento, Los Angeles/Tampa (tied), and Denver.

The bottom ten cities for recreational walking and bicycling: Atlanta, Cincinnati, New York, Chicago, Houston, Phoenix-Mesa, Cleveland, Miami, Las Vegas, and Virginia Beach.

The top 10 cities for "utilitarian" walking and bicycling: New York, Philadelphia, Baltimore, Minneapolis-St. Paul, Boston, San Francisco, Chicago, Portland, Cincinnati, and Oakland.

The bottom 10 cities for "utilitarian" walking and bicycling: Memphis, Columbus, Cleveland, Virginia Beach, Milwaukee, St. Louis/Atlanta (tied), San Jose, San Diego, and Sacramento.

The top 10 cities for parkland as a percentage of city acreage: San Francisco, Washington, D.C., New York, San Diego, Boston, Minneapolis-St. Paul, Portland, Cincinnati, Philadelphia, and Phoenix-Mesa.

The bottom 10 cities for parkland as a percentage of city acreage: San Jose, Atlanta, New Orleans, Tampa, Miami, Houston, Cleveland, Memphis/Sacramento (tie), and Columbus.

We should be paying attention to what some other countries are doing in terms of reforestation in heavily built up areas.

I was surprised, for instance, to learn that in Mexico City, where green space is at a premium, rooftop gardens are turning heat traps into natural filters that cool the city and clean the air. The Mexican capital is also planting 175 million trees around its perimeter to improve air quality and create a natural barrier to further urban expansion.

I believe many urban areas in America have been moving in the right direction—but the example of Mexico City is a clear indicator that we could, and should, be much more aggressive in not just preserving our green spaces and urban forests, but more aggressive in enhancing the ones we do have and endeavor to create new ones.

We need more Vitamin G!

Wise Use of Our Lands

What Do We Put Where?

"If you really love the country, live in town."
Randy Craft
Nature Conservancy specialist

Just as our use of, and reliance on, fossil fuels is fundamentally flawed, so too is some of the past two centuries of land use in America.

We have buried some of our finest farmland under concrete and asphalt and, we've drained—and destroyed—some of our prime marshes, swamps, creeks, and rivers as we've let greedy developers run wild with their addiction to the sprawl of suburbs rippling outward from urban centers like a stone thrown into a pond.

As I've discussed earlier, and as many urban planners, scientists, environmentalists, and conversationalists think, continued urban sprawl is not smart growth.

We in the western world enjoy the highest quality of life ever known to humankind. We have, in some cases, caused almost immeasurable damage to our own environment to achieve this—but what's worse is that we have not set a great example for the rest of the world, most of which aspires to have what we have.

Politically, it's causing enormous difficulties as developing nations with appetites to achieve "western" standards of living quite rightly scream that we are imposing an impossible and unfair double standard on them requesting, or even insisting, through sanctions, that they adopt "green" technologies and not contribute to the greenhouse gas problems that WE started.

There is no simple answer, and I won't pretend to even have a complicated one.

But here are some cold, hard facts: In May 2010, the UN reported that twentieth-century, American-styled, economic growth of, and appetite for, raw materials in countries such as China, India, and Brazil is quite simply threatening the entire world's biodiversity.

One third of our planet's animals and plants are "at risk of extinction," the UN says.

The latest report—the third edition of the UN's *Global Biodiversity Outlook*—is based on data obtained from studies in more than 120 countries across the world.

Ahmed Djoghlaf, the executive secretary of the Convention on Biological Diversity, said in a media conference on the UN's report that "The magnitude of the damage (to ecosystems) is much bigger than previously thought. The rate of extinction is currently running at 1,000 times the natural historical background rate of extinction."

If mankind does not stop its unsustainable pattern of growth, production, and consumption, he warned, "If the nine billion people predicted to be with us by 2050 were to have the same lifestyle as Americans, we would need five planets."

At this point, the only truly smart growth is no growth, but that is not a reality, although, as I've discussed, we're already experiencing the oft-shockingly rapid decline of some of the most unsustainable developments in American history—Detroit is the most-cited example, where an estimated ten thousand homes and entire neighborhoods of abandoned strip malls are being torn down and their impermeable concrete and asphalt surfaces torn up and returned to once-natural states.

Yet the reality is our population is growing—not as rapidly as the developing world, but growing nonetheless. While we are, by many accounts, fast reaching the point of no return in terms of a stable global climate, we are, in a sense, being given a second chance when it comes to the growth of our towns and cities: And it can be either "smart" growth or further unsustainable development; same mistakes, different locations.

It's an oft-used quote in many contexts but as the highly regarded land-use specialist and managing partner with the Arcadia Land Use Company in New Mexico, Christopher Leinberger repeats, "We have met the enemy, and he is us."

The key, I believe—and has been not only illustrated but proven true by people like Serenbe community founder Steve Nygren—is to not try to reinvent the wheel, as it were, but to look to the past at what has worked and stood the test of time. In the case of Serenbe, it's been the English village model. I think, and have read many books by credible urban planners and scientists who have devoted their lives to this subject, that to some degree smart growth is going to take the courage of politicians worried more about doing the right thing than risking not being re-elected, the big-picture ethics of developers such as South Carolina's Poplar Grove founder Vic Mills, and a paradigm shift in the flawed version of the "American dream" that is based on a huge house on a large lot and three cars in every garage—a "dream" that has played out to actually be a nightmare of low-density sprawl and unrelenting, ever-worsening dependence on roads and highways and fossil fuels, traffic congestion and pollution, and the loss of precious green spaces and forested lands.

As smart growth advocate Douglas Porter of the Urban Land Institute has lamented, there is a "gap between the daily mode of living desired by most Americans and the mode that most city planners believe is most appropriate." To the dismay of smart growth proponents, locally elected officials are generally unwilling to approve and embrace smart growth policies for fear of the wrath of voters. Porter and others have suggested one solution, which in itself raises the wrath of more conservative voters: Give regional, state, and federal governments a mandate to ensure smart growth—taking some of the responsibility and political vulnerability out of the hands of locally elected officials.

This may seem like a conservationist's utopian fantasy, but the fact is that it has already begun, at least in some small measure. Ray LaHood, whom President Obama appointed Secretary of Transportation in January 2009, started a blog (fastlane.dot.gov/) in which he announces his intentions to revolutionize and refocus many aspects of how goods are transported and how, indeed, Americans themselves get to and from work and places of commerce. As part of Obama's massive American Recovery and Reinvestment Act of 2009, which ambitiously aims to boost the economy while "helping to rebuild America from coast to coast," Secretary LaHood announced that the federal government is embracing a "major policy revision" that aims to give bicycling and walking the same policy and economic consideration as driving.

"Today I want to announce a sea change," he wrote on his blog. "This is the end of favoring motorized transportation at the expense of non-motorized."

I don't want to get partisan or pick on any individual politician, but Congressman Steven LaTourette, an Ohio Republican, shot back that "I don't even understand how you get a bang for the buck out of a bicycle project. I mean, what job is going to be created by having a bike lane?"

Humbly and respectfully, I think he's missing the point.

Just about everything we've done over the past sixty years has been without a great deal of forethought. Much of it has been simply wrong. It is as if we were in a huge hurry to build, build, build, without a great deal of concern for the integrity of what we are building and without the long view in mind. So many corners have been cut in all kinds of projects for various reasons, to meet a schedule or to save a buck here and there, that the outcome has clearly resulted in a lot of developments that are unsustainable and hardly what one could argue as smart, much less sustainable or strong.

While certainly not ill-intentioned, the way our fathers and grandfathers brought about a change in transportation, in zoning laws, mortgage financing (which alone has crippled the world's economy, essentially, for more than two years now and shows little sign of recovery), housing construction, and a damn-the-torpedoes (or, more correctly damn the environment) land-use policies has brought us to where we are today: Vast highway systems and suburbs separate people from their workplaces; farmers are further separated from their customers; and suburban strip malls and shopping malls have decimated traditionally commercial downtown cores.

The reality is that we have what we have at this point, but we also have the opportunity at this juncture to take a long, hard look at the best options for how we grow going forward. The future is, obviously, in planning. It will be either good planning or flawed planning.

That's where I think good Regional Planning Councils or Regional Commissions might play an increasingly important role. Some have been around for decades, helping individual community governments come together with their strengths to help solve each other's weaknesses, and some have only been instituted in recent times. Whether well established or new, the purpose of these entities is to keep good data on things like existing infrastructure, roads, areas already developed, areas that are best kept in green spaces or parks, and a close eye on proposed development. Therefore, they can help a community best decide where and how to grow.

Such councils or commissions are essentially inter-governmental agencies comprised of both elected and appointed officials and help multiple-county regions—such as the Atlanta Regional Commission, which coordinates with ten area counties as well as the city of Atlanta. Their goal, and crucial role, I believe is to assist regional leadership on planning initiatives for town planning, educational programs, emergency preparedness and hazard mitigation, transportation concerns, outdoor recreation planning, solid waste processing and, among the most important long-term goals, land-use issues. This is especially important for the challenges faced—in everything from land use, land protection, transportation, and other issues—in such a rapidly growing region as Atlanta.

Ideally, the commissions work off the strengths of the individual regions as a catalyst for reaching the most suitable problem solving for the quality of life of its residents, and the quality of preservation of its regions.

There are some similar councils and commissions that, in fact, straddle state lines, such as the Bear Lake Regional Commission, which helps local governments with issues and planning in two counties under the direct jurisdiction of local governments in Bear Lake County, Idaho, and Rich County, Utah.

Atlanta is trying to redefine itself with its BeltLine and the development of "village" neighborhoods within the metropolis, while cities such as Detroit have surrendered to the reality that the unsustainable growth they have experienced will require their partial deconstruction into "new" small cities. And that's where I think part of the answer lies: "new" small cities. They have some assets that large cities lack, and if the designs are well thought out, the results can be very smart, strong, and sustainable. In the meantime, we can certainly make our existing metro areas better as well, through intelligent renovation, thoughtful placement of public transportation, putting businesses, schools, and residential spaces in the right places, and using other techniques for re-thinking our inner cities.

This, too, is where Regional Commissions can play vital roles as they are more likely to be more objective and posses the ability to look at the "big picture" of a larger region than, say, just one individual township or county.

Whether we are talking about new townships or existing communities and cities, achieving "grid parity"—that is, the point at which renewable energy is as cheap as or cheaper than power from traditional fossil fuel or nuclear sources—is going to be exceptionally difficult without broader thinking.

But we don't have a long-term choice.

By simply thinking how to source our energy, like putting small (20-50 megawatt, for instance) power sources, whether biomass, wind, solar, or other renewable sources, in rural areas that will use that power locally, we will have come a long way toward grid parity. Smaller "new" communities could consider these options as well, and could be located near a source of renewable energy, benefiting from being close to new, next-generation power sources such as biomass plants and leave the massive grids that they are usually on—grids that can suffer energy losses of up to 10 percent purely by the inefficiency of transferring power along tens, or even hundreds, of miles of high-voltage power lines, which themselves are proven to be detrimental to both the environment and people's health.

If energy production were localized all over the country in what experts describe as a "first-world energy grid," then renewable energy could truly become predominant.

As the *Washington Post* reported, "Hydrokinetic power harvested from underwater ocean currents shows promise in coastal areas. Hydropower from rivers would generate the most electricity in the West and Midwest, where the drop is higher and the water rush more forceful than in other parts of the country. Solar power on a large scale works best in sunny climates, and wind power on the coasts and in the Great Plains. And geothermal energy tapped from the thirteen Western states that sit within the trans-Pacific 'Ring of Fire' could provide up to half of the nation's current level of electricity output."

In other places, such as the Southeast, Pacific Northwest, and even parts of the Midwest, biomass energy production is likely to make the most sense given the amount of wood and other cellulosic renewable resources available.

As smaller cities develop and embrace new energy, just think of their potential for local job creation.

As Catherine Tumber points out in her excellent *Boston Review* piece "Small, Green, And Good: The Role of Neglected Cities In a Sustainable Future":

"A 2007 American Solar Energy Society report claimed that renewable energy and energy-efficient industries had already created nearly 8.5 million jobs in the United States, a little more than half in indirectly related fields such as accounting, information technology, and trucking. Many are blue-collar jobs in maintenance and manufacturing. A September 2008 proposal from the Apollo Alliance estimates that its New Apollo Program—a renewable energy proposal on a scale akin to that of the Kennedy administration's space program—could create five million "high-quality" green-collar jobs over the next decade. Indeed, many have pointed out that bold low-carbon policy initiatives could launch the next Industrial Revolution."

Deron Lovaas, a representative of the Sierra Club's Challenge to Sprawl Campaign, told a CNN panel that city dwellers are becoming evermore aware of how unsustainable our cities are: "They may not call it sprawl, but they talk about the symptoms, like traffic congestion, like pollution, loss of green space, loss of a traditional neighborhood feeling, loss of quality of life. Now that there's an awareness that all these are problems, we're at a tough point where we have to deal with solutions. Some realize they're part of the problem, but others don't."

Christopher Leinberger, who was on the same panel, agrees, saying "that we are experiencing a tragedy of commons, whereby the quality of life that we all aspire to, by all of us running towards it, we destroy that quality of life. I do believe there's a greater understanding, though it's certainly not prevalent, but growing."

And as much as there is an increasing movement against "big government," I think federal involvement in developmental policy in some cases is a good idea, as it could supersede regional squabbles and perhaps serve a greater good.

As Leinberger says: "Some of the greatest cities on the globe are Canadian. So it's depressing to hear a Canadian saying they have the same problems we do. Most of our metropolitan areas have a jumble of government. In Chicago, there are more than 300 jurisdictions—cities, towns, and counties planning land use. What they do is push the negative consequences of sprawl onto their neighbors. It's obviously self-defeating. Canadians have done a better job, and we should learn from them. We have many governments trying to optimize their own citizens' needs and, in the process, they destroy the quality of life for the whole metropolitan area.

"Jane Jacobs' *The Death and Life of Great American Cities*, was obviously one of the seminal books regarding this issue. What she was pointing out was that there are really only two approaches to urban planning. It may sound simplistic. One is car-dominated, which is what we've been following for the last 50 years. The other is pedestrian- and/or transit-oriented, which is what we've forgotten how to build over the last 50 to 100 years. The former approach, the car-dominated approach, basically means we'll devote the vast majority of our land to asphalt. For every 1 percent population growth, we're looking at a 10 percent increase in the growth of our metro areas. That's what's happened in the last 50 years. The latter approach, which is what Jacobs was trying to persuade us to understand, certainly leads to more mixed use, and much more choice for Americans. Right now, today, we're following that first approach, without much choice in our metro areas. It will be car-dominated. The second question that you posited lays out yet another lack of choice. As much as I believe in transit-oriented development, and more pedestrian orientation, to take such a draconian approach will never work. But fundamentally, it is opposed to the choice that we have always held as our ideal, as a people."

Leinberger is one of the smartest experts on how we need to redesign our cities and realign our zoning practices to ensure schools, hospitals, shops, and services are located appropriately —along with renewable-resource energy plants and agricultural areas that best serve local populations.

As he said on CNN: "It's important to note that zoning ordinances were driven predominantly by traffic codes. Basically, traffic and how we park our cars has driven development over the last 50 years. Many of those traffic codes came into the books the good, old-fashioned way—they xeroxed them. They tended to xerox them from the traffic institute at Michigan State University, which happens to get much of its funding from General Motors. In other words, our zoning has primarily made the world safe to park and move cars. I was just involved in the drafting of a new development code for downtown Albuquerque, New Mexico. They threw out all the old zoning, and put in place some very simple principles, such as the front door of the building must face the sidewalk. If you follow those principles, you get your building permit in three weeks. We need that kind of code throughout the country, and I think we will in the next decade."

Lovaas agrees: "Smart growth is development that protects open space, mixes land uses, so people can shop, work and live in areas near one another, so they don't have to travel far, that offers transportation choices, so people can drive, take rail, take the bus, can walk or bike in their community, and smart growth contributes to revitalizing one or more existing communities. I missed the most important part—location. Smart growth is located near or in an existing community and an existing transportation system."

Both experts agree that, quite simply, public transportation and the availability of pedestrian- and bicycle-friendly options is the best option for the future—and that high gas prices through taxation is one way to force the change. Says Leinberger: "I do believe higher gas prices will help contribute to a more smart growth, pedestrian-friendly future. It will take time, however. It's taken us 50 years to put ourselves in this position where we have little choice: We can either drive or we can drive."

"Transferable Development Rights is a useful tool," says Lovaas. "It's underused in this country. The concept is that you split the right to develop from property rights, and you use that as a tool to preserve open spaces, to preserve farmland and green spaces and, at the same time, to allow for greater density and more development in designated areas."

Says Leinberger: "In this country, we have too much land. We value it very cheaply, therefore. So farmland, like we saw in the show—farmers can't afford to pay more than $5,000 per acre for land. Suburban subdivision land starts at about $40,000 per acre. You have a large gap between the farmer and the subdivision developer as to what they can pay. It seems to me that the only way an effective Transfer of Development Rights system will work is that once we understand that we need to impose urban growth policies on our metro areas beyond which development can't take place and therefore the undeveloped land within those boundaries will begin to be developed properly. By the way, we only have a few examples of urban growth boundaries in this country, including Seattle, Portland, Oregon, and a few other metro areas, but there are many examples in Canada, Europe and Japan."

When the farmland is protected in this way, it's far easier for farmers to succeed, and succeed on a local level. The closer food is grown or raised (in the case of cattle, poultry and pork, etc.) to its destination the more sustainable it is, and the healthier.

While we're talking about how to plan growth, it is of paramount importance that we also look at protecting certain natural lands, and take measures to make sure some lands avoid substantial development of any kind. Among the most useful tools we have available for these purposes are land trusts and conservation easements—such as the huge easement Vic Mills arranged through Ducks Unlimited for his South Carolina Poplar Grove development. Rose Lane and I have also put part of Charlane Plantation under easement. Much of the massive (more than 2 million acres!) tracts of land that media mogul Ted Turner owns is under conservation easement, assuring that they will never be developed.

I don't want to get too technical, but it's important to give a full explanation of how easements and land trusts work. So...

Conservation easements provide landowners a means of protecting the conservation values of their property while simultaneously maintaining ownership, retaining certain uses of their land and earning significant tax benefits. A conservation easement is a legal agreement between a landowner and another party by which the landowner imposes permanent restrictions on the way the property is used in order to protect its conservation values. Property rights, such as certain kinds of mining or future subdivision and development, are removed or limited and conveyed to the easement holder while remaining rights, such as recreation, agricultural, and forest uses, are retained by the property owner.

Within reasonable limits, there can be some rights reserved for minor additions or certain activities. For instance, in our easement we wrote in the right to build up to four cabins on a twenty-five-acre footprint of where we have some existing buildings. The entire easement covers about three hundred acres. The reason I wanted to maintain that right was that we have existing houses on the tract that we use for our hunting and retreat guests. So if we wanted to expand that business in the future, we wanted to maintain the right to do so in the same area (the twenty-five-acre "footprint") that the existing houses are on. This will have little impact on the three-hundred-acre easement in terms of staving off real development, while giving us the opportunity to do a reasonable expansion if we so desire. But the bottom line is that when you put a property under easement, you are promising, in perpetuity, never to allow a shopping mall, residential development, office buildings—whatever—to be built on the property. The owner of the property gets a fairly significant tax benefit from the federal government—and some states also have tax credit programs for easements (Georgia is one) that make it even more attractive.

As to the benefit to the landowner who donates an easement on his or her land, under the regulations set forth in 170(h) of the Internal Revenue Code those landowners are eligible for a federal income tax deduction equal to the value of their donation. The value of the easement donation, as determined by a qualified appraiser, equals the difference between the fair market value of the property before and after the easement takes effect.

To qualify for this income tax deduction, the easement must be: a) perpetual; b) held by a qualified governmental or non-profit organization; and, c) serve a valid "conservation purpose," meaning the property must have an appreciable natural, scenic, historic, scientific, recreational, or open space value. As a result of legislation signed by President George W. Bush in 2006, for that year and 2007, conservation easement donors may deduct the value of their gift at the rate of 50 percent of their adjusted gross income (AGI) per year. Further, landowners with 50 percent or more of their income from agriculture may be able to deduct the donation at a rate of 100 percent of their AGI. Any amount of the donation remaining after the first year can be carried forward for fifteen additional years (allowing a maximum of sixteen years within which the deduction may be utilized), or until the amount of the deduction has been used up, whichever comes first. With the passage of the Farm Bill in the summer of 2008 these expanded federal income tax incentives were extended such that they also apply to all conservation easements donated in 2008 and 2009.

There are basically two ways to set up a conservation easement. One is for the landowner to donate the development rights—resulting in the previously mentioned tax benefits. The other is an outright sale of the rights to a third party. That's how my friend Vic Mill's easement worked. In doing the easement for his Poplar Grove development, he was able to raise substantial capital from the sale of his easement to Ducks Unlimited, which he used to reduce the debt he would have owed on the overall project, thus giving him more capital to devote to building things like his equestrian center or to build ponds and such.

Conservation easements offer great flexibility. An easement on property containing rare wildlife habitat might prohibit any development, for example, while an easement on a working farm might allow the addition of agricultural structures. An easement may apply to all or a portion of the property, and need not require public access. Each conservation easement is carefully crafted to meet the needs of the landowner while not jeopardizing the conservation values of the land.

So easements are a way to encourage families and property owners to keep their land in a natural state, or to keep it in agriculture, or in forests. It is not a perfect tool; I take exception under the current rules that govern conservation easements that when donating an easement, the person donating gets a one-time benefit out of it while he or she is agreeing not to develop it "in perpetuity." In other words, the landowner gets the one significant tax break (which as explained above, under current rules can be spread over sixteen years) and that's it. So, a hundred years up the road, the property is still not to be developed, but the landowner at that time (whether still in a family or is sold) receives no benefit. I believe that there should be some re-visitation of benefits in reasonable time frames—shall we say for the sake of argument, every hundred years—as long as the property stays in the easement. That's just my personal opinion—but having put part of our place in this situation, that phrase "in perpetuity" certainly gave me pause. We followed through with the easement because in the long run we felt it was simply the right thing to do. But I personally think it's unfair not to get some kind of incremental benefits within reasonable time frames instead of just one. Hey—perpetuity is a long time!

Land trusts are another way that lands can be protected in their natural state, but in a different way.

Land trusts, sometimes called land conservancies or more rarely, conservation land trusts, have been in around since 1891, but only in the last two decades have land trusts truly been used on a larger scale, and they now are one of the fastest-growing and most successful conservation movements in our country.

The first regional land trust, the Trustees of Reservations, was founded in 1891. Since then, the number of land trusts has steadily increased, and there are now more than 1,667 land trusts operating in every state. Some of the most popular entities that handle trusts that folks may be familiar with include the Nature Conservancy, the Conservation Fund, the Trust for Public Lands, and the World Land Trust.

Land trusts conserve all different types of land; some protect only farmland or ranchland, others forests, mountains, prairies, deserts, wildlife habitat, urban parks, scenic corridors, coastlines, wetlands, or waterways. Each organization decides what type of land to protect according to its mission. Some parcels protected by land trusts have no, or extremely limited public access, for the protection of sensitive wildlife, or to allow recovery of damaged ecosystems. Many protected areas remain under private ownership, which also limits access as well. However, in many cases, land trusts work to eventually open up the land in a limited way to the public for recreation in the form of hunting, hiking, camping, wildlife observation, or other responsible outdoor activities. Some land is also used for sustainable agriculture, ranching or logging.

Like conservation easements, they have various tools to work with. They can buy or accept donations of land in fee. Landowners may also sell or donate a conservation easement to a land trust.

As nonprofit organizations, land trusts rely on donations, grants, and public land acquisition programs for operating expenses and for acquiring land and easements. Donors often provide monetary support, but it is not uncommon for conservation-minded landowners to donate an easement on their land, or the land itself. Some land trusts also receive funds from government programs to acquire, protect, and manage land. According to the latest National Land Trust Census, 31 percent of land trusts reported having at least one full-time staff member, 54 percent are all volunteers, and 15 percent have only part-time staff.

In between selling land or an easement to a land trust is an option called a bargain sale. A bargain sale is where a landowner sells a property interest to an organization for less than the market price. The amount of value between the market price and the actual sale price is considered a donation to the organization.

The important thing to know about conservation easements and land trusts are that they are tools that can be used to help keep natural lands in their natural state, and in many cases allow farming, forestry practices, and other related activities to continue, and can also allow for recreational use, sometimes by the public. And, that there are benefits to be had by the landowners that place their lands in these programs.

So as we grow, we need to be sensitive not only what we put where—but also to make sure we set aside some lands to assure they will stay in a natural state—some to be permanently preserved, and some that will avoid development but continue sustainable working activities in agricultural, managed forest, and recreational usages.

As Michael Pollan wrote in his hugely successful book, *The Omnivore's Dilemma*, food production has an enormous carbon footprint, particularly in a country as geographically large as America. "Sustainable agriculture and animal husbandry not only produce more nutritious food and less cruelty to animals, they are also far less dependent on petroleum for long-distance transportation, fertilizer, and neurotoxic pesticides (not to mention antibiotics)," he says.

The UN, which has for years declared that local agriculture and food production is key to famine reduction in third-world nations, recognizes that localized, sustainable food production and consumption by "locavores" is also a boon to the environment in terms of the carbon cost of transportation and, ultimately, dependence on foreign oil.

Sounds Green

Artists Finding Harmony Nurturing Nature

"If we don't have a clean planet, then what do we have—
all the causes in the world can't be handled if we
don't have water, if we don't have food,
if it's too hot to even walk outside."

Sheryl Crow

When I was in Japan on tour with Eric Clapton's Unplugged band, backing George Harrison on what would turn out to be all but two of his final public performances (I played with him on a benefit show at the Royal Albert Hall a few months later, and he played the Bob Dylan tribute concert about a year after that), I can't say that I was on the inside track on some of the behind-the-scenes moves that Eric, particularly, was making.

But I knew that it had taken quite an effort on Eric's part to get George to agree to go back on the road in the first place, and there was constant talk—a great hope among the fans, not to mention us in the band—that the tour would last beyond Japan and go around the world.

George wouldn't have it, though. He said the experience of the Dark Horse (George Harrison & Friends North American) tour of Canada and the US in 1974 was too painful to think about reliving. The press had been hostile to him—though, as history has shown, there were some incredible performances by George on that tour, and he was extremely well received by fans—but he also mentioned that it bothered him how much trash and waste was left in the wake of him being on the road. He was aware of the ecological impact of taking a large show on the road, and he told me that it was one reason he was limiting the tour to Japan. I have to say that it was probably one of the first times it struck me, too, what an enormous toll such large tours can have on the environment.

I'm proud to say that the Rolling Stones have been credited as being one of the first major bands to embark on showing off some green sensibility when the UK portion of our 2003 Licks tour was carbon neutral, after the band's organization struck a deal with T-Mobile and Future Forests to fund two new highland forests in Scotland.

There are varying estimations, but most of the emissions from music tours come from not just the bands traveling between gigs, but also from the fans themselves, getting themselves to the shows. On the Licks tour, we were told that it would take one tree to offset the emissions from fifty-seven fans—and we played to more than 160,000 people on just nine UK dates. That meant us planting more than 2,800 trees.

The president and founder of Future Forests, Dan Morrell, was pleased with the arrangement, but told the press that it was a small step that was valid, if still symbolic, as: "Everything we do, from going to a gig through driving a car to boiling a kettle, creates carbon dioxide yet there is still a lot of inertia in the public's attitude."

Many artists are aware of their impact on the environment and are showing their sensitivity. The reissue in 2010 of the Stones' album *Exile on Main Street*, for instance, was released by a multinational company that aims to offset emissions related to the manufacture and transportation of their product.

Pink Floyd has followed suit with its tours and releases, and Pearl Jam has partnered with the Cascade Land Conservancy (CLC) to mitigate carbon-equivalent emissions from its ongoing world tour. Pearl Jam will donate $210,000 to plant thirty-three acres of native trees and plants in four Puget Sound communities: Seattle, Kirkland, Redmond, and Kent.

"We're going to store carbon where it should be," said Pearl Jam guitarist Stone Gossard in several interviews, including one with the Mother Nature Network, "in our urban forests."

The *Seattle Times* reported that Pearl Jam had its tour's carbon footprint measured by Michael Totten, chief adviser of Climate, Freshwater & Ecosystem Services at Conservation International. The band's fourteen trucks, six buses, and other shipments rack up some 1,600 metric tons of emissions. The band and crew travel 899,525 passenger miles, creating another 1,182 metric tons of carbon. Hotel rooms add up to 3,183 nights for band and crew, and cost 114 metric tons of carbon. The 32 venues use 484,800 kilowatt hours of electricity, and generate 187 metric tons of carbon. And then there are the fans, responsible for 2,339 metric tons of carbon, generated by car trips to and from the shows. Calculating carbon emissions isn't pretty, Gossard said, but it has to be done. Sort of like cleaning out the bathroom drain, I thought. Once you do it, you do all you can to make sure it never gets that bad again.

"I'm trying to be a responsible business owner," Gossard said. "I've traveled enough to realize that there's not a lot of places that look like Washington State."

The carbon partnership is the largest CLC has ever had, and one CLC president Gene Duvernoy would like other businesses to imitate.

There's no reason not to, he said. Carbon offsets are not only good for business, they preserve habitat and bring communities together, since the plantings in the four Puget Sound cities will be done by volunteers.

"Learning how to do this responsibly is a great strategic benefit for any business," he said—not just for a rock band.

Gossard told the Mother Nature Network that, "Since 2003, we've been identifying our carbon footprint and calculating how much carbon we put out into the atmosphere as part of our business. When we tour we have freight, we have a lot of trucks, shipping, there's chartered flights, fans going to and from the venue, etc. It's a very energy-intensive process for us to tour."

Gossard told Mother Nature Network Pearl Jam's investments aim to offset carbon from the band's use of fossil fuels linked to trucks, ships, planes, hotels as well as estimated emissions by

480,000 fans traveling to and from concerts in 2009. According to calculations from the CLC, the band's 32-date tour produced 5,474 metric tons of CO_2." There's been a lot of effort put into making sure this is a clear and verifiable project," Gossard said. "And we hope that everybody scrutinizes it closely so that you can help us show that we really put the work into it; identifying why it has so many multiple benefits to our business, the band, and the local community."

With Pearl Jam's donation, plantings and restoration of the native natural beauty around Puget Sound will begin immediately. The project is expected to be complete by 2013. "This sort of approach has an enormous impact on improving forest health, connecting people to nature, and activating communities to engage in the restoration and stewardship of natural open spaces," said Duvernoy.

When discussing what Pearl Jam is doing to reduce emissions while on tour, Gossard said the group doesn't tour much or with a big production like so many other groups. "We tour with about five or six semi trucks compared to, say, the Rolling Stones that might have a hundred semis. Our particular focus is on analyzing our fuel and energy and acknowledging that."

As well as offsetting its carbon footprint, Pearl Jam donated $100,000 to organizations that are working on climate change, and other green causes. On one tour, the band donated funds to help preserve Madagascan rainforest. I applaud this extraordinary effort by my friends in Pearl Jam, and in a lot of cases, other artists that are like-minded are doing work for the environment and making donations that they eschew publicity for and do anonymously.

Grammy-winning hip-hop group The Roots is an ardent supporter of Organix, an organization started in 1992 to encourage the food industry to create better food choices for babies and children and raise standards in general within the food industry. The band members are animal lovers, working with PETA on a campaign to "Stop the Violence: Go Veg." The group also hosts an annual Pre-Grammy Jam & Green Carpet Bash, inviting fellow artists and friends to jam with them and raise awareness about green issues.

Green Day partnered with the Natural Resources Defense Council on a Move America Beyond Oil campaign, and has made a number of YouTube videos voicing support for environmental protection and smarter energy policies.

There have been some rockers who've taken severe criticism for their touring—particularly U2, whose last "360 Tour," according to the *Belfast Telegraph* newspaper, was larger than even the biggest of the Stones' tours, requiring nearly 140 transport trucks to haul a half-million pounds of equipment to each venue. That tour emitted three times more carbon than Madonna's 2006 world tour or any of the Stones' outings, according to the media.

Guitarist The Edge told the BBC that the band would "love to have some alternative to big trucks bringing the stuff around but there just isn't one. U2 will offset whatever carbon footprint we have."

According to Helen Roberts, an environmental consultant for carbonfootprint.com, the band would need to plant 20,118 trees a year to offset its tour impact.

Among the most vocal critics of large tours such as U2's (and, by default, I would assume, Madonna and the Rolling Stones) is Talking Heads frontman David Byrne. On a blog, he slammed the band and said the U2 world tour costs were "excessive," considering the band's stance on world hunger.

Byrne wrote: "$40 million to build the stage and, having done the math, we estimate 200 semi trucks crisscrossing Europe for the duration. It could be professional envy speaking here, but it sure looks like, well, overkill, and just a wee bit out of balance given all the starving people in Africa and all."

The Edge responded that, "I think anybody that's touring is going to have a carbon footprint. I think it's probably unfair to single out rock 'n' roll. There's many other things that are in the same category but as it happens we have a program to offset whatever carbon footprint we have."

I don't want to get in the middle of an argument between such great artists, but I will say that I think it's vitally important that artists, whether in the rock world or from any other genre, should pay attention to their carbon output and be willing to do something about it.

One artist I can think of who deserves nothing but praise for the way he runs his show, so to speak, is Willie Nelson. For decades he's been a leader in the music world of being environmentally conscious, and has gone so far as to start selling his own biodiesel—BioWillie. He runs his family vehicles on biodiesel, and all his tour buses and trucks run on diesel made from any number of crops. "It could get as big as we can grow fuel or find different things to make fuel from, such as chicken fat, beef fat, add that along to soybeans, vegetable oils, peanuts, safflower, sunflower," he has said.

"As long as the idea progresses because all I'm caring about is getting it out there and maybe helping the country, the farmer, the environment. I knew we needed to have something that would keep us from being so dependent on foreign oil, and when I heard about biodiesel, a light come on, and I said, 'Hey, here's the future for the farmers, the future for the environment, the future for the truckers,'" Willie told the *New York Times* in an interview in 2005. "It seems like that's good for the whole world if we can start growing our own fuel instead of starting wars over it."

As he wrote in his song "Whatever Happened to Peace on Earth?":

"So many things going on in the world,
Babies dying, mothers crying.
Just how much oil is human life worth?
And whatever happened to peace on earth?"

"That upset a lot of people, as you can imagine," he says, "I've been upset about this war from the beginning and I've known it's all about oil."

Willie, of course takes his work with Farm Aid very seriously, promotes a "buy local, sell local" theme, and has been active in supporting the use of hemp in clothing and fuel, and protecting horses from slaughter.

Add Bonnie Raitt to the list of environmentally active artists: Since about 2005, her tours have offset their carbon footprint, she has insisted that all her buses and tour trucks run on biodiesel, and she tries to offset her energy consumption by using wind energy.

"Our economic life must run in harmony with the sanctity of the natural environment," she says. None of this is new to Bonnie—she's known for her lifelong commitment to social activism as she is for her music.

Back in the 1970s, in fact, she began doing concerts to protect American old-growth forests (she's been arrested twice at forestry demonstrations!) and water supplies and to counter destructive mining operations. She's a founding member of MUSE (Musicians United for Safe Energy, www.musemusic.com), which produced the historic concerts, album and movie, NO NUKES in 1979.

On her 2002 Summer Tour, Bonnie initiated Green Highway, a traveling eco-village that provides information to concertgoers about alternative energy solutions (solar and wind power), displays Honda Hybrid vehicles, and connects fans to local environmental issues and organizations. Carrying the message of change to the national energy policy, Bonnie participated in the historic Vote For Change tour, co-headlining a bill along with Jackson Browne and Keb' Mo'.

Like Willie Nelson, Bonnie is using biodiesel made from whatever is available in terms of sustainable crops—not just feed stocks such as corn or soy. Switchgrass, Jerusalem artichokes, even industrial hemp, and, of course, used cooking oil are viable to power vehicles.

More recently, Bonnie helped start the Green Highway nonprofit (www.greenhighway.net), which is a great information resource for environmentally concerned fans and was a considerable part of the 2009 Bonnie Raitt and Taj Mahal BonTaj Roulet Tour.

As Sheryl Crow told CBS in an interview supporting the Nature Conservancy, "I was raised with this idea that you leave the campground better than how you found it. We were brought up to shut off the water when we were brushing our teeth, only ran the dishwasher when it was stuffed, never took forty-five-minute showers. I have a little boy now, so my concern is what kind of planet are we leaving."

Sheryl also tours in biofuel buses. "I have spent the better part of this tour trying to come up with easy ways for us all to become a part of the solution to global warming," she said, "Although my ideas are in the earliest stages of development, they are, in my mind, worth investigating." In 2007 she launched an effort to urge college students to become part of the movement to stop global warming, with her Stop Global Warming College Tour with Laurie David: "I find that all my causes fall under the umbrella of environmentalism. Even cancer, to a certain extent, is correlated to environmental issues. (Sheryl is a cancer survivor.) I also feel that, if we don't have a clean planet, then what do we have—all the causes in the world can't be handled if we don't have water, if we don't have food, if it's too hot to even walk outside."

Neil Young, who has long helped with Willie Nelson's Farm Aid, among other charitable causes, is an ardent believer in alternative fuels. "You're out there putting American farmers to work with a renewable fuel and taking away our dependence on foreign oil and our need to go through all these wars and tap dances we do over economics in the Middle East," he told *Rolling Stone* magazine. "Why should we do that when you have everything we need right here and we can put our own people to work?"

Actor Woody Harrelson has received an honorary doctorate from Canada's York University for his work on environmental issues.

"Mr. Harrelson's understanding of why we each need to reduce our ecological footprint is authentic, and his efforts to inspire others to grasp and act on this concept provide an object lesson for those of us who teach," said associate professor Dawn Bazely, director of the Institute for Research and Innovation in Sustainability at York. Woody told the press at the time that, "I don't consider myself much of a role model at all. The reason they're giving me this doctorate has to do with my getting a hold of a principle that I believe in and sticking to it. Otherwise, I can't think of any other aspect that I would even want my own children, much less other people's children, to follow."

He doesn't publicize his environmental efforts much, but Woody, like Willie Nelson, is one of the honorary directors on the Sustainable Biodiesel Alliance, founded in 2006 by biodiesel pioneer Kelly King, Annie Nelson, and Daryl Hannah. They're joined on the board by acclaimed musician Adam Gardner, who, with his wife, environmentalist Lauren Sullivan, founded the

REVERB non-profit group, which has helped with eco-tour support for John Mayer, Red Hot Chili Peppers, Sheryl Crow, Barenaked Ladies, Avril Lavigne, Dave Matthews Band, as well as Doobie Brothers founding member Pat Simons and Hawaiian-born singer-songwriter-environmentalist Jack Johnson. (I'll get to him in a minute!)

REVERB also runs a Campus Consciousness Tour (in 2010 it featured Drake and Ben Harper and Relentless 7), which hit universities around the country as a combination music and fan education outreach, with biodiesel-fueled buses and trucks, CO_2 offsets, recycling and composting stations, biodegradable catering supplies, co-friendly cleaning supplies, organic, local food in catering, sustainable merchandise, as well as an onsite eco-village at each concert featuring national, environmental, non-profit partners and local student groups.

Alanis Morissette is also a considerably high-profile activist on the environmental scene, involving herself in Live Earth concerts and doing activism with Adam Yauch from the Beastie Boys.

"It's a great way do it through music and art," Alanis has said in interviews. "I think I have some social activism by default in some of lyrics. Rather than trying to control people outside and tell them what to do, I'd rather take responsibility for my own life," she explains, hoping that her celebrity status helps at least on an inspirational level for her fans and others.

"We run our tour buses on biodiesel, recycle, use solar panels, I drive a hybrid car, I paid for my CD covers to be made of eco-friendly materials when they weren't doing it. They wouldn't pay, so I paid for it myself at the beginning. Now it has become a sort of a commonplace thing, but a few years ago the Red Hot Chili Peppers and myself were paying for it ourselves—so that was cool."

Alanis also narrated with Keanu Reeves a dramatic film about climate change, *The Great Warming*, which some have described as the best film on global warming yet, as it's particularly harsh with hard-hitting comments from leading scientists on America's lack of leadership and it's reacting to global warming as a political issue, instead of one threatening the very life of the planet.

In late 2009, the Canadian-born singer took up a challenge from actors Ed Norton and Anthony Edwards and ran the New

York City marathon to raise money for the Maasai Wilderness Conservation Trust, benefiting the endangered African tribe and its lands.

Sting is another superstar who has used his celebrity and profile to move green into the spotlight. In 1989, Sting and his wife, Trudie Styler, established the Rainforest Foundation, which has worked collectively with several different governments, both in South America and Europe, to protect land and native cultures, particularly of the Kayapo Indians in Brazil.

When the Police held its final concert in New York in August 2008, the organization announced, along with Police band members Andy Summers and Stewart Copeland, a $1 million donation to a program in New York City to plant one million trees by 2017.

"We have a long history here," Sting told a press conference. "We wanted to leave a gift with our last performance that would keep on giving year after year, decade after decade—the gift of trees does do that."

While I can't say this was exactly practical, I loved it when Rufus Wainright launched his Blackout Sabbath campaign with a 2003 show at a New York synagogue—using no electricity whatsoever—just a thousand candles. If nothing else, at least it made a few people think!

Radiohead is another band that does all it can to bolster the environment and lessen and offset its impact while making music and taking it to its fans.

"I think it's important for everyone to understand the consequences of our economic activity. You must be aware of the level of exploitation that's going on," frontman Thom Yorke stated during an interview with looktothestars.com website, "It's part of our Western life, and one we should accept responsibility for. There's no such thing as a free lunch or a free ticket to another country."

"Climate change is indisputable, and we have to do something dramatic. You have a certain amount of credit you can cash in with your celebrity and I'm cashing the rest of my chips in with this," Yorke continued. "The music industry is a spectacularly good example of fast-turnover consumer culture. It is actually terrifying.

Environmental considerations should be factored in to the way the record companies operate."

John Mayer is another artist who uses biodiesel buses and trucks, sells eco-friendly merchandise, and does carbon offsetting.

Pete Seeger, Country Joe McDonald, Tom Paxton, and many, many others who got together and started MUSE and spend their time working on the faculty of the Institute for Deep Ecology, crewing on the *Clearwater* and *Sea Shepherd*, creating benefit CDs for Arctic conservation and California coastal habitat, and performing in hundreds of Earth-oriented celebrations and actions.

The environmental awards received by this group are many, including an Outstanding Achievement Award from the Environmental Protection Agency, and Award of Excellence from the United Nations Environment Program.

Dave Matthews is another of the most environmentally considerate musicians out there. In fact, he and his band have done everything from scattering free bicycles around their hometown of Charlottesville, Virginia, to teaming up with NativeEnergy and Clean Air-Cool Planet, and are working to fully offset 100 percent of the fossil-fuel pollution the Dave Matthews Band has created with its tours since 1991—a pretty admirable undertaking.

Matthews, Emmylou Harris, Patty Griffin, Buddy Miller, Kathy Mattea, Big Kenny, and many others were on the bill 19 May 2010 to perform at the Music Saves Mountains Concert at Nashville's historic Ryman Auditorium to benefit the Natural Resources Defense Council's (NRDC) campaign to bring an end to the destructive practice of mountaintop removal coal mining. The project was launched by the Heartwood Forest Council, which has been working with singer/songwriter Jason Wilber (the guitar player for John Prine) on a compilation CD of music by nationally known recording artists to raise awareness about, and help stop, the tragedy of mountaintop removal coal-mining.

Emmylou Harris told a series of reporters that, " Mountaintop removal coal mining burns me up inside worst than any current environmental issue. I just can't fathom that something so obviously self-destructive could go on so close to home and for those in Appalachia, in their own backyard. I have written a number of times about the devastating nature of mountaintop removal coal mining, and most recently, the socially conscious musicians who are doing everything in their power to stop it.

She kicked the show off by singing about the "Green Rolling Hills" of West Virginia—"the nearest thing to heaven I know."

When Patty Loveless took the spotlight, she shared her story of being a coal miner's daughter. Loveless dedicated "You'll Never Leave Harlan Alive" to her father (who died of black lung disease) and the twenty-nine miners who died in the April 2010 West Virginia mine disaster.

According to the NRDC, entire mountaintops are blown up to get at the thin seams of coal below. Already five hundred peaks have been leveled, forests have been clear cut, and mountain streams polluted beyond repair. Countless communities in Appalachia have been devastated by the practice. According to Mountain Justice, mountaintop removal coal mining has already transformed some of the most biologically diverse temperate forests in the world into biologically barren moonscapes.

"The mountains of Appalachia are responsible for countless folk, country, and bluegrass songs. Now, the home of that rich tradition is being destroyed," Emmylou Harris told *The Tennessean* newspaper.

WyClef Jean has raised tens of millions for food and improved farming techniques in his native Haiti and throughout the third world.

The more and more I dug, the more and more surprised I was, and the more proud I felt about so many of my fellow artists. It seems that there's a whole book just in what actors and singers and musicians are doing for the environment.

The Eagles' Don Henley, for instance, has helped create the Walden Woods Project and Institute as well as the preservation of Caddo Lake, a rich wetland between the Texas and Louisiana border.

Moby goes so far as to limit his touring to cut down on his environmental impact. Also a vegan, he's a big supporter of PETA and the Humane Society, and in 2002 he opened Teany, a vegetarian tea café in New York City.

Hollywood has long been seen as one of the ground zeros for progressive social change, but according to a report from a UCLA study, the television and film industry is actually the state of California's second-largest polluter—after, ironically, the oil industry.

As a report in the Associated Press put it: "No amount of public service announcements or celebrities driving hybrid cars can mask the fact that movie and TV production is a gritty industrial operation, consuming enormous amounts of power to feed bright lights, run sophisticated cameras, and feed a cast of thousands."

But people are stepping up to the plate. According to an article on Hollywood going green on thedailygreen.com: Actress Cameron Diaz requested that her film *In Her Shoes* meet the standards for a "green seal" (as set by the Environmental Media Association, and she insisted on flying commercial for filming and promotion. Leonardo DiCaprio set strict eco-rules for production on his *11th Hour*, as did Al Gore for *An Inconvenient Truth*.

Producers Dean Devlin and Roland Emmerich turned things green with their 2004 *The Day After Tomorrow*, when the studio paid $200,000 to offset the set's emissions by planting ten thousand trees. *The Matrix* movie sets saw a whopping 97.5 percent of materials recycled; its steel and lumber were reused for low-income housing in Mexico. ReUse People of America, a nonprofit that deconstructs film sets, claims it was cheaper to dismantle and reuse the material than the fee a contractor would charge for demolition.

Producers of Fox's TV show *24* used wind and solar energy to power their sound stages, used biodiesel fuel for set cars and onset generators, and recycled everything possible. Fox Studios as a whole aims to be carbon neutral in the near future.

Tom Shadyac's *Evan Almighty* laid down some "green prints" for how to run an environmentally conscious set. Besides the usual recycling during filming, driving eco-friendly vehicles and using solar power and diesel fuel, Universal offset the production's greenhouse gasses by donating two thousand trees to the Conservation Fund.

Crosby, Stills, and Nash have long had a commitment to peace, social change and environmental activism, including non-nuclear energy protests, and they are also—along with Jackson Browne and David Lindley—ardent supporters of the charitable Guacamole Fund, a California organization that helps entertainment companies generate nonprofit revenues and stream them to worthy causes.

In fact, Jackson Browne won the 2010 Duke LEAF Award for Lifetime Environmental Achievement in the Fine Arts. Duke University's Nicholas School of the Environment presented the award to Browne in April 2010. According to the school, Actor Robert Redford received the inaugural award, which was established by the Nicholas School in 2009 to "honor artists whose works have lifted the human spirit by conveying our profound spiritual and material connection to the Earth, thereby inspiring others to help forge a more sustainable future for all."

"Jackson Browne is no pretender. While inspiring a generation to work for a better life and a better future for our children through his music, he has advocated for environmental stewardship and has a house that runs entirely on wind and solar power," said William L. Chameides, dean of the Nicholas School, "Browne exemplifies what the Duke LEAF Award is all about. We are thrilled to have him come to the Duke campus to receive the award."

In 2002, Jackson was the fourth recipient of the John Steinbeck Award, given to artists whose works exemplify the environmental and social values that were essential to the California-born author. In a 2008 interview with *Rolling Stone* magazine, Browne said, "We're all in the same boat. That's always been the subject of my songs. We only have a little time. It's a mess, so you do everything you can."

Of all the celebrities who have turned their life's work away from their callings of music or acting or writing or filmmaking or art to that of helping save our environment and move to a sustainable lifestyle, Ed Begley, Jr., stands out as one of the leaders.

Environmental lawyer and a close friend of Ed's, Bobby Kennedy, Jr., says "Ed has a greater sense of social obligation than anyone I know. He's like a West Coast cadet who gets up every morning and says 'reporting for duty.'"

Ed is well known for showing up at Hollywood functions on his bicycle, has served, or is serving, as chairman of several different environmentally leading groups, as well as the Thoreau Institute, the Earth Communications Office, Tree People, and Friends of the Earth, among many others.

The home he shares in the LA area with his wife, Rachelle Carson Begley, is entirely self-sufficient, powered by solar energy. He's installed economical water-filtration systems and a greywater recovery system for gardening. His home and office are nearly 100 percent post consumer—in terms of paper, office supplies etc. The family recycles everything possible—as has been seen on his popular *Living With Ed* television show on Discovery Channel's Planet Green.

The crew has also adapted to Ed's ways—even when they travel to other locations to film they use hybrid vehicles and charge all their equipment and batteries from the solar power at Ed's home. There's little need for me to be any more specific about his work and the challenges he proposes, as in addition to the now-multiple seasons of his excellent show, Ed has an ongoing series of books written expressly for the average homeowner to improve his or her relationship with the environment and encourage sustainable living practices.

It is worth mentioning that Ed's work in encouraging our attention to the environment and our impact on it has earned him awards from some of the nation's most prestigious environmental groups, including the National Resources Defense Council, the Coalition for Clean Air, the California League of Conservation Voters, and others.

I said I'd get to Jack Johnson. He deserves a book on his own for the amount of positive environmental work he has done, and is doing—in his native Hawaii, California, and throughout the world.

When his recent album, *Sleep Through the Static* was released, Jack issued a statement that sums up what he's all about—well, maybe not as succinctly as his surfer pal Mark Cuningham, who says "People see Jack as the anti-bling. He's a backlash to all that crap."

What Jack told his fans was: "My friends and I have just finished recording a new album called *Sleep Through the Static*. At this point in my life I weigh about 190 lbs and my ear hairs are getting longer. I also have a couple of kids. My wife popped them out, but I helped. Some of the songs on this album are about making babies. Some of the songs are about raising them. Some of the songs are about the world that these children will grow up in; a world of war and love, and hate, and time and space. Some of the songs are about saying goodbye to people I love and will miss. We recorded the songs onto analog tape machines powered by the sun in Hawaii and Los Angeles."

No doubt Jack is one of the pioneers from our music industry who is taking ecologically sound touring to a new level, as well as recording.

Jack has toured on a biodiesel bus since 2005, and he requires that performance venues buy carbon offsets for every show and compost the organic waste from his concerts. He's staged the *Kokua Festival* in Oahu each spring since 2004—playing with friends such as Eddie Vedder, Ben Harper, and Willie Nelson—and donates proceeds to the Kokua Hawaii Foundation, which he started to support environmental education in schools.

With the remodeling of his Brushfire offices, he and his business partner, Emmett Malloy—cousin of the pro-surfer Malloy brothers, Chris, Keith, and Dan—now operate one of the most eco-minded record companies in the industry. The Brushfire studios run on electricity provided by 32 rooftop solar panels; the building is insulated with blue-jeans scraps and outfitted with compact fluorescent lighting and low-flush toilets. Johnson even recorded *To The Sea*, his latest album, which hit stores last June, in solar powered studios.

While he seems all right with his celebrity, Jack is, just like his pal Cunningham says.

"I'm not trying to act like I've got all the answers and that I'm greener than everyone else," he told one interviewer. "I want to do what I can to help, but sometimes it starts to overwhelm me. It's hard, because as soon as you put your voice in there, all of a sudden you're the guy the newspaper wants to talk to. I accept the fact that I'm a somewhat known person for good things, but I ultimately don't want to run for president."

Jack Johnson and his Brushfire label are members of 1% for the Planet and they encourage their Brushfire artists to do the same. In 2004, Jack Johnson became the 50th member of 1% For The Planet. Jack's 2005 Brushfire Records release of *In Between Dreams* became the first album to carry the 1% label and his 2005

Hawaiian-born folk rocker Jack Johnson - here on the roof of his solar-powerd Los Angeles studio - is one of the leaders of sustainability in the music business, using recycled materials for his CDs and posters and even moving toward corn-based plastics instead of traditional petroleum-based plastic. *Photo courtesy Brushfire Records*

world tour promoted the 1% For The Planet mission and brand and helped to launch the organization. Today 1% For The Planet is a growing global movement of more than 1,100 companies that donate 1% of their sales to a network of more than 1,700 environmental organizations worldwide. In the process, these companies pave the way for more corporate responsibility in the business community.

On the CD packing front, Brushfire convinced Universal (their manufacturer/distributor) to use FSC-certified recycled paper for all their Brushfire music and movie releases, developed the first 100% recycled plastic tray, and piloted a new form of environmental packaging called Eco-Pac. Brushfire is currently challenging Universal to develop a biodegradable corn-based shrink wrap and soy-based inks, and are developing a recycled plastic slimline or paper replacement for all radio singles.

Jack has also worked extensively to protect the world's oceans with the Surfrider Foundation. He founded the Kokua Hawaii Foundation in his home state of Hawaii to support environmental and social work in the islands. This benefit concert has provided some great programs with publicity and much needed funding.

A model of recording studios of a greener future is the extremely popular and successful Tree Sound Studios in Atlanta, owned and run by Paul Diaz and his family. Paul's always had a proactive approach to ecologically responsible business, but, like Jack Johnson and others, he is taking it in steps as far as he's able, and as quickly as he's able.

"I was always really into nature," Diaz said. "I wanted to grow up and be an activist or even an environmental lawyer. But I always wanted to do music." During a live Dave Matthews broadcast from Tree Sound Studios, one of the audience members asked Matthews what political agendas he supported.

"Dave said, 'Green things, I support anything green. The reason to focus on green is because I don't want our great-great-great-grandchildren to look back at us and say I hate you because this is what you left us,'" Diaz said.

"It was like a light bulb went off, and I was like 'Man, I've got to get back on point, I've got to get on this mission.'"

Diaz and his wife, Sunshine, buy carbon credits to offset the pollution caused by the operation of their home and the travel of their employees to and from the studio. They use biodegradable soaps, cups and plates, and run biodiesel in all their vehicles.

"We've got rainwater catchment for the gardens, dual-flush toilets, we remodeled with cork floors, used non-toxic paints, LED lighting, reusable glasses … any plastic that's around this place is made out of corn, so even our disposables are biodegradable."

Paul's Tree Leaf record label is also as petroleum-product free as he can make it. "We use no plastic," he says. "It's all corn-based, organic cotton or hemp T-shirts and hats."

At one point, he says, "half of our power bill was coming from methane, from landfills. Green power. We were paying a premium for it and happy to pay that premium knowing we were taking steps in the right direction. Really, we were all about paying that extra money but sat down and figured in the long run we'd be better off taking that $500 or so every month and buying extra solar panels, and putting that money into our mobile systems."

Tree Sound is a large studio, which at any one time can accommodate two full bands in full production. "You think about

The control room at the inventively "green" Atlanta recording studio Tree Sound.
Photo courtesy Tree Sound

it," Paul says, "that can be, like twenty people or more ... we've got two kitchens, seven bathrooms, large showers, people doing laundry ... we go through a lot of hot water!"

So his first leap was to take the studio to total solar-powered water heating:

"When I started thinking about green options, the first thing I thought of was that $15,000 or so wasn't a cheap way to go just to heat water and have

Tree Sound Studio co-owner Paul Diaz with one of his ingenious solar- and wind-power-driven portable power systems for operating live performances. *Photo Chuck Leavell*

zero (natural or methane) gas consumption. But you know, we've got an electric backup for those really cold days in winter if we've got a lot of people in the studio, and it's taken only a couple of years to totally recoup. I mean, the gas company really sticks it to you just to have gas running to your house. I was spending, without using any gas, $400 a month in service fees. And I wasn't even using it! We just told them we didn't want it—take us off that grid.

The gas stove in the kitchen I converted to run off a propane tank. Now we're looking at running solar thermal baseboard heating around the edges of our main room … just a couple more panels on the roof will heat a pretty good chunk of that space."

Tree Sound also has a permit to put up a wind turbine at the studio, and Paul says he's "chomping at the bit" to get the most he can out of Georgia's green energy rebate program, which by all accounts would seem to be the best in the country—with 65 percent of all green-energy expenditures coming back to the consumer in cash—35 percent from the state and 30 percent from the federal government.

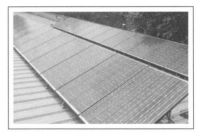

Solar panels on the roof of Tree Sound Studios' roof supply the energy for hot water and, in the future, will run heating systems and more. *Photo Chuck Leavell*

Paul has also taken his green approach mobile: He has two trailer units that are solar and wind-power generators that charge battery banks. "It's a pretty good system," Paul says. "We can run a show big enough for about a thousand people: Lighting, backline (all the amplifiers and sound equipment). Right now we can run a show from noon until about one or two in the morning and stay completely off the grid. I've got a biodiesel generator for backup but haven't had to use it yet."

In the coming year or so, Paul says, he hopes to build an 18-to-21-panel solar array on a bigger trailer, with a bigger battery bank, two or three inverters and a mobile recording studio.

He's also hoping to use government programs to assist in taking the entire Tree Sound Studio into carbon-negative territory. "The goal is that four or five years down the road, once the system has paid for itself, we start getting checks from selling power back to the utility company.

Not only does Paul and his family grow organic vegetables and herbs in gardens right at the studio, but they bring water from the well on Rockstar Farms, where the family has begun growing as much of their own food as possible. "Food that doesn't travel doesn't pollute," Paul says.

The Diaz family has a long-term goal of building an educational center for kids to get out in the country and learn about gardening and livestock: "We've got an orchard and we're already selling produce to a restaurant in Atlanta."

Paul says that in his efforts, he's encountered a sense that "People feel like they can't afford to be part of the green movement because they can't afford a hybrid. It's an us-and-them mentality. You have to go after the blue-collar average guys and get them involved in the green movement. You have to give them the knowledge and tools. It doesn't have to cost you money to be green—you don't have to be a tree-hugger or left-winger. We need to bring green to the common man because we are all in this together.

"We're trying to move away from hippy image. There's a lot of that going on realize the real ability and resource we have. If I can get a facility like this off the grid or carbon negative rather than offset, don't have to be living in a teepee, you can be kicking ass and still be green!"

Another studio that is still on the grid for those days when it can't produce its own power, but, instead, feeds into the grid when its solar panels produce an excess of energy is Evergroove in Colorado. The studio was built from the ground up with construction methods intended to reduce the building's reliance on electricity and gas, the company fully recycles and composts, and even boasts that, by large, it uses used recording equipment and recycles gear in return, "we recycle gear in turn, which keeps electronics and other environmental nasties out of landfills," says studio manager Jenny Smalling, "Because we used a lot of insulation to keep sound in, and outdoor noises out, the studio is as energy efficient as it is sound proof."

"Our initial calculations tell us we will generate about as much as we use, but we can always add more panels if we need more power," says Jenny. "And if we generate more than we use, at the end of the year we get a check from Xcel (Energy, the local power company), and other customers get to use our solar power."

Colorado also boasts the alternative-energy studio of Todd Park Mohr, frontman for the band Big Head Todd and the Monsters.

Mohr—the band's songwriter, guitarist, keyboardist, and vocalist—built a solar-powered recording studio in his off-the-grid log cabin near Steamboat Springs, Colorado. "I like to tell people in fun that audio equipment powered by alternative energy sounds better because it has good karma," says Mohr. Big Head Todd also donates time to causes including EarthFest, the Taos Solar Music Festival, and the RiverReach Rendezvous. Says Mohr, "I think it's pretty easy to come to the conclusion that renewable, clean energy is the most pressing issue of our age."

Overseas, the London, England-based The Premises began transforming its Studio A to solar power back in 2006 and now boasts the first fully solar-powered professional studio in Europe.

It's cool to see that this is more than just a fashionable trend.

Will Benoit, a founding member of the New England band Constants, has always dreamed of building a studio and isn't going the traditional route. He says he's trying to construct the first solar-powered, echo-friendly studio in New England. To do so, he's launched a page on Kickstarter.com (www.kickstarter.com/projects/964070251/a-solar-powered-eco-friendly-recording-studio) to help raise funds, offering bands a day of free recording time for every $100 contributed.

He says: "I already own a 2,000-square-foot barn, its solar panels have already been installed, and now it's time to insulate, frame, build walls, soundproof, install flooring, install plumbing, heating, doors, and windows as well as purchase audio gear. My wife and I have spent the past six months updating our 250-year-old home with all new, low-demand, energy-efficient appliances—from the water heater and dual-flush toilet down to energy-rated light bulbs. Now it's time to bring that approach to the barn. I want to build it using recycled materials wherever possible—insulate with recycled denim and BioBased spray foam, purchase used furniture and equipment (which keeps it out of landfills), rely on renewable resources like cork and bamboo and use low demand, energy efficient heaters and electronics as much as possible."

Will says that Constants tours run as eco-friendly as they are able, using waste vegetable oil in their bus. He and his wife are vegetarians who grow as much of their own food as possible and compost—basically, they're shining examples of an ordinary family (other than being a musician!) doing exactly the right thing. "The point," he says, "is we aim to keep our carbon footprint low, and live as sustainably and environmentally conscious as possible."

I was sitting one day while working on this chapter and began to think of not just the artists, musicians, and actors who dedicate their time and their money toward environmental causes, but those who actually have constituted the environment in their work. Just for fun, I went looking for what some consider the most relevant "environmental" songs and came across a surprising number of conflicting lists (of course—everyone's taste in music is different no matter what a song's message!) When J. Marshall Craig and I ran out of ideas, we asked friends and also went searching the Web for ideas that we hadn't come up with—some of which were embarrassed we'd omitted. In particular, I need to mention Mark Jeantheau's terrific www.grinningplanet.com environmental site for mentioning a few songs we'd missed.

Bruce Cockburn, "If a Tree Falls" (1988): Songwriters and environmentalists love Cockburn equally, for his music represents unflinching activism. I have to say I take some exception to the song if taken out of context, since I am an ardent supporter of sustainable forestry and know that trees are a renewable resource, and again remind readers that more of America is forested in 2010 than it was in 1910. However, in the context of clear-cutting the Amazon jungle and some old-growth areas, Cockburn's right on the money.

Joni Mitchell, "Big Yellow Taxi" (1970): This is probably the best anti-sprawl song ever. (Of course, Chrissie Hynde's "My City Was Gone" certainly touches a similar tone.) Written about the view Joni's Hawaii hotel room—a vista that was part pavement, part tropical nirvana—inspired Mitchell to write one of her most famous songs. Whether describing the Hawaiian islands or the old-growth forests of Vancouver Island, the theme behind "Big Yellow Taxi" is universal.

Cat Stevens, "Where Do the Children Play?" (1970): A dreamy tune upheld by Stevens's softly sung queries. Stevens smartly hung his concerns over blind industrial progress on the fate of our children.

Jackson Browne, "Before the Deluge" (1974): There are Biblical overtones, to be sure, but "Before the Deluge" is about our mistreatment of the environment as much as anything else—and who can forget his "Doctor My Eyes," which is a general commentary on the state of things, and actually one of his earlier hits, which shows how long Jackson's been thinking smart, strong, and sustainable.

Tracy Chapman, "The Rape of the World" (1995): Tracy Chapman was everywhere, musically and emotionally, on her album *New Beginning*. During one tune she's singing about heaven on earth, and the next, how humankind has "clear-cut, dumped on, poisoned and beaten up" Mother Earth. Blind anger isn't always pretty. However, "The Rape of the World" proves it can be profound.

I won't go on and on with an analysis of songs that have come to mind that spill over with ecological messages, but even I was surprised at the number of tunes that Jeff and I came up with in a relatively short period of time—and more surprised, perhaps, at the diversity of the artists with the same message, spanning more than forty years, from folk and country singers to rockers and crooners, pop stars, and reggae stars. The message remains the same while the songs couldn't be more different. Here's a few more:

"Mercy Mercy Me (The Ecology)"—by Marvin Gaye

"Clear Blue Skies"—by Crosby, Stills, Nash & Young

"Death of Mother Nature Suite"—by Kansas

"Nature's Way"—by Spirit

"The 3 Rs (Reduce, Reuse and Recycle)"—by Jack Johnson

"Don't Go Near The Water"—by the Beach Boys

"Earth Anthem"—by the Turtles

"Only A Dream"—by Adrian Belew

"Earth Day Every Day (Celebrate)"—by John Denver

"Earth Song"—by Michael Jackson

"Wond'ring Again"—by Jethro Tull

"The Sun Is Burning"—by Simon & Garfunkel

"Fresh Garbage"—by Spirit

"Rain on the Scarecrow"—by John Cougar Mellencamp

"Om"—Moody Blues

"Saturn"—Stevie Wonder

"Only So Much Oil In The Ground"—Tower of Power

"A Gallon of Gas"—The Kinks

"Dirty Business"—New Riders Of The Purple Sage

"Apeman"—The Kinks

"Saltwater"—Julian Lennon

"Poison In The Well"—10,000 Maniacs

"Men In Helicopters"—Adrian Belew

"I'd Love To Change The World"—Ten Years After

"Don't Kill The Whale"—Yes

"Vapor Trail"—Rush

"Underground"—Wishbone Ash

"(Nothing But) Flowers"—Talking Heads

"The Last Resort"—Eagles

"Pass It On Down"—Alabama

"Garden Of Eden"—New Riders Of The Purple Sage

"Goodbye To A River"—Don Henley

"Hey You"—Madonna

"Dragonfly"—Ziggy Marley

"Song For A Dying Planet"—Joe Walsh

"Silent Ruin"—Olivia Newton-John

"The Eagle And The Hawk—John Denver

"To The Last Whale: a) A Critical Mass b) Wind On The Water"—Crosby & Nash

"Ecology Song"—Stephen Stills

"Cement Octopus"—Pete Seeger

"Don't Go Near The Water"—Johnny Cash

"Last Lonely Eagle"—New Riders Of The Purple Sage

A lot of artists have been echoing what the scientists have been saying for decades, and acting on it in their own ways. We've run out of time, as a society, of just listening instead of taking action. We can't all live like Jack Johnson does, but we can take a few lessons from how he lives, the things he and all these artists keep reminding us, and apply them even in the smallest ways and we WILL have a collective positive impact for ourselves and generations to come.

Wake-up Call

What Happens If We Don't Change Our Ways?

*"I really wonder what gives us the right
to wreck this poor planet of ours."*

Kurt Vonnegut

In chapter two I discussed the "awakening" of American politicians and business leaders to the fact that a new, sustained way of living our lives and reducing as much as possible our impact on the environment is not just fashion—it's a necessity.

But are things really more serious than the prospect of $10-a-gallon gasoline?

Yes.

Even most of the naysayers of global warming have come around to the fact that the climate is changing—despite horrid winter storms in Europe and our own northeast in recent years, the average monthly and annual temperatures are at centuries- and all-time highs. In the early winter of 2009/2010, in fact, people were outright questioning the idea of global warming—a common joke being "where's Al Gore when we need him."

But by the summer of 2010, a different song was being sung. Many records for hottest days across the US were set, and June was the hottest on record worldwide. January 2010 was one of the warmest on record, and the decade 2000-2009 was the hottest on record, according to the World Meteorological Organization.

Weather, in general, is unstable planet-wide, with hurricanes increasing in strength all over the world, according to studies published in *National Geographic*. "Category Four and Five—the most powerful, damaging hurricanes—has nearly doubled over the past 35 years." The study finds that the increase in hurricane intensity coincides with a rise in sea surface temperatures around the world of about 1°F (0.5°C) between 1970 and 2004, according to the journal *Science*.

The study's lead author, Peter Webster, said, "I'm prepared to make an attribution to global warming."

Even destructive cold snaps that make some believe global warming is a myth, are as a result of a climate out of control.

The observed climate changes that we report are not opinions to be debated. "They are facts to be dealt with," said one of the report's chief authors, Jerry Melillo of the Marine Biological Laboratory in Woods Hole, Massachusetts. "We can act now to avoid the worst impacts."

Among the things Melillo said he would like to avoid are more flooding disasters in New Orleans and an upheaval of the world's food supply. The scientists softened the report from an earlier draft that said "tipping points have already been reached and have led to large changes." Melillo said that is because some of the changes seen so far are still reversible—but only with an immediate 60-80 percent reduction in greenhouse gas emissions.

The only way to do that may be a challenge, but it's not impossible: A smart and sustainable approach to living. Hey, America put man on the moon in less than ten years from when it began as a dream. We're now facing a nightmare—surely we can summon the drive and ingenuity to reduce our energy consumption, adopt sustainable energy generation on a wide scale and make mass transit a way of life. Perhaps high-speed trains will become more of an option for us over the increasingly ridiculous delays, security demands, and environmental impact of air travel. I'm not going to get into an argument about the need for heightened security or the debate that some measures have reached downright ludicrous levels—but given the amount of travel I do, unless I'm headed for an overseas destination or have no choice but to be across the continent within twenty-four hours, I tend to lean toward alternative travel methods than flying—and not just for environmental reasons. Practically speaking, it's faster, in some cases, to drive or take a train or bus to certain destinations than it is to fly, given lengthy check-in times, flight delays, and ever-increasingly invasive security measures. If I have a choice between high-speed, environmentally friendly mass transit and a flight, I'll miss the plane every time!

But even if President Obama's dream of a nationwide high-speed rail system (which is perhaps comparable to President Kennedy's space program in ambition) were to become reality in the next five or six years—or, in fact, TOMORROW—we have already passed the point of no return for one of our crucial environmental tipping points, according to Tom Karl of the National Climatic Data Center: The world's sea levels are rising, irreversibly. The center, in Asheville, North Carolina, is the world's largest active archive of weather data and reports that glaciers all over the world are retreating (melting) rapidly—fact, not theory, as "satellite imagery of polar melting doesn't lie," Karl says.

Still, there remains some disagreement from some as to what role man has played in this shift.

I'm not sure why, frankly.

It's simple. As scientists explain, global warming is due to an increase in what is known as the greenhouse effect: Certain gases in the atmosphere act like glass in a greenhouse—allowing sunlight through but trapping its heat from radiating back into space. One of the main greenhouse gases is carbon dioxide. As trees grow, they absorb CO_2 and produce oxygen, but when the trees die—or are cut and then burned in forest clearance—they release their CO_2 back into the atmosphere. And fewer trees mean less CO_2 being sequestered. So, just imagine: in 1987, according to the Sierra Club, an area the size of Britain was burned in the Amazon rain forest, adding an estimated 500 million tonnes of CO_2 to the atmosphere.

Ten years later, more than a million hectares of forest in Indonesia was burned.

However, less than half of the yearly total of CO_2 released into the atmosphere is from deforestation; the rest comes from burning fossil fuels such as coal and oil in our power plants and our cars and factories.

The concentration of CO_2 has increased 25 percent since the Industrial Revolution; half of this rise has been in the past thirty years. It is expected to double within decades.

Can we do anything about this? The Kyoto Protocol, a United Nations effort to fight global warming, called for the top thirty-seven industrialized countries to reduce their greenhouse gas emissions by 5.2 percent of 1990 levels, but the United States failed to ratify the agreement.

The Copenhagen Climate Conference in late 2009 similarly sought a legally binding pact among world nations to reduce greenhouse gas emissions sufficiently to prevent global temperatures increasing by no more than 2 degrees by 2020. It ended with a whimper, beset by political and economic problems and failed, as I mentioned earlier, to be a legally binding replacement for the Kyoto Protocol, which expires in 2012.

Even in a best-case scenario, some leading scientists say, we're not going to make it.

Research by Australian National University environmental law and policy expert Andrew Macintosh indicates that, "based on most industrialized nations' stated mid-term commitments, limiting warming to 2 degrees Celsius simply won't work."

"It's simply not enough if you want to prevent warming of more than 2 degrees," Macintosh told the Australian Associated Press.

"They know this. But what they're trying to tell everybody is no, it's fine; we can go for moderate cuts by 2020 and still stay within the limit. Even if a 20 percent cut were achieved by 2020, emissions would have to fall by an additional 5 percent a year in order to reach the next target. That's just extremely unrealistic (unless) we find some magic technology."

Macintosh's computer simulations, according to the news agency, ran models for 45 different climate change scenarios. His research indicates that cuts on the order of at least 30 percent by 2020, with reductions of at least 50 percent by 2050 compared to

1990 levels, and larger reductions soon afterward will be required to prevent runaway global warming.

One UN panel has estimated that we need to reduce global fuel use by 60 percent immediately if we have any hope of stabilizing the climate.

With the inertia of not wanting to alter our lifestyle, the quality of life the Western world has, and the developing world aspires to—along with a long-stalled global economy—the chance of significant and lasting change seems all but impossible.

In fact, for the first time in Gallup's twenty-five-year history of asking Americans about the trade-off between environmental protection and economic growth, a majority of Americans say economic growth should be given the priority, even if the environment suffers to some extent.

In 1984, more than 60 percent of Americans picked the environment over the economy. But in 2010, for the first time ever, the percentage of Americans choosing the environment fell to 42 percent, while the percentage choosing the economy jumped to 51 percent.

Sadly, there is a distinct partisan spread. Two-thirds of Republicans say they prefer energy to environmental protection, while two-thirds of Democrats hold the opposite view.

So while there seems to be universal acceptance of global warming, if not its cause, the question of whether we will do anything about it is in high dispute—and it's not looking good.

NASA scientist James Hansen, widely considered one of the world's premiere climate researchers, has given us five years or less to reverse global warming. According to Hansen: "If we don't act, ice sheets will melt ever more quickly, causing a rise in sea levels that would put most of Manhattan (and London, half of Florida, and all the world's coastlines) under water.

"While a mere 2 percent of the world's land is less than 10 meters above the mid-tide sea level, it is home to 10 percent of the world's population—630 million and counting—and much valuable property and vital infrastructure," Hansen says, "Without mega-engineering projects to protect them, a five-meter rise would inundate large parts of many cities—including New York, London, Sydney, Vancouver, Mumbai and Tokyo—and leave surrounding areas vulnerable to storm surges. In Florida, Louisiana, the Netherlands, Bangladesh and elsewhere, whole regions and cities may vanish. China's economic powerhouse, Shanghai, has an average elevation of just four meters."

Hansen is an outspoken critic of cap-and-trade carbon-market plans, such as are being adopted in Europe and proposed in America—in which permits to pollute are bought and sold—and believes there is no room for compromise with it comes to addressing climate change immediately.

"This is analogous to the issue of slavery faced by Abraham Lincoln or the issue of Nazism faced by Winston Churchill," he said. "On those kinds of issues you cannot compromise. You can't say: 'Let's reduce slavery; let's find a compromise and reduce it 50 percent or reduce it 40 percent.' We don't have a leader who is able to grasp it and say what is really needed. Instead we are trying to continue business as usual."

A possible consequence would be more prolonged droughts and heat waves, powerful hurricanes in new areas, and the likely extinction of a high percentage of species.

"We cannot burn off all the fossil fuels that are readily available without causing dramatic climate change," Hansen said. "This is not something that is a theory. We understand the carbon cycle well enough to say that."

For instance, when explorers went into the Himalayas in the 1950s to map, measure, and photograph the Imja Glacier, they found a mass of glacial ice that was thousands of years old.

Fifty years later, that glacier is gone—reduced to a giant alpine lake that now threatens to burst.

American mountain geographer Alton Byers returned to the precise locations of the original pictures and replicated forty panoramas taken by explorers Fritz Müller and Erwin Schneider. His results were published in the *Himalayan Journal of Sciences*.

"Only five decades have passed between the old and the new photographs, and the changes are dramatic," says Byers.

"Many small glaciers at low altitudes have disappeared entirely and many larger ones have lost around half of their volume. Some have formed huge glacial lakes at the foot of the glacier, threatening downstream communities in case of an outburst."

Today, the Imja Glacier, which is just a few miles from Everest, continues to recede at a rate of nearly 250 feet a year—the fastest rate of all the Himalayan glaciers. Partly to blame is that Nepal's average temperature has increased by 1.5 degrees Celsius since 1975, according to the UN Environment Program. The mountain glaciers will melt another 75 percent by 2030 at this rate, UN scientists warn.

What's of immediate concern is that Imja is one of twenty-seven glacial lakes in Nepal classified as potentially dangerous; if breached, thousands of lives in the most densely populated Sherpa valley in Nepal are at risk from flooding and landslides. What's more, the Himalayan glaciers also feed the major Asian river systems, and should they slow to a trickle, more than a billion people who depend on that water could face drought.

"Scientific evidence shows that the effects of globalization and climate change are being felt in even the most remote Himalayan environments," Byers said. "While climate change is mostly caused by the highly industrialized parts of the world, the effects are taking their toll in the sensitive mountain areas. The signs are visible, but the in-depth knowledge and data from the Himalayan region is largely missing. What happens in this remote mountain region is a serious concern for the whole world."

Many scientists back him up, declaring that in the ten, twenty-five, and fifty years to come, extinctions will occur at a thousand times the natural background rate, and many ecologists believe we are entering a period of global mass extinction similar to the one that wiped out the dinosaurs—only this time the cause is not otherworldly, like a comet, but due to human impacts.

"It's the next annihilation of vast numbers of species. It is happening now, and we, the human race, are its cause," warns Dr. Richard Leakey, the world's most famous paleoanthropologist, on a piece in www.well.com."Every year, between 17,000 and 100,000 species vanish from our planet, he says. "For the sake of argument, let's assume the number is 50,000 a year. Whatever way you look at it, we're destroying the Earth at a rate comparable with the impact of a giant asteroid slamming into the planet." The statistics he has assembled are staggering—he estimates half of the planet's species will vanish in the next hundred years.

Some of the most alarming indicators that mankind is having a major negative effect on the planet can be found in changes in ocean ecosystems all over the world. *Smithsonian Institution*

The first mass extinction, about 440 million years ago, and the four succeeding extinctions were the result of physical shocks to the planet like volcanic eruptions, plate tectonic shifts, and at least one major asteroid strike, which is blamed for the mass extinction that claimed the dinosaurs.

"Scientists now refer to a sixth major extinction crisis that's under way," says the head of the United Nations Environmental Program, Achim Steiner.

The oceans are a good place to start looking at this effect: The most pessimistic sources, quite alarmingly, have declared that this is "the last century of wild seafood," according to Dr. Stephen Palumbi of Stanford University, part of a global team on ocean health.

Award-winning Canadian environmental reporter and author Alanna Mitchell turned heads with her 2008 book *Seasick: The Hidden Ecological Crisis of the Global Ocean*. In that, she argues, the condition of the planet's oceans, which cover 71 percent of the Earth's surface and contains 90 percent of all life, is even more critical than climate change. The human use of fossil fuels, she writes, is changing the chemistry and temperature of the water.

"In the atmosphere it's very dangerous because it's changing our climate," she says of the greenhouse gas. "When carbon dioxide goes into the global ocean … it is not inert. It mixes with the ocean and changes the chemistry." If we don't stop burning fossil fuels and pumping CO_2 into the air, the oceans will die, she warns, as will most life on the planet.

Mitchell visited five continents in the course of her research and details cases of aquatic "dead zones," changing acidity, rising sea levels, plankton and fish deaths, and coral bleaching.

Australia's Great Barrier Reef also features as a central part of the equation. In the book, Mitchell describes the Great Barrier Reef as a potential "Noah's Ark" for the world's coral reefs and, in turn, life.

As documented on www.theage.com.au, Mitchell says that in previous mass extinctions, tiny clusters of coral reef-based genetic material that survive have provided the seeds of entire new reefs, which eventually brought the oceans back to life. With healthy oceans, new life could populate the earth. "Coral reefs are the most important ecosystem on the whole planet," she says. Mitchell continues:

"They hold hope for the rest. It's clear that the ocean is more important for the future of the planet than the land. Within the ocean the Great Barrier Reef is by far the most complex and important ecosystem.

"But even though that's happening, it's still clear that forces that are larger than a single country's ability to protect (it) are at play. So, parts of the reef are changing … because the chemistry of the ocean is changing, the temperature of the ocean and the atmosphere are changing and are harming the reef already.

That's why, she says, as the custodian of this key and crucial ecosystem, Australia has a particular responsibility to act on climate change. "In order to protect the Great Barrier Reef the Australian Government needs … to take a very, very strong, passionate voice in global climate talks, and say if carbon dioxide concentration is increased any more, by a single unit, it's terrible for the reef and terrible for life on Earth."

What has to change, she argues, is the entrenched nature of our exploitative attitudes towards the sea.

Despite the book's grim message, Mitchell says it's not too late. "I think there's still time to bring it back ... but we have a very, very small window of time in which to act." Her book quotes scientists as pinpointing between 2015 and 2030 as the "drop dead point for action" to save the seas.

One very specific example of this I've found is how the waters around the North Pole are reacting to an increase in carbon dioxide in our environment by absorbing CO_2 at a higher rate than normal—which is exactly what cold water does, compared to warmer waters.

While that might seem like a good thing—sequestering more CO_2—it's ultimately not. Especially for some of the wildlife, such as sea creatures that live in shells: The rate of absorption could, in due course, start dissolving the creatures' shells.

The resulting turmoil this poses the entire food chain is frightening. Research professor Jean-Pierre Gattuso of the Centre National de la Recherche Scientifique, and his team predicts that the Arctic is headed toward being 10 percent more acidic than natural, becoming 50 percent above normal in 2050. By 2100, the entire Arctic Ocean will be inhospitable to shellfish, they predict.

"This is extremely worrying," Gattuso told the Oceans of Tomorrow conference in Barcelona.

"We knew that the seas were getting more acidic and this would disrupt the ability of shellfish—such as mussels—to grow their shells. But now we realize the situation is much worse."

It could spark the collapse of the entire ecosystem of the food chain of life in the Arctic. Taken to the end, up the food chain, that means seals and polar bears—already threatened—disappear, and an entire human civilization, the Inuit, extinct or displaced.

This prediction is seen by many as the most pessimistic possible, but even naysayers don't have the data—at least that I could find—to back up a defense that it's not true. It seems that we could see, within the next century or so, the end of ocean life as we know it. This seems like a really alarmist statement, but a major international scientific study is saying exactly that.

Stocks have collapsed in nearly one-third of sea fisheries, and the rate of decline is accelerating.

The journal *Science* has, since its 17 January 2003 edition, published a series of articles by an international team of researchers who, as recently as July 2010, say fishery decline is closely tied to a broader loss of marine biodiversity, while a greater use of protected areas could safeguard existing stocks.

"The way we use the oceans is that we hope and assume there will always be another species to exploit after we've completely gone through the last one," said research leader Dr. Boris Worm, from Dalhousie University in Canada.

"What we're highlighting is there is a finite number of stocks; we have gone through one-third, and we are going to get through the rest," he told the BBC News website.

Numbers from the fisheries themselves entirely back up the pessimistic predictions. In 2003, 29 percent of open sea fisheries were in a state of collapse, defined as a decline to less than 10 percent of their original yield.

Bigger vessels, better nets, and new technology for spotting fish are not bringing the world's fleets bigger returns—in fact, the global catch fell by 13 percent between 1994 and 2003.

Zones of biodiversity loss also tended to see more beach closures, more blooms of potentially harmful algae, and more coastal flooding.

"The image I use to explain why biodiversity is so important is that marine life is a bit like a house of cards," said Dr. Worm, "All parts of it are integral to the structure; if you remove parts, particularly at the bottom, it's detrimental to everything on top and threatens the whole structure. And we're learning that in the oceans, species are very strongly linked to each other—probably more so than on land."

According to Carl Gustaf Lundin, head of the global marine program at the International Union for Conservation of Nature (IUCN), says "The benefits of marine-protected areas are quite clear in a few cases; there's no doubt that protecting areas leads to a lot more fish and larger fish, and less vulnerability." He continued that,"you also have to have good management of marine parks and good management of fisheries. Clearly, fishing should not wreck the ecosystem, bottom trawling being a good example of something which does wreck the ecosystem."

The trouble is that it takes strong political initiative to protect fishing stocks—at this point, instituting total bans, and before it's too late.

The Canadian government, for instance, instituted a total ban on the Atlantic cod fishing industry in 1992. By that time, the estimate for northern cod was the lowest ever measured. According to Greenpeace, "The Canadian Minister of Fisheries and Oceans had no choice but to declare a ban on fishing northern cod. For the first time in four hundred years the fishing of northern cod ceased in Newfoundland. The fisheries department issued a warning in 1995 that the entire northern cod population had declined to just 1,700 tonnes by the end of 1994, down from a 1990 survey showing 400,000 tonnes, and showed no sign of recovery—just 1,700 tonnes remained in a fishery that had, for more than a century, yielded quarter-million tonne catches year after year. The fisheries department also predicted that, even in the unlikely event that the fish stock started to recover immediately, it would take at least fifteen years before it would be healthy enough to withstand significant fishing.

"Following the 1992 ban on northern cod fishing, fisheries for cod in other areas and for most other species of groundfish around eastern Canada also had to be either severely curtailed or closed altogether because of serious depletion. An estimated thirty thousand people who had lost their jobs after the 1992 Northern Cod Moratorium took effect, were joined by an additional twelve thousand fishermen and plant workers following these additional cutbacks and closures. With more than forty thousand people out of jobs, Newfoundland became an economic disaster area as processing plants shut down, and vessels from the smallest dory to the monster draggers were made idle or sold overseas at bargain prices. Several hundred Newfoundland communities were devastated."

Imagine, a whole province of the country of Canada facing the end of an entire way of life, much like Detroit was faced with the collapse of the domestic auto industry, as we'd known it.

As of 2010, there remains no hope that the fishing industry in Newfoundland will recover, although the Canadian government has been listening to recommendations that a minor catch of

5,000-8,000 tonnes be allowed—entirely against scientific advice. Marine biologist Robert Rangeley, Canada's Atlantic vice president at the World Wildlife Fund says it's "a lighting rod for everything that's wrong with international fisheries management."

Rangeley fears that without a cautious approach to rebuilding fish stocks, they could collapse again. Rangeley agrees there are "encouraging signs," but worries that "it implies rebuilding is inevitable. And it's not."

The dwindling cod fishing industry could disappear on the other side of the Atlantic, too, if Irish Sea stocks of the species do not recover, Agriculture Minister Michelle Gildernew warned in January 2009.

Cod stocks have "virtually collapsed" in the Irish Sea, warns a story in the *Irish Independent* newspaper, while stocks of cod, whiting, and haddock are "severely depleted" in Irish fishing grounds west of Scotland according to a wide range of fishing, environmental and oceanographic sources.

The Marine Institute says the cod stocks show "little sign" of recovery, and warns that stocks could become so low that the fish will disappear from dinner plates because it will not be commercially viable to catch.

But the Marine Institute's Stock Book, which gives an overview of the state of Irish fish species, says there is good and bad news for the fishing industry. While cod, whiting and haddock stocks are in trouble, stocks of mackerel are up by 33 percent because of the introduction of young fish.

Prawn stocks are also in a healthy state, which is good news for the industry.

Compiled from scientific surveys, port landings and observations by industry, the Stock Book contains management advice on more than eighty fish stocks, many of which are managed by the EU under the Common Fisheries Policy.

"The role of science in supporting a sustainable fishing industry is to answer the fundamental question of how many fish can we safely remove from any particular stock today while leaving enough fish in the sea to reproduce and support the fishery into tomorrow," said Marine Institute CEO Dr. Tony Heffernan to the *Irish Independent*.

Protecting stocks demands the political will to act on scientific advice—something which Boris Worm finds lacking in Europe, where politicians have ignored recommendations to halt the iconic North Sea cod fishery year after year.

Without a ban, scientists fear the North Sea stocks could follow the Grand Banks cod of eastern Canada into oblivion.

"I'm just amazed, it's very irrational," he said.

When some of the Canadian stocks showed signs of recovery, restricted fisheries were re-opened and the small increase in stock size was quickly wiped out, and a full ban was reinstituted in 2003—again to the strong objections of the fishing industry. The difference this time, researchers say, is that there is no expectation of a comeback of the cod. It's now regarded as in "terminal decline."

"You have scientific consensus and nothing moves," Dr. Worm says. "It's a sad example; and what happened in Canada should be such a warning, because now it's collapsed and it's not coming back."

The National Fisheries Institute, a trade group representing seafood producers as well as suppliers, restaurants and grocery chains, has declared that its members could meet the rising global demand for seafood in part by relying on farmed fish: "To meet the gap between what wild capture can provide sustainably and the growing demand for seafood, aquaculture is filling that need."

And while even the most optimistic sources acknowledge that a full third of international fishing stocks—such as the Atlantic cod industry, which has ceased to exist—have been exhausted beyond the point of no return, even they are confident that the brakes can be applied to save the oceans.

"We've got the message," says Dr. Steven Murawski, chief scientist for the National Marine Fisheries Service. "We will continue to reverse this trend."

I couldn't find data to support that claim, however.

The contention that the oceans are following the fisheries into decline is the subject of a well-regarded documentary film, *The End of the Line*, which echoes the sentiment that natural, wild fisheries will be exhausted by the middle of this century.

This isn't to say there will be NO FISH in the seas, but that "if things go on as they have in the past we shall run down all the major fisheries in the world to below a 10th of what they were in 1950 by some time around the middle of this century. That doesn't mean no fish, just a fraction of the fish we have today, when the human population will have increased by a third," according to the film.

According to CNN, 50 percent of the world's catch is caught by 1 percent of the fishing fleet. These industrial boats have gigantic capacities, and incredibly sophisticated technology, including ultrasound. The largest trawl net in the world would hold three 747s. As an expert in the film *The End of the Line* says, "Our fishing power outweighs our ability to control ourselves."

The film goes on to explain that not only is there the obvious problem of a lack of fish, but that this lack of fish will cause a cascade collapse of the ocean ecosystem, resulting in oceans clogged with algae and jellyfish, or an ocean that will not be able to absorb carbon dioxide, thereby worsening global warming.

Journalist Charles Clover, the correspondent for *The End of the Line*, and author of the book of the same name, explains that seafood that contains a Marine Stewardship Council-certified sticker is safe, environmentally speaking, to purchase and eat. Varieties of sustainable fish include Alaskan wild salmon, Pollack, and finfish. These fisheries harvest far less of the stock and so there's less risk they will collapse. Properly harvested mackerel and tilapia are other varieties that have been sustainably harvested, traditionally.

It's simple, Clover says: None of us should be eating fish that is endangered or threatened in areas where it is harvested—such as bluefin tuna, big eye tuna, shark, and sturgeon. For you caviar lovers out there, you'll know that the legal trade in caviar and sturgeon products from the Caspian Sea went into international effect back in 2006, though there is still a brisk black market trade that continues the threaten the species. As well, domestic harvesting of caviar remains unchecked, and the sturgeon, which enters rivers to spawn, has long faced threats to its survival, including dams that block access to spawning grounds, pollution, and overfishing.

The fish are especially vulnerable to pressure because they take several years to reach sexual maturity, and in some cases spawn only once every few years.

The value of their eggs, briny and dark, has become their curse. The best caviar now fetches more than $250 on ounce, or 28 grams, on Western retail markets. This has made fishing for them lucrative and encouraged corruption, according to the *New York Times*.

Even the most optimistic sources acknowledge that a full third of international fishing stocks—such as the Atlantic cod industry—have been exhausted beyond the point of no return. But they are confident that the brakes can be applied to save the oceans.

There really isn't any data to back up their optimism, but let's hope they're right.

Let's take a look at our situation with gas and oil. Now, I'm not suggesting that we're facing an easy task: We can't just turn off the gas valve. Our very civilization right now depends on oil. And, what's even worse, our thirst for oil is yet another threat to the oceans and fish and seafood stocks, as was shown with the devastating oil spill off the delicate wetlands of the Gulf coast in 2010.

Caltech's vice provost David Goodstein's 2004 book, *Out of Gas: The End of the Age of Oil*, considers how an ill-prepared world would cope with an irreversible fuel shortage in the near future. The answer: Not very well. As his book begins: "The world will soon start to run out of conventionally produced, cheap oil. If we manage … (to shift) the burden to coal and natural gas … life may go on more or less as it has been—until we start to run out of all fossil fuels by the end of this century … Civilization as we know it will not survive unless we can find a way to live without fossil fuels."

In the 1950s, Shell Oil geophysicist Marion King Hubbert developed a bell curve chart, called the Hubbert's Peak curve, in which he predicted US oil production would peak in the early 1970s. He had many critics at the time but turned out to be correct.

Experts have no consensus, with optimistic ones believing that oil production will peak around 2020, while pessimistic ones believe it's already occurred. But there is an agreement that Saudi Arabia's Ghawar, which is the largest oil field in the world and is responsible for approximately half of Saudi Arabia's oil production over the past fifty years, has peaked. The world's second largest oil field, the Burgan field in Kuwait, entered decline in November 2005.

It's important, experts agree, because governments need to base their energy policies on shifting from conservation to alternative sources, such as solar, wind, nuclear, and others—and alternatives must be firmly established decades before we run out of oil.

(Technically, we will never actually run out of oil, scientists say, but we will run out of practical and economical methods of extracting remaining oil from oil fields.)

But there is a growing, general consensus that we've had a wake up call: Our climate is changing unnaturally, species are dying off at a record rate, and we are running out of the fossil fuels that are at the heart of our climate change—yet those fuels are at the heart of our civilization, too.

It's easy to find alarming statistics.

A network of scientists came together in 2000 in Denver, Colorado, and called itself the Association for the Study of Peak Oil and Gas, or ASPO. Led by retired British Petroleum geologist Dr. Colin Campbell, its stated purpose is to determine the approximate date of peak oil production and raise awareness of the inevitable decline and impact on humans.

The worst-case scenario is that an irreversible global depression will result, initiating a chain reaction in the global market that might stimulate a collapse of global industrial civilization, potentially leading to large population declines within a short period, through war and starvation.

The theory, as alarming as it is, is not new, and it is not restricted to the environmental or alternative-fuel movements.

In 2005, the United States Department of Energy published a report titled *Peaking of World Oil Production: Impacts, Mitigation, & Risk Management*. Known as the Hirsch report, it stated, "The peaking of world oil production presents the US and the world with an unprecedented risk management problem. As peaking is approached, liquid fuel prices and price volatility will increase dramatically, and, without timely mitigation, the economic, social, and political costs will be unprecedented. Viable mitigation options exist on both the supply and demand sides, but to have substantial impact, they must be initiated more than a decade in advance of peaking."

Are we already past that point?

In April 2006, the leading Saudi oil company, Saudi Aramco, admitted that its oil fields are declining at a rate of 8 percent a year. Of the largest twenty-one fields, at least nine are declining their output. This information, endorsed by the oil industry itself, has been used to argue that Ghawar has peaked and, as I mentioned, that the Burgan field in Kuwait is in decline.

Ultimately, climate change has the potential to be the greatest long-term threat faced by humanity. It could cause more human and financial suffering than the two world wars and the Great Depression put together. All countries will be affected, but the poorest countries will be hit hardest.

It's not that we haven't taken action in the past. An international treaty to tackle the hole in the Earth's ozone layer eliminated roughly 95 percent of our emissions of ozone-damaging chemicals.

That time, it worked.

Brazil deserves praise for promising to roll back deforestation in the Amazon. But how are we going to sustain a global population, which by some counts—such as the United Nations World Population 2300 forecast—is expected to stabilize at between eight billion and ten billion people?

As terrible as this sounds—we can't, at least according to the UN's Achim Steiner.

"The human population is now so large that the amount of resources needed to sustain it exceeds what is available at current consumption patterns," Steiner told the *New York Times*. Efficient use of resources and reducing waste now are "among the greatest challenges at the beginning of 21st century," he said.

"Life would be easier if we didn't have the kind of population growth rates that we have at the moment," Steiner continued in the *Times* piece, "But to force people to stop having children would be a simplistic answer. The more realistic, ethical and practical issue is to accelerate human well-being and make more rational use of the resources we have on this planet."

According to the *Times*, Steiner said other tipping points triggered by climate change could occur in areas like India and China if Himalayan glaciers shrank so much that they no longer supplied adequate amounts of water to populations in those countries.

One hundred eighty-two nations are now parties to the Convention on Biological Diversity. The United States is the only industrial country that has failed to ratify it, but there is wide agreement that the treaty has had virtually no impact on continuing mass extinction.

So, what is the worst-case scenario if we continue, essentially, to do nothing to protect the planet's wildlife, its oceans and, particularly, its stable climate?

A comprehensive piece published in *USA Today* reported that researchers in the US Virgin Islands fear more than half the world's coral reefs could die in less than 25 years and say global warming may at least partly to blame.

Sea temperatures are rising, weakening the reefs' resistance to increased pollutants, everything from runoff from construction sites to toxins from boat paints. The fragile reefs are hosts to countless marine plants and animals.

"Think of it as a high school chemistry class," said Billy Causey, the Caribbean and Gulf Mexico director of the National Oceanic and Atmospheric Administration (NOAA).

"You mix some chemicals together and nothing happens. You crank up the Bunsen burner and all of a sudden things start bubbling around. That's what's happening. That global Bunsen burner is cranking up."

"Last year's coral loss in the Caribbean waters supports predictions that 60 percent of the world's coral could die within a quarter century," said Tyler Smith of the University of the Virgin Islands.

"Given current rates of degradation of reef habitats, this is a plausible prediction," Smith said.

"Up to 30 percent of the world's coral reefs have died in the last 50 years, and another 30 percent are severely damaged," said Smith, who studies coral health in the US Virgin Islands and collaborates with researchers globally.

"US Virgin Islands coral today is likely at its lowest levels in recorded history," Smith said.

"Climate change is an important factor that is influencing coral reefs worldwide," said Mark Eakin, director of NOAA's Coral Reef Watch. "It adds to the other problems that we are having."

It all adds to a nightmare scenario: widespread coastal pollution, bleached coral reefs, acidification, and the imminent loss of wild foods depended upon by millions of people. As reported in www.allbusiness.com, "The world's farmers face a steady shrinkage in both per capita cropland and irrigation water. The likely result is higher food prices, leading to economic and social disruptions.

"The environmental deterioration of the last few decades cannot continue indefinitely without eventually affecting the world economy. Until now, most of the economic effects of environmental damage have been local: the collapse of a fishery here or there from overfishing, the loss of timber exports by a tropical country because of deforestation, or the abandonment of cropland because of soil erosion. But as the scale of environmental damage expands, it threatens to affect the global economy as well.

"The consequences of environmental degradation are becoming ever more clear. We cannot continue to deforest the earth without experiencing more rainfall runoff, accelerated soil erosion, and more destructive flooding. If we continue to discharge excessive amounts of carbon into the atmosphere, we will eventually face economically disruptive climate change. If we continue to over pump the earth's aquifers, we will one day face acute water scarcity.

"If we continue to overfish, still more fisheries will collapse. If overgrazing continues, so, too, will the conversion of rangeland into desert. Continuing soil erosion at the current rate will slowly drain the earth of its productivity. If the loss of plant and animal species continues at the rate of recent decades, we will eventually face ecosystem collapse."

And we will either put the brakes on because we should—or, the economy and global stability becomes so adversely affected that we act, at which point it could be too late for millions of people, mostly in the third world.

There are some experts who believe that it's our food system that will fail first and spark worldwide economic decline. Historically, this has played out.

According to one UN report: "The decline of the early Mesopotamian civilization was tied to the waterlogging and salting of its irrigated land. Soil erosion converted into desert the fertile wheatlands of North Africa that once supplied the Roman Empire with grain.

"Rising grain prices will be the first global economic indicator to tell us that we are on an economic and demographic path that is environmentally unsustainable. Unimpeded environmental damage will seriously impair the capacity of fishers and farmers to keep up with the growth in demand, leading to rising food prices. The social consequences of rising grain prices will become unacceptable to more and more people, leading to political instability. What begins as environmental degradation eventually translates into political instability."

When grain and corn prices doubled in the mid 1990s, it had little effect on the developed nations, since, according to the UN we spend only a small share of our income for food and our food expenditures are dominated more by processing costs than by commodity prices: "But for the 1.3 billion in the world who live on a dollar a day or less, a prolonged period of higher grain prices would quickly become life-threatening. Heads of households unable to buy enough food to keep their families alive would hold their governments responsible and take to the streets. The resulting bread or rice riots could disrupt economic activity in many countries. If the world could not get inflated food prices back down to traditional levels, this could negatively affect the earnings of multinational corporations, the performance of stock markets, and the stability of the international monetary system. In a world economy more integrated than ever before, the problems of the poor would then become the problems of the rich.

Again, according to the UN: "The consequences of environmental abuse that scientists have warned about can be seen everywhere: In the European Union, the allowable fish catch has had to be reduced by 20 percent or more in an effort to avert the collapse of the region's fisheries.

In Saudi Arabia, overreliance on a fossil aquifer to expand grain production contributed to an abrupt 62 percent drop in the grain harvest between 1994 and 1996.

The soil degradation and resulting cropland abandonment that invariably follows the burning off of the Amazon rain forest for agriculture has helped make Brazil the largest grain importer in the Western Hemisphere."

The report continues: "If the price of grain were to double (again), as it already has for some types of seafood, it could impoverish hundreds of millions more almost overnight. In short, a steep rise in grain prices could impoverish more people than any event in history, including the ill-fated Great Leap Forward in China that starved some 20-30 million people to death between 1959 and 1961.

The world's farmers also face water scarcity. "The expanding demand for water is pushing beyond the sustainable yield of aquifers in many countries and is draining some of the world's major rivers dry before they reach the sea. As the demand for water for irrigation and for industrial and residential uses continues to expand, the competition between countryside and city for available water supplies intensifies. In some parts of the world, meeting growing urban needs is possible only by diverting water from irrigation," the UN says.

"One of the keys to the near tripling of the world grain harvest from 1950 to 1990 was a 2.5-fold expansion of irrigation, a development that extended agriculture into arid regions with little rainfall, intensified production in low-rainfall areas, and increased dry-season cropping in countries with monsoonal climates. Most of the world's rice and much of its wheat is produced on irrigated land," the UN says.

"A critical irrigation threshold was crossed in 1979. From 1950 until then, irrigation expanded faster than population, increasing the irrigated area per person by nearly one-third. This was closely associated with the worldwide rise in grain production per person of one-third. But since 1979, the growth in irrigation has fallen behind that of population, shrinking the irrigated area per person by some 7 percent. This trend, now well established, will undoubtedly continue as the demand for water presses ever more tightly against available supplies."

"Though this is hardly a politically correct topic, population policy is a very real concern.

"For a large part, European countries have stabilized their populations, though third world populations continue to expand unchecked. Obviously, the best-case solution to stabilizing world population is for emigration from third to first world countries—again, not such an easy or politically popular task.

As Earth Day organizer Doug La Follette wrote in a 1996 commentary: "We occupy a very small niche in the ecology of nature; that we cannot continue to pollute our finite world and destroy other species and their habitats; that we are just one interrelated link in a complex system of living things; and that we are totally dependent on our environment for our survival comes as a rude awakening to many people. Change frightens most people, especially those who are getting rich exploiting our finite resources for very short-term gain. The recognition that "growth" cannot continue and that there must be serious limits to human activity is a paradigm shift many refuse to accept.

"Saying no to polluting projects, products and technologies is a far better solution than trying to "clean up" expensive and life-endangering messes after they have been created. This idea upsets both the polluting industries and the regulatory systems they have learned to manipulate or buy off. Suggesting that the over-consuming first world nations cut back and learn to find happiness in something other than more and more electric toys, diet dog food and second homes on five-acre lots upsets those in power. And finally, telling people that they should consider having no more than one child per family is not the way to get elected to high office."

As for stabilizing our carbon emissions, it's easy, in theory: Stop burning fossil fuels. This is less easily achieved when one considers that 85 percent of our energy comes from oil, coal, and natural gas. Yes, hydrogen, wind, and solar—even nascent tidal technologies—are emerging as possible replacements, but not at rates necessary.

Still, there is room for optimism. The outline of a solar/hydrogen economy that is likely to replace the fossil-fuel-based economy of today is beginning to emerge. Wind energy, for instance, remains minor compared to fossil fuel use, but it is expanding at a double-digit rate, as is the use of solar cells, particularly in Europe. A new analysis by the National Audubon Society reveals that "populations of some of America's most familiar and beloved birds have taken a nosedive over the past forty years," with some down as much as 80 percent. The dramatic declines are attributed to the loss of grasslands, healthy forests and wetlands, and other critical habitats from multiple environmental threats such as sprawl, energy development, and the spread of industrialized agriculture.

A study reported in www.audubonohio.org notes that these threats are now compounded by new and broader problems including the escalating effects of global warming. In concert, they paint a challenging picture for the future of many common species and send a serious warning about our increasing toll on local habitats and the environment itself.

"These are not rare or exotic birds we're talking about—these are the birds that visit our feeders and congregate at nearby lakes and seashores and yet they are disappearing day by day," said Carol Browner, Audubon chairperson and former EPA Administrator. "Their decline tells us we have serious work to do, from protecting local habitats to addressing the huge threats from global warming."

"The director of the Center for Biodiversity and Conservation at the museum, Eleanor Sterling remarked that, 'we've lost sight of the biodiversity crisis because of other global challenges like climate change. But now we need to step back, understand the causes and consequences of our continued impact on life on the planet, and develop realistic and comprehensive strategies that allow dynamic human communities, economies, and life to thrive.'

"Increasingly scientists and policymakers have underlined the link of biodiversity preservation to the economy. A rich biodiversity provides a number of environmental services, such as pollination, food security, pest control, freshwater, medical breakthroughs, and carbon sequestration.

"In 2002 nations pledged that by 2010 they would achieve a 'significant reduction' in biodiversity loss. They have failed: if anything the extinction crisis today is worse than it was eight years ago."

The gathering was hosted by Conservation International, Fordham University, United Nations Development Program (UNDP), United Nations Foundation, and the Wildlife Conservation Society.

Their findings including the disturbing news that few species have faced: "Such vitriolic hatred from humans as the world's top predators. Considered by many as pests—often as dangerous—they have been gunned down, poisoned, speared, 'finned,' and decimated across their habitats. Even where large areas of habitat are protected, the one thing that is often missing are top predators. However, new research over the past few decades is showing just how vital these predators are to ecosystems. Biologists have long known that predators control populations of prey animals, but new studies show that they may do much more. From controlling smaller predators to protecting river banks from erosion to providing nutrient hotspots, it appears that top predators are indispensable to a working ecosystem. Top predators sit at the apex of an ecosystem's food chain. Wolves in Alaska, tigers in Siberia, lions in Kenya, white sharks in the Pacific are all examples of top predators."

So between the shift in global climate—what most experts agree is unlikely to be arrested—as well as its specific effects on the ocean and the land and the global ecosystem, as well as overpopulation, and even the Mid-East's admission that oil reserves are in a decline (and our civilization will need a decade or more to prepare for its end), this really is, as my co-writer and I started out in jest as describing as the "doomsday" chapter.

To bring it home, here's what you, personally, could suffer as a result of global warming—ignoring the possibility you live in a coastal area that could no longer exist a decade or two down the road.

According to the US government's Food and Drug Administration, here is how climate change could affect your health.

1. Stepped-up sniffling. Allergies, from ragweed in the fall to tree pollen in the spring, are predicted not only to become stronger but also to enjoy lengthened seasons because of less frost and earlier blooming. Fungal spores (those outdoors and in moist basements) will most likely thrive, tickling the throats of many.

2. Algae-related complaints. Cyanobacteria, or blue-green algae, thrive and bloom in the rising temperatures of bodies of water, from municipal water systems to the Great Lakes and Florida's Lake Okeechobee. The algae have been linked to digestive, neurological, liver, and dermatological diseases.

3. Painful kidney stones. Because of higher temperatures and more dehydration, the crystallized calcifications that must be passed—often painfully—through the urinary tract could plague an additional 2.2 million people a year by 2050, researchers estimate. The current "kidney stone belt," which includes southern states like Florida, the Carolinas, and Arkansas, could extend up into Kentucky and northern California.

4. Exotic infections. Dengue fever, malaria and encephalitis, while not exactly household names, have seen U. S. outbreaks and upticks in incidence in recent years. Mosquitoes and plankton, which flourish in warmer water temperatures, play a key role in transmitting such diseases.

5. Itchier cases of poison ivy. Poison ivy appears to become more potent as carbon dioxide levels rise, research has suggested.

6. Surplus of stings. Alaska's warming has heralded a six-fold rise in severe stings reported, and the buzzing bees, wasps and yellow jackets are showing up in spots never before seen. Alaska may be a harbinger for the rest of us, as its temperature changes have been the most significant in the United States.

7. Fewer fruits available. The value of crops produced in the Yakima River Valley of Washington State—more than 6,000 square miles of orchards and farmland east of

Seattle—may drop almost a quarter as temperatures rise over the coming decades. Less water for irrigation from nearby mountain snowpack could drive down fruit availability and drive up the cost of the produce.

8. Upsurge in summertime hacking and wheezing. Cool breezes coming down from Canada could diminish, driving up ozone pollution at ground level—particularly in the Northeast and Midwest—say some Harvard University scientists. Possible result: irritated lungs, especially in people with respiratory illness.

9. Deluge of heat-wave deaths. Already a risk to the very young and the very old in the summer months, strings of hot and humid days are expected to become more frequent and more severe, says the Intergovernmental Panel on Climate Change. In California, for example, such deaths could double by 2100. In the summer of 2010, more than 2,000 cattle in Kansas died from excessive heat exposure.

10. Bigger coastal storms. The flooding associated with the likes of hurricanes Katrina and Ike, and the physical and mental stresses that ensue, are expected to occur more frequently as storms surge around the world. By 2050, a one-foot rise in sea level is predicted, which could worsen flood damage by 36 percent to 58 percent as well as radically changing the structure and nature of much of our fragile wetlands that are in coastal areas.

Most of the information we've discussed so far in this chapter has centered on things that are going on in other parts of the world. What about the pressure of growth and development right here in our own country? As I pointed out in the introduction, as of this writing, the population of the US has reached 310,000,000. Any way you look, that is a lot of pressure on our natural lands and on our environment. The best statistics I could find indicate that there are about 258,000,000 registered passenger vehicles in the US and about 2,735,000 miles of paved roads; some 230,000 general aviation aircraft and 19,600 airports; 12,095,000 recreational boats; 131,000,000 housing units; 5,000,000 commercial buildings; 133,000 elementary and secondary schools; 450,000 churches. I could go on and on, but you get the picture. And don't forget, this is just in the US (which is currently about 4.52 percent of the world population). Now, imagine how all of those numbers will increase when we are estimated to hit a population of 400 million by the year 2039—not really that far off when you think about it.

A recent study by the USDA called *Forests on the Edge* indicate that many private forests—particularly in the East, where most are located—are likely to see substantial increases in housing and other development in the next three decades. More than 44 million acres of private forest are projected to experience increased development by 2030. Projections are that we will hit 439 million in population by 2050; and 1 billion by 2100. Think of how our country will look given those increases, and how it will look if we don't address all of the things connected to that incredible growth. How much more asphalt and concrete can we afford to spread out over our American soil? How many more trucks, cars, buses, and other fossil-fueled vehicles can we support? How many more airplanes can we fill the skies with and still have safe airways? How many more boats can our rivers and lakes support? How much more pollution can our air and water withstand? How much more waste can our landfills absorb? With that in mind, isn't it time that we address these things NOW? Would not that be the prudent and smart thing to do? Can we really stand up to that kind of pressure on our country if we don't start making better choices and finding better answers to our growth issues?

We would like to be wrong. We would like all of our sources to be wrong. But even if some of the numbers and statistics we cite are off by a few percentage points here and there—what we have found is at best troubling and disturbing. And even if things are not as bad as what we have uncovered, by most accounts, our own country and planet Earth in general is under a tremendous strain and faces serious and severe challenges.

Now is the time to act.

The Challenges of Change

What Can We Do?

"We generate our own environment.
We get exactly what we deserve.
How can we resent a life we've created ourselves?
Who's to blame, who's to credit, but us?
Who can change it, anytime we wish, but us?"

Richard Bach
Author of *Jonathan Livingston Seagull*

Before I get into some day-to-day things we can all do to reduce our carbon footprints, I'd like to address some issues that are more community based. Let's face it—it's not easy to change the world, but we all can make a difference if we try. Having our voices heard concerning growth in our communities, in our neighborhoods, and throughout our states is so important. How do we do this? The old fashioned way: Write or call your government representatives, go to town meetings, attend some planning and zoning meetings in your area, talk to your neighbors and community leaders about these things.

Yes, it takes time and effort, and it takes getting involved. But it's worth it because each of us can have an impact. Do you really want to see another strip-mall-type shopping center just down the road from you? Do you think the new school being proposed in your neighborhood is really up to the best current standards of energy use and generally well-designed? Does the plan take into account the traffic situation, parking, adequate sidewalks, and safety features for the students and teachers walking? Is it really best to tear down that old courthouse or is it worth considering renovating it?

Is it the right thing to do to build those condos so close to the beach? Should your community explore expanding or changing your mass-transit system to be more efficient? Are our landfill and recycling programs as good as they should be? Do you have some car-pooling options in your area that would help save energy and traffic problems (and money)? Should we add some green space to our community, and if so, where is the best place to do so? Is that new residential project taking up too much land? Will the homes being proposed be built to high energy-efficient standards, using the best materials? Should your town look into using natural gas in its city vehicle fleet?

There are hundreds of questions I could get into, but I think you get the picture. This is your town, your community, your life, and your choice. If there is something being done that you don't agree with or don't like, then it's up to you to do something about it. Write a letter to the editor of your newspaper—call your representative's office to express your concern. Talk to your friends and neighbors. Go to city council meetings.

The alternative is complacency, not really caring or doing anything to make sure what's being done is being done right, being thought through carefully and all the options explored. It's well worth the time and effort to stay informed about the growth and changes in your own backyard. It goes back to that old saying: "If it's worth doing at all, it's worth doing right!"

So don't hesitate to speak up on matters that will affect your neighborhood, community, town, and state. It's our right—and our responsibility. I can tell you from repeated, personal experiences my wife, Rose Lane, and I have been through with local authorities over various concerns or issues or suggestions we've had, or our neighbors and friends have had, that getting involved works! I believe it's a little irresponsible not to stand up and offer your opinion, speak your mind, or take whatever civic-minded actions you are able to take to help, even in the smallest manner, to make your home, your community, your county, state—your country—a better, safer, more economically and ecologically sound place.

Now, when we're talking about "carbon footprints" and what steps governments and corporations are taking, or could be taking, to reduce the amount of climate-changing gases being released into the atmosphere, there are things you and I, and each of our families, can do that can make a difference.

Collectively, we can make a surprisingly huge difference. Each day, on average, each American, directly or indirectly, is responsible for about fifty-seven pounds of carbon dioxide being released, according to the Environmental Protection Agency. What is that, exactly? You can imagine fifty-seven pounds of, say, potatoes, but what would fifty-seven pounds of CO_2 look like? Here's one way I've heard it described: Think of a balloon. One pound of CO_2 would fill a balloon the size of one of those big exercise balls; now consider that each of us releases fifty-seven of those "balloons" of CO_2 into the air every DAY.

You can measure your own carbon footprint easily by, for example, going to the Nature Conservancy's website calculator (www.nature.org /initiatives/climatechange/calculator/). Once you know what your impact on the environment is, it makes it easier to find ways of lowering your contribution to greenhouse gases, to polluting our rivers and streams and crop fields, live healthier lives—and, if possible, save money.

Even more user friendly is the very cool GoodGuide's iPhone app (www.goodguide.com) that lets you scan the barcode of any product and then gives you a head's up on where it ranks on the green scale!

First up, we contribute an enormous amount of greenhouse gas pollution by the way we move around, which I have addressed in another chapter—but remember that you can make a surprising contribution to the planet's health by choosing an alternative form of transportation even one day a week if you are able—be it walking, bicycle, public transportation, or carpooling.

Increasingly, residents of some areas, such as New York City; Santa Monica, San Diego; Austin, Texas; and more actually have the option of purchasing "green" power, albeit at a slightly higher cost.

But in terms of what each of us can do, I'll make the initial focus on our homes, which are the largest, single cost in our lives, and where we can individually have a positive impact immediately. Remember that roughly two-thirds of your household's garbage can be recycled. Make sure you separate the garbage and use recycling bins. Use your own shopping bags when you go to the grocery store, and opt for paper over plastic if you don't have your own bags with you.

I recommend you visit the Department of Energy's Home Energy Saver site (hes.lbl.gov/hes), which contains not only a calculator that will serve to give you a basic guideline to the efficiency of your own home based on zip code and an online survey, but also contains invaluable information on insulation, windows, doors, skylights, and everything else from appliances to lighting. There are dozens of terrific tips: Just off the top, using shades or curtains to provide natural relief from the sun, and utilizing ceiling fans to circulate air, effectively replacing air conditioning on those less-scorching days.

In the course of general research, one interesting tidbit I discovered, which was supported in research from numerous sources, including the federal government's Energy Savers website (www.energysavers.gov/), is that the use of small electric room heaters can be a wise choice.

Like many people, we have areas of the house we don't use on a daily basis and it doesn't make sense to have a single heating or air conditioning system. Valuable heat (or cold air) is lost in the ducts before it even reaches the living areas of the home. This is why it's wise, if you can afford it, to have an assessment made of the condition of all the heating and cooling ducts in your home. You might be surprised that some have gaping holes or ducts have partially separated with time.

There are some technologies on the horizon, such as a new aerosol being developed at Lawrence Berkeley National Laboratory, which would seal ducts without the need for a laborer to manually reach and plug every leak, increasing their efficiency.

And if you are able to retrofit during renovations, as our family did, and install regional heating and cooling systems, you make the most efficient use of the energy you're consuming, especially if your insulation and windows and doors are up to the highest possible codes of efficiency. But I certainly won't feel so guilty about pulling out a small electric heater for under my desk in my study during cold mornings, since research clearly supports that it's a wiser choice than heating an entire room.

One conflicting contention is whether it's better to turn down your heat or turn up your air conditioner if you're leaving the home for a few hours, or whether it's more energy efficient to keep your home at a constant temperature. Some people think it takes more energy to cool (or heat) your home back to a comfortable temperature than if you leave the temperature settings unchanged. Well, according to the federal government's Home Energy Saver program, there is actually no simple answer because we live in quite divergent climates all over America. But, as the program illustrates, "The rate of heat transfer from your house to the outside, or vice versa, is dependent partly on the temperature difference between your house and outside. More heat is transferred when the difference is greater, so it takes more energy to keep your house at 72°F when it is 40°F outside than to heat your house back up to 72°F after you return."

As for air conditioning, according to these experts, "Cooling your house back to the comfortable temperature will use less electricity than the unit would use cycling on and off for short periods to maintain the set temperature."

So what's the answer? A digital programmable thermostat, which Home Energy Saver says "can reduce the energy used for air conditioning or heating by 5 to 30 percent … if they are properly programmed. Just installing the thermostat isn't enough; you need to enter a schedule designed to be sure the heating and cooling systems do not run when not needed, and are set back when the comfort needs are more flexible."

You can also program them to start heating or cooling your house an hour or so before you return, which, in the long run, will save energy—and money.

Another thing people are becoming a little more widely aware of is the problem of all the "vampire" energy suckers in our homes. Your television(s), DVD players, stereos, microwave, and that whole home office of electronic equipment drains electricity even when it's not turned on—even leaving your cell phone charger plugged in when it's not charging your phone is drawing a small amount of energy. In fact, according to the Grist.org environmental organization, all of these devices consume $1 billion a year in electricity in the United States. Their recommendation is to keep devices plugged into power strips that can easily be turned off when not in use.

There are so many little things you can do around the house to improve your overall efficiency—which means money AND carbon emission savings. Don't think you need to do this all at once, but it isn't difficult to replace conventional light bulbs one or two at a time with compact fluorescent light (CFL) bulbs, which are more expensive to begin with but which use about a fifth of the energy as regular bulbs and last up to twelve times longer.

I went to the Natural Resources Defense Council, which runs and excellent website for homeowners (www.simplesteps.org), and found some of the most accessible, and sensible, advice on lowering each of our contributions to greenhouse gases. The Mother Nature Network (mnn.com) site I'm involved with also contains an ever-evolving database of excellent tips on how each of us can lower our carbon footprints. And of course I highly recommend visiting the site regularly for our updates.

For instance, a single 75-watt incandescent bulb burning for two hours a day generates six pounds of carbon dioxide a month. There are alternatives—right now, there are CFL bulbs, which cost up to $19 each, and LEDS, which can cost $30 or more. There has been some concern that the CFL bulbs are not necessarily a foolproof option since they contain small amounts of mercury. But the NRDC has concluded "CFLs are the clear choice for everyone concerned about protecting their health and saving energy. CFLs are a welcome and necessary change from outdated incandescents because the energy savings in CFLs are dramatic, while the quantity of mercury contained in the bulb, and the opportunity to be exposed to the mercury, is quite small."

If you were to replace just six bulbs at once in your home—the lights most often used daily—you would likely see an immediate, though admittedly conservative, savings on your next power bill; replace all the bulbs in your home and add motion-detector switches so that lights are never left on accidentally, and you'll see a much more significant impact on your power bill and you will be lowering your carbon footprint by, according to the NDRC, possibly as much as .21 tons a year!

The future in lighting, most likely, however, is very likely LED, or light-emitting diode lighting. Durable and very small, they last up to sixty thousand hours, which is about sixty times longer than our outdated incandescent bulbs. You use them every day, whether you know it or not, since LEDS are the lights in all your small electronic devices. They use so little power that some of them don't need to be plugged in at all! They are excellent candidates for running on solar power or other alternative energies. As I say, they are considerably more expensive, but much more efficient. In time, we'll be seeing a transition to these alternative lights. As a matter of fact, the American government has plans to implement new energy standards in 2012 that will phase out incandescent bulbs as we know them.

The federal Department of Energy has set a $10 million prize for the first company that develops a high-quality, high-efficiency, solid-state lighting replacement for conventional light bulbs. Philips has come up with its Master LED bulb, which is on sale in Europe and has recently become available in the States. But whoever comes up with the new standard for lighting will land a massive government contract; those bulbs will become standards in government offices all over the world, and the chosen company may also receive subsidies to reduce consumer prices of the bulbs.

We're seeing LEDs show up more and more in products such as strings of holiday lighting, but the technological forward thinking hasn't stopped with LEDs. There are numerous companies which are trying to quickly make OLED (organic light-emitting diode) lighting that would be brighter, use less power than even conventional LEDs—and could come in the form of thin sheets. Imagine a massive, high-definition TV that's not much thicker than a sheet of wallpaper, or a laptop computer that you can roll up like a magazine!

The bottom line as of this writing: CFLs are the most cost-effective and environmentally sound choice. Some consumers are avoiding them for lights that they want to be able to dim, as most CFLs don't offer that option. However, everyone should know that there is at least one company that is making dimmable CFLs; Pure Spectrum out of Savannah, Georgia, has been making them for some time now. Their website (purespectrumlighting.com/) even has a section that tells you where you can purchase their products.

Aside from the obvious, initial cost of your home, the biggest expense is going to be its energy use, just a small example of which are the aforementioned light bulbs. This energy, and cost, translates into an impact on the environment and your pocketbook annually.

Companies are also developing ways of making LCD and plasma screens more efficient, but it will take time. And manufacturers are aware of their impact on the environment at least through negative publicity and, in turn, the positive publicity they can receive with "green" efforts. For instance, Sony has developed a 32-inch model HDTV that's not only energy efficient, but also constructed entirely out of recycled materials from other Sony operations. It's a test, available only in Japan, but the company asserts that it's an "environmentally-conscious offering sure to act as a guide for future HDTVs all over the globe."

While lighting is a major contributor to our energy use, it's the most easily and cheaply addressed—a bulb at a time if you wish. Major appliances, however, are the most serious energy drains in our homes.

Number one on the list is your refrigerator. It's often the prime energy user in your home—hey, it needs to keep your food cold or frozen 24 hours a day, 365 days a year. The Department of Energy, in fact, estimates that 14 percent of your power bill comes from just one refrigerator. And of course many families have two fridges, and stand-alone freezers. The latter two are often kept in a garage, which is fine during colder months but in hot summer weather puts an extra strain on your energy consumption and costs. The only way to combat that is to either forgo the convenience of extra appliances or to purchase the most energy-efficient model—in the smallest size possible to meet your needs.

Energy Star refrigerators, for instance, use 15 percent less energy than current federal law requires and 40 percent less than conventional models sold in 2001.

In general, according to the Environmental Protection Agency, which created the Energy Star rating along with the Department of Energy, you will more than make up for the upfront cost of an energy-efficient appliance over the life of the product. There are a number of sites, such as the Consumer Reports greenerchoices.org that can assist you in making an informed decision.

In general, the consensus is that Energy Star-rated bottom-freezer fridges are the best choice—without energy-draining ice machines but with internal water filtration systems, which discourages wasteful bottled water purchases.

Washing machines—it should go without saying that an Energy Star-rated model is preferable—are next on the list. Unlike refrigerators, however, they don't have to be the energy drain they are, since most sources indicate that 90 percent of the energy that goes into doing our laundry is from heating the water. I've yet to find a source that says we can't wash all our clothing with cold water, and we get the most efficiency from our washing machines by doing full loads at a time.

I'll get into home-cleaning products soon, but while we're on the subject of laundry, there is no reason not to use an environmentally friendly biodegradable detergent when washing clothes. If you have a front-loading washer, it's recommended that you use high-efficiency green detergents that don't create as many suds as traditional detergents.

Clothes dryers, whether they're electric or gas, are certainly convenient: But they're also energy hogs that are far more a luxury than a convenience. Whenever possible, air-drying clothes instead of using a dryer not only saves energy, but also helps clothes last longer.

This may seem obvious, but we're also in the habit of washing clothes even when they don't need it. The United Nations Environment Program came up with the statistic that if you wear your jeans three times without washing them (this is assuming you don't get them dirty!) and then washed them in cold water, skipped the dryer and iron, you'd conserve five times the energy you'd normally consume by washing your jeans after every wear. It is also far better for your jeans to treat them this way—clothes last far longer the less they're washed, and especially if they're not put through a dryer.

While we're on the subject of clothing, it's worth considering just how "green" your jeans are. Actually, let's look at our entire wardrobe. First of all, don't buy clothes that need to be dry-cleaned. The majority of commercial dry cleaning businesses in the US use a solvent called perchloroethylene, or perc, according to the National Cleaners Association—and the chemical is classified, outright, by the Environmental Protection Agency as a hazardous air pollutant. Just about every fabric can be safely washed or spot cleaned at home.

According to *Consumer Reports* greener choices website (www.greenerchoices.org/), only angora sweaters and garments such as lined suits need to be sent to a professional cleaner, while all other clothing can be cleaned at home.

"Plain (no embroidery, embellishments, fancy stitches), solid-color sweaters can often be hand washed or machine washed on a gentle/delicate setting," *Consumer Reports* says. "Be sure to turn cotton and cashmere inside out. If you have a top-loading machine, you can often extract excess water from hand washing using the spin cycle only. It's best to lay sweaters flat to dry, because that allows you to reshape them."

"Lightly colored plain-weave rayon and silk blouses labeled 'dry-clean' or 'dry-clean only' have been successfully hand washed in *Consumer Reports* tests. Note that deep or saturated colors had a tendency to bleed, or lose color, with washing. Washable wool labeled as such can be both machine washed and dried," *Consumer Reports* says.

When it comes to purchasing "green" clothing, it's difficult to find a consensus on what the wisest consumer choices are. Polyester, for starters, is made from oil—a non-renewable resource; it is also non-biodegradable, and requires large amounts of energy to produce and results in the undesirable release of greenhouse gases. Further, according to the EPA, about six billion pounds of polyester textile waste ends up in landfills every year. If that's not enough for you, guys, listen to this: Polyester develops significant electrostatic charges while being worn, and these charges have been associated with, ahem, negative effects in men who wear polyester underwear.

Cotton is among our favorite and most historical textiles. We think of cotton as being an eco-friendly material, and granted, it is certainly a "natural" product. Yet it may come as a surprise to many that depending on the exact conditions, it is, in some cases, hardly environmentally friendly in its growth and management. It requires massive amounts of water, which evaporates and leaves mineral deposits such as salt behind, eventually rendering soil unusable. Some estimates rate worldwide cropland destruction through over-cultivation of cotton at a hundred million hectares, although figures vary wildly. Cotton's biggest environmental impact worldwide is water use, and even growing cotton organically doesn't always save water. In California, for example, according to the www.simplesteps.org site, "organic cotton can actually use more water than conventional cotton, more than 780 gallons per pound of fiber—enough to make a single t-shirt. However, a rain-fed organic cotton farm in India could use about 528.3 gallons of irrigation water to grow a pound of fiber. Organic cotton grown in Brazil is almost entirely rain-fed, and would use only about 10.6 gallons to make a t-shirt. Some manufacturers include a rain-fed claim to help you find low-water cotton."

According to the Environmental Protection Agency, conventional cotton consumes 11 percent of the world's pesticides and 24 percent of the world's insecticides. It takes a third of a pound of pesticides and fertilizers to produce enough cotton to make just one T-shirt.

So, clearly, organic cotton is the most desirable option if it is available to you—although it still requires an enormous amount of cotton to make the products we demand, and that puts a strain on our lands. It's like I say, no process comes without a cost. As the EPA says, "Organic cotton is definitely a huge improvement as it removes synthetic pesticides, insecticides and synthetic fertilizers from the equation. However, water use is not considered in organic cotton certification so in a sense organic cotton production is not even truly sustainable as it stands right now."

Bamboo has gained enormous popularity in recent years since it's a grass rather than a tree and grows quickly, is naturally pest and disease resistant, and is one of the world's most sustainable resources—plus, bamboo plantations are great at sequestering greenhouse gases.

The story gets a little murky beyond the harvesting stage of bamboo, however. While bamboo can be turned into fabric via a mechanical process, it's not economically viable, so a chemical process is the most common method of converting bamboo into fabric. The trouble is that this is basically the same process as used to make rayon—the leaves and woody parts are cooked in very poisonous solvents. And since much of this is done in the third world, the chemicals often end up directly in waterways and the atmosphere.

A newer method of turning bamboo into textile is through the use of nanotechnology, which has its strong opponents since the technology is so new and ultimately unpredictable.

So, best advice? If you purchase products that have "organic, sustainable" certification from an independent watchdog such as Oeko-Tex, you'll at least be getting fabric that's safe for you to wear and for your kids to be around—but there's no guarantee that it was manufactured using environmentally friendly methods.

Hemp is also an attractive alternative for our clothing, as hemp growth requires no pesticides, fungicides, or chemical fertilizers. The fibers are three times as strong as cotton, and hemp is naturally mold and mildew resistant. Even better is that no part of the plant is wasted during its production into fiber and other products. The seeds are full of Omega-3 fatty acids, which can be used to make health supplements, and it's a terrifically renewable resource that can be used to create everything from paper to clothing to mattresses.

In his 1997 book *Hemp Horizons: The Comeback of the World's Most Promising Plant,* John W. Roulac wrote that hemp requires up to thirty times less than cotton for cultivation. It doesn't require the use of pesticides and can be grown in the same spot repeatedly as it naturally fertilizes the soil (compared to cotton, which depletes soil). When hemp is harvested, the leaves are left on the ground, replenishing the soil with nutrients. Hemp has long roots that prevent erosion and can be grown in a variety of different climates. It often yields more fibers and is a fast-growing plant that absorbs lots of CO_2. Hemp can typically be harvested about 120 days after it is planted. This also produces a lot of biomass in a short period of time, which can be used to great advantage for biofuel or of building material.

Hemp clothes are amazingly tough. The strength of the fiber is three times that of cotton, yet the garments are lightweight. In conclusion, hemp clothes are a great alternative to the traditional, cotton clothing that most people wear. First and foremost, hemp clothing is much better for the environment than cotton.

Hemp can be used as a raw material for making (besides environmentally friendly clothing) things like rope, bags, and nets. Oil extracted from the fruits can be used in cooking as well as a lubricant, or as a component in soap and shampoo. Further uses include biofuel, insulation, and building material.

It's an amazing crop that can even be used as a "mop crop" to clear impurities out of wastewater, such as sewage effluent, excessive phosphorus from chicken litter, or other unwanted substances or chemicals. Hemp is being used to clean contaminants at the Chernobyl nuclear disaster site, according to a report in the *Wall Street Journal*.

For some, hemp has a negative reputation due to its correlation to marijuana and led to its being banned as a crop, which is so sort-sighted. Most countries around the world are growing hemp. China, North Korea, most all former Soviet Union countries, most European countries, South America, and even Canada grow hemp. France is Europe's largest producer. Canada, the United Kingdom, and Germany all resumed commercial production in the 1990s. Hopefully our US lawmakers will wake up and lift this ban that is keeping us from engaging in a proven crop with many positive uses.

Ultimately, much of our clothing these days is made in foreign countries and is not terribly eco-friendly. But with a bit of research and the desire you can find more locally manufactured garments, though often at a premium price.

Although there aren't eco-friendly ways to produce synthetic fibers, purchasing recycled polyester goods extends the life of the fabric and keeps it out of landfill.

Look for fabrics that bear the Global Organic Textile standard. When GOTS-certified products aren't available, look for Oeko-Tex. Oeko-Tex is a little less stringent, but primarily ensures that any chemicals used in dyeing or finishing are not lingering on the finished product. Look for either heavy-metal-free or vegetable-based dyes. "GOTS-certified" products are free of heavy metals. Again from the simplesteps.org site, recommendations are that you:

Choose recycled fibers whenever possible, and look for fleece made from post-consumer recycled materials.

Look for cotton that is either unbleached or bleached with hydrogen peroxide instead of chlorine bleach.

Avoid textiles labeled permanent press, no-iron, crease-resistant, shrink-proof, stretch-proof, water repellent, or water-proofed. Some finishes, such as those to prevent stains and wrinkles, can release formaldehyde into the air.

Look for products that are machine-washable to keep dust and allergen levels at a minimum (wool is naturally inhospitable to dust mites).

Coming back to our general household: Here's something that surprised me: When it comes to dishwashers, I was a little surprised to learn that in most cases, washing dishes by hand uses more water than even an outdated and inefficient dishwashing machine, and certainly more energy than an Energy Star machine. Again, just like your washing machine, run the cycles only when there's a full load and skip the dry cycle—let your dishes air-dry. And, just like our laundry, there's no reason to use hot water over warm or even cold water—along with that biodegradable detergent free of petroleum and phosphates—which I'll get to shortly.

Our demand for hot water and how we're used to achieving it is not at all efficient. It's recommended that we install low-flow showerheads and also aerators on all faucets, which saves not just hot water but conserves water overall. Generally, according to MetaEfficient, an organization that tests products to rate their efficiency:

"Low-flow aerators will generally pay for themselves in only a few months. Standard faucet aerators will allow flow rates of 2.5–5 gallons of water per minute. But for bathroom faucets, low-flow aerators that deliver between a half and full gallon of water per minute will deliver the same force of spray, but often in a more pleasing fashion. Kitchen faucets may require a higher flow rate of two to four gallons per minute if you regularly fill the sink for washing dishes. Fifteen percent of an average household's daily water consumption is through faucet use. In a family of four, where each person uses the bathroom sink for six minutes each day, using a half-gallon-per-minute aerator (instead of a 2.5-gallon-per minute aerator) would reduce the daily household water consumption by 48 gallons per day, which totals 17,520 gallons annually."

According to the EPA, replacing old toilets saves even more water. New federal mandates say toilets can not use more than 1.6 gallons of water per flush; some pre-1994 models use up to 3.5 gallons.

As for our actual water heaters, the initial recommendation from every source I can find is that you lower the temperature of your water heater to 120 degrees and insulate the tank. Of course, if you can afford it, the wisest thing to do would be to install tankless water heaters. Almost a standard in Europe for years, tankless or "instant" or "on demand" water heaters make so much sense. Rather than heat water and keep it in a tank, these heaters flash heat water as it's needed when you turn on a tap—so you'll never "run out" of hot water—you're getting clean, fresh water every time you use hot water rather than water that's being stored in a tank, which has to keep water at a certain temperature. Some estimates are they can save up to 40 percent on annual energy bills compared to, say, a forty-gallon electric tank heater.

What's more is that even with these tankless heaters, there is energy lost by transporting hot water through pipes from the heater to the desired source. So point-of-use water heaters make the most sense, such as a heater installed immediately under a sink or near a shower. No longer would you be paying to heat a large tank of water, keep it hot, and then lose energy transporting it via pipes to a far-off room, where you waste gallons for water waiting for it to warm up: You'd have hot water instantly right at the location where it's desired.

Incentives are constantly being added. For instance, if you purchased and installed a tankless system before 31 December 2010, you would be eligible for a tax credit equal to 30 percent of the full purchase and installation price up to a maximum of $1,500.

We've already installed a couple of these units in our Charlane plantation buildings—such as our hunting lodge, where it's a pure waste of energy and money to have water kept heated in a building that is used only at specific times of the year and for short periods of time. As time goes on, we will eventually replace all of our old tank units in favor of the tankless system, or perhaps in some buildings with the solar option.

A less radical alternative is solar water heating, which requires less of a retrofit and is less expensive. Solar water heaters can save homeowners as much as $500 a year on energy costs, according to the Environmental Defense Fund:

"The initial cost, including installation, is usually higher than for conventional water heaters, but after the payback period of two to five years, homeowners can realize substantial savings (even more than $500 a year if energy prices continue to increase). The economics are even more convincing if you're buying a new home or refinancing. You can include the price of a solar water heater in your mortgage. For a 30-year mortgage, the amount is usually between $13 and $20 per month"

As for home-cleaning products: First up, it's better to choose products sold in bulk to save on packaging, and keep in mind that powdered detergents are lighter and so require less energy to ship than liquids. Of course, you really don't need to be purchasing specific cleaning products to begin with, aside from a quality earth-friendly laundry detergent.

Your home can be properly, cheaply, and safely cleaned with natural products such as vinegar, lemon juice, baking soda, or Borax—the latter of which is a good natural insecticide to kill ants, cockroaches, and fleas, though keep in mind that just because you use a natural insecticide rather than a synthetic one does not mean it is any less harmful to animals or humans. Application of any type of natural insecticide should be performed safely and only at the frequency necessary to maintain a healthy crop of fruits or vegetables. For truly safe insecticides, use botanical oils. Those derived from chrysanthemum, garlic, sweet flag, and clove kill garden-dust. Not only do these natural avengers zap the bad bugs, they are also harmless to humans and the environment. Many of the newer green pesticides have a unique effect that targets neurotransmitter sites that only insects have—so there's no harm to mammals, birds, or fish.

But as you stock up on vinegar and baking soda, don't just clean out your cupboard or dump all those cleaning products that are lurking under your sink. As the EPA points out, if they're too toxic to be a wise choice for your home, they're just as bad going down the drain or ending up in a landfill. Most communities hold events during which staff will take obsolete electronic equipment as well as toxic substances, and have them disposed of appropriately and safely.

Antibacterial soaps have become common place in most homes, but they are not only a waste of money, according to the FDA, they're actually dangerous. They don't work any better than regular soap and water in terms of killing germs, the government agency asserts, and they add to the risk of breeding "super germ bacteria that survive the chemical onslaught and have resistant offspring."

As newspaper writer Priya Giri Desai described in her *Boston Globe* environmental column: anything you use to clean floors or counter tops can also be inhaled and ingested, and ends up going down our sewers and sending harsh chemicals into our environment accordingly. As Barbra Batshalom, executive director of The Green Roundtable says, "The key issue is getting people to understand that you don't need toxic chemicals to clean your home." So take a little vinegar or baking soda, mix it with a little warm water and, with either one, you've got an all-purpose cleaner that is safe to both the environment and you and your family and your pets.

In one of her excellent posts, Mother Nature Network contributor Chanie Kirschner backed up this contention, saying that baking soda or vinegar mixes are strong enough—while still safe—for toilet bowls, soap scum, and kitchen sinks.

Going one step further, Chanie recommends that you also don't need that horribly corrosive and poisonous (not to mention expensive) drain cleaner.

"Have a clogged drain?" she writes on mnn.com: "Pour one cup vinegar, then one cup baking soda down the drain. Let it sit for a few minutes and follow with a cup of boiling hot water. Usually this'll be just as effective as the most expensive drain cleaners, and drain cleaners can be one of the most toxic things in your cleaning cadre. They can be bad for your pipes, and they are the last thing you want your toddler mistakenly guzzling down when he can't find his sippy cup (shudder).

"What about everyday household cleaning? Mix one cup vinegar with one cup water in a spray bottle and you're ready to go. For more serious disinfecting, try having one spray bottle of vinegar around and one spray bottle of hydrogen peroxide (make this one a dark bottle since light can change the properties of hydrogen peroxide). Research has shown that spraying these two nontoxic ingredients on your countertops can kill 10 times more bacteria than peroxide alone."

It's difficult sometimes not to appear "preachy" when it comes to all these standard things a lot of us grew up with and suggesting that they are not, indeed, the proper direction for us to be taking. But ultimately, no manufacturing process is without impact of some sort. Fortunately, industry, governments, and individuals are beginning to consider the full-life cycle of products in assessing how eco-friendly they are and weighing the negatives and the positives.

Just to illustrate this, even wax candles aren't ultimately a wise choice when we have the option to purchase soy candles.

I know, you're probably thinking that I'm going way overboard now by saying you shouldn't even burn candles! Rose Lane and I still buy and burn wax candles, but we've become more aware and try to by soy-based ones now. I'm not suggesting this is a major concern we're facing, certainly, but all these little things can add up, and I think it's important that we learn about the options we have for purchasing and using products that are connected to our daily lives. As for the candles and some of the other products and items mentioned in this chapter, I use them as an example of where, fundamentally, a product is flawed and we're just learning there's a better way. So to explain further on the candles, paraffin is manufactured from waste in the oil-refining process, and while it's good that it's a waste product being used, it's still not a renewable product, and soot from paraffin contains carcinogens, and can eventually muck up your walls over the course of time.

Just as cursory examination of our house at Charlane shows that with upgrades to heating, cooling, water heating, major appliances, lighting and small appliances—ensuring that everything is Energy Star rated, we could save more than $1,000 a year but, more importantly, we could save nearly 10,000 kilowatts of energy and reduce our carbon footprint by nearly 14,000 pounds of CO_2 a year.

Here are some handy resources of government incentives to assist you in upgrading your appliances and weatherization of your home.

State incentives: The Alliance to Save Energy: (ase.org/content/news/detail/2609).

Federal incentives: The Tax Incentives Assistance Project (energytaxincentives.org/) contains terrific info on improvements you can make to your home, some of which may qualify for federal income tax deductions. Depending on income, some families may be eligible for free energy audits and weatherization assistance through the Weatherization Assistance Program (apps1.eere.energy.gov/weatherization/), which is available to renters as well as homeowners.

President Obama instigated a "Cash for Caulkers" home-retrofitting rebate. The program, dubbed Home Star, would offer rebates to homeowners who make energy-efficient upgrades to their homes. Based on the popular "Cash for Clunkers" old-car program, Home Star would offer homeowners rebates of up to $3,000 for renovations such adding energy-efficient windows or better insulation, sealing ducts and upgrading to energy-efficient water heaters. As of this writing it has not been passed into law, but it is promising.

Now let's move into how we feed ourselves—probably a much more contentious subject matter!

Michael Pollan created quite a stir with his book, *Omnivore's Dilemma*, and he's back with another book on food that is certainly less controversial.

Like many folks who live in the country or spend a lot of time outdoors, I am a dedicated and ethical hunter, and here on the plantation we enjoy what we cull from our hunts. Quail, venison, wild turkey, and the like are staples of our own consumption, as well as being on the menu that we serve our guests. Of course, we also include the wonderful organic vegetables that Rose Lane grows in our garden as well as the nuts and fruits that we're blessed to have here. I enjoy a good steak now and then, too, but recognize that there is a thing as too much meat—just as there's a thing as too much mercury-laden seafood, which is otherwise very healthy.

At a public event in the fall of 2009, Pollan was asked to sum up his new book, and he said he wrote it for its simplicity, "They wanted simple rules of thumb. They don't want to know the whole back-story, the science of nutrition. They're very commonsense rules to get you onto real food."

And the advice he offered is very much in tune with sustainable, local farming.

> "Eat food that your grandmother or great-grandmother would recognize.
>
> "Don't eat foods that have ingredients you can't picture in their natural state.
>
> "Avoid foods with more than five ingredients or ingredients a third grader can't pronounce."

In other words, eschew "edible food-like substances" and beware of bogus health claims on packaging, marketing ploys to get us to buy.

"Don't buy cereals that change the color of the milk," Pollan said in an interview with *Womans Day* magazine. "Shop the periphery of the supermarket," where the produce, fish and meats are located. "Don't eat foods that are pretending to be something else. I tend to avoid mock meats," he said. "And eat foods that will eventually rot because it means they're not treated with chemicals."

Pollan even jokes that it's OK to "eat all the junk food you want as long as you cook it yourself. I love french fries, but if I go to the trouble and mess of cooking them, I'm only going to do it once a month."

Pollan is aware that he's fortunate to live in California where he has year-round access to a farmers' market two blocks away, but he stresses the importance of eating in season for environmental and health reasons. "We've forgotten that there are winter salads made of root vegetables like carrots and beets," he noted. He buys mostly organic, but he does so judiciously, based on which crops have the most pesticide residue—information that is searchable online. "You have to be strategic about your organic dollars. Blueberries and strawberries are worth it. Broccoli and bananas, not so worth it."

He also thinks we need to stop judging produce always by appearance, something it's bred for "at the expense of taste, and that makes growing organic more difficult because to make produce look that good can take a lot of pesticides." He's encouraged, however, that consumer demand has given rise to alternatives to the mainstream food system, evidenced by the fact that the number of farmers markets nationwide has doubled twice in the past ten years and that food chains are stocking more local and organic food.

"The key ingredient of industrial food—inexpensive meat and processed food—is fossil fuel," noted Pollan. "It takes 10 calories of fossil fuel energy to produce one calorie of processed or fast food." Then add the billions we're now spending to treat obesity, diabetes and other results of eating unhealthful food. "Healthcare spending has gone from 5 percent of national income to 18 percent."

Pollan, who teaches courses on food writing and science writing at the University of California at Berkeley, began writing about food as a natural outgrowth of his interest in gardening, the environment, "and how humans engage with the natural world. If you care about that, you're going to end up looking at food. It's through food, through agriculture, that we change the landscape more than anything else we do."

Not only are we changing the composition of species via our behavior, "We're learning through our food choices we're affecting the atmosphere as much as anything else we're doing with the greenhouse gases that come out of it. To solve the environmental crisis, the healthcare crisis, the fuel crisis, will require us to confront the food system," he stated, hopeful that with *Food, Inc.*'s DVD release and PBS debut in April, "We're going to see some real change."

The meats Pollan eats are from free-range, grass-fed, not hormone-filled, corn-fed animals. "We spend a lot more money—good alternatives cost more," he acknowledged. "I put more time into preparing food than I did before. But I think it's time and money very well-spent.

"We all have the power to make small changes that can alter the bigger picture, starting with what we choose to eat," Pollan said. "Taking back control of our diet in every possible way is a vitally important project for our health, for the health of the environment."

As I've described, I enjoy the bounty from my hunting here on Charlane—but according to various sources, skipping meat one meal a week can help the environment. Again, according to the Grist organization, "Meat production takes a lot more energy and resources than growing vegetables or grains, and 18 percent of human-generated greenhouse gases come from the livestock industry. If every American had one meat-free day per week, it would reduce emissions as much as taking 8 million cars off the roads."

An interesting statistic, indeed.

Some simple tips that I've discovered from many sources that have a consensus on food issues: We should buy organic when we can, particularly peaches, apples, bell peppers, celery, nectarines, and strawberries, which commonly contain the most pesticides. Organic is also often locally grown, which our families should concentrate on—it not only is fresher, more likely organic, but it is a huge savings in transportation costs and also helps support our local farmers and, in turn, our local communities.

From a health standpoint, here are some tips that make total sense, but I recognize that they're a little more difficult and unreasonable to entirely adhere to: We shouldn't buy canned foods with tomato bases, and we should drink less soda. The linings of the cans leach chemicals into their contents, while canned vegetables (generally) contain too much sodium and sodas (generally) contain too much corn syrup or sugar. But unless you can preserve your own homegrown tomatoes each fall, it is a little difficult to find alternatives to conventional, canned tomatoes and tomato-based products, aside from prepared pasta sauces in glass jars.

We know that fish is an excellent source of lean protein, is very nutritious with B vitamins and Omega-3 oils but, according to various experts (Natural Resource Defense Council [NRDC], the FDA, the EPA, and the American College of Preventive Medicine), shark, king mackerel, swordfish, tilefish, grouper, and orange roughly should be avoided because of their high levels of mercury. Tuna, sea bass, halibut, and even lobster are recommended to be eaten no more than three times a month, according to some sources, and should be avoided entirely by pregnant women. For middle-aged and older men and postmenopausal women, the benefits of fish consumption far outweigh the potential risks.

I'll try not to linger on the bad news, but it would seem that we have drastically overfished Chilean sea bass and bluefin tuna, and scientist Tim Fitzgerald from the Environmental Defense Fund begs us not to eat them at all.

In fact, the bluefin tuna is so prized that it sells for hundreds of dollars a pound (a 512-pound bluefin sold for $175,000 in January 2010, according to media reports in Japan). Marine experts, however, are asserting that the species is being overfished faster than it can replace itself. Among the troubling notions is that the more rare it becomes, the more its price rises, the more of a delicacy it becomes and actually the more it is in demand by some consumers and certainly by some fishermen, who can earn a year's salary or more from one fish. The fact is that the International Commission for the Conservation of Atlantic Tunas (ICCAT) affirmed in October 2009 that Atlantic bluefin tuna stocks are declining dramatically, by 72 percent in the Eastern Atlantic, and by 82 percent in the Western Atlantic.

Monaco is one of the leading nations that have proposed that the Atlantic bluefin tuna be added to a list of fish illegal to catch and keep. While European nations seem divided on the issue, Japan is opposed to a ban. The United States supports the end of trade in wild-caught bluefin tuna until stocks recover.

It would take another full chapter to explore fully what fish are the best, and the least eco-friendly for us to be eating but there are some excellent resources on the Web, among them the Environmental Defense Fund (www.edf.org).

But the bottom line is, avoid fish high in mercury and choose fish that are sustainably caught to ensure a steady supply for years to come. Look for the Marine Stewardship Council seal that certifies seafood is caught or raised in a sustainable, environmentally friendly manner.

According to the Natural Resources Defense Council, a typical American meal contains ingredients from at least five countries outside the United States. For instance, you might have garlic from China, asparagus from Peru, peppers from the Netherlands, tomatoes from Mexico, and raspberries from Chile. In fact, most food has traveled thousands of miles to reach your grocery store's produce aisle. By choosing local produce, you can reduce fuel consumption and global warming pollution associated with transporting food, support local farmers, strengthen the local economy, and protect the environment—all by eating fresher, tastier fruits and vegetables.

Local produce offers better flavor for less money. You might find at your local farmer's market fresh-picked berries, Brussels sprouts on the stalk, tomatoes that have ripened on the vine and eggs that were laid yesterday. When it only takes an hour to drive food to market, food arrives fresh, ripe, and bursting with flavor. Buying directly from family farmers in your area helps them stay in business, and by buying local, it means that your food isn't traveling long distances by planes, trains, trucks, and ships, which all consume energy and spew pollution that contributes to global warming and unhealthy air quality.

If you're not fortunate enough to have a large garden (and the patience, if not outright love of gardening like Rose Lane has!) and can't find a farmers' market within a reasonable distance to you, at least make an effort at your local grocer to find out what products are coming from where. Why buy grapes from Chile if there are California-grown grapes in the next bin? It's a small gesture, but if there's a slow paradigm shift in the way shoppers shop, we can change how the markets react: Retailers respond to customer demands and actions, and if we start insisting on locally grown (or at least as local as possible) produce and meats, they will become more readily available.

At the grocery store, try to avoid buying produce that has been flown in from abroad. Cherries, blueberries, blackberries, raspberries, tomatoes, bell peppers and asparagus are the main fruits and vegetables most frequently shipped by air. Instead, look for local produce. Use NRDC's online guide (www.simplesteps.org) to find out what fruits and vegetables are in season in your area.

NRDC is working to reduce the health and environmental costs of food transport by cleaning up dirty diesel ships, trucks, and

Taking advantage of locally grown seasonal food—such as this local market in the Serenbe community in Georgia—no matter where you live, is more economical, better for the environment and better for your health, and supports the local economy. *Photo courtesy Serenbe*

equipment; encouraging energy efficiency; collecting fees on shipping containers to help reduce the health and environmental impacts of shipping; and promoting local agriculture.

In recent years, Community Supported Agriculture (CSA) has become a popular way for consumers to buy local, seasonal food directly from a farmer. Here are the basics: a farmer offers a certain number of "shares" to the public. Typically the share consists of a box of vegetables, but other farm products may be included. Interested consumers purchase a share (aka a "membership" or a "subscription") and in return receive a box (bag, basket) of seasonal produce each week throughout the farming season.

This arrangement creates several rewards for both the farmer and the consumer. Of course local farmers markets and typical roadside fruit and vegetable stands can also offer foods grown in your community. A great website to visit about these issues is: www.localharvest.org.

When I was discussing refrigerators, I mentioned that the best model to purchase was one with a built-in water filtration system to encourage family members to drink "from the tap" via the filtration system. While there is an energy impact on this, via the electric pump in the fridge for the water, it is a more convenient solution to most of us lazy folks than using filtered containers that need constant refilling. Filtering your water directly at the tap is a handy alternative. Make sure that the filter you buy has NSF certification. NSF is the National Sanitation Foundation, which was founded in 1944 to establish a standard for human-safe food water and consumer goods. (The organization now has expanded into certification for all sorts of eco-friendly products, including flooring.)

I'll try to avoid getting too technical, but an NSF 53 standard for a filter will remove or substantially reduce many hazardous contaminants, including heavy metals such as copper, lead and mercury; disinfection byproducts; parasites such as Giardia and Cryptosporidium; pesticides; radon; and volatile organic chemicals such as methyl-tert-butyl ether (MTBE), dichlorobenzene, and trichloroethylene (TCE).

Reverse osmosis filters are the most outstanding of the water filtration systems, but they are expensive, waste water, and are truly necessary only if your tap water is contaminated with substances that can't be removed by a carbon filter, such as perchlorate, which occurs naturally but is most often used in fireworks, explosives, flares, rocket propellant, lubricating oils, matches, aluminum refining, rubber manufacturing, paint and enamel manufacturing, leather tanning, paper and pulp processing. It has been found, according to the Environmental Protection Agency, in about 4 percent of the country's community water systems.

As far as I can tell, this hasn't received wide media exposure, but the EPA, citing experiments on rats and epidemiological studies in Arizona and California, says perchlorate is dangerous in drinking water at levels above one part per billion. Most perchlorate contamination in the United States, including the Colorado River, range between four and 100 ppb.

"To date, the EPA has identified 75 perchlorate releases in 22 states, including Arizona, Texas, Nebraska, Iowa, New York, Maryland and Massachusetts, as well as California. The Colorado River, the main water source for about 15 million homes across the Southwest, contains perchlorate at roughly seven parts per billion." That's seven times the level that the EPA's National Center for Environmental Assessment says is safe.

Still, some environmentalists claim that chlorine, added to drinking water as a disinfectant, is far more dangerous than perchlorate—so it's an issue that currently is being debated back and forth with no end in sight.

Very broadly speaking, however, an inexpensive carbon filter will remove most contaminants.

Finally, if you're one of those water lovers who is leaving a trail of twelve ounce plastic bottles in your wake, purchase an aluminum bottle instead, which is not only more environmentally friendly but is also healthier for you as it can be reused—where most officials recommend that plastic water bottles NOT be washed and reused.

Besides, US studies show that total energy required for bottled water production is as much as two thousand times the energy needed in producing tap water. As for the water used by bottling industry: It takes 3 liters of water to produce 1 liter of water in the standard PET plastic, according to the Pacific Institute.

So, we've had a look at the water you're drinking—or should be drinking—now let's have a look at the air you should be breathing. We've all been well aware of outdoor air pollution for years—acid rain, ozone, methane, carbon monoxide, etc., but I was a little alarmed, honestly, to learn that our indoor air, which most Americans breathe 90 percent of the time, is 25-65 percent more toxic than the outdoors. Fumes from paints, tobacco smoke, cooking, cleaning products, heating the home, and outgassing fumes from building materials are just a few of the many pollutants we are taking in with every breath in our homes and our offices.

Excellent ventilation helps, but can be a heat- or cooling-exchange roll of the dice, and filtration systems can be expensive and must be properly maintained or they can actually increase the problem by concentrating molds and bacteria that are circulated throughout your indoor environment.

As a farmer and lover of nature, I simply adore what one of the simplest and most commonsense solutions for indoor pollution has turned out to be: plants.

In the 1980s, NASA and the Associated Landscape Contractors of America teamed up to find ways of purifying air in space facilities. Plants turned out to be one of the most economical and cheapest methods. And the plants, of course, can be used just as easily in your living room as on a space station!

More recently, the *Journal of American Society of Horticultural Science* published a study of the science further asserting that it's a well-founded method for air purification.

I poured through a series of sources, including NASA, the MetaEfficient website, and www.webecoist.com, as well as Mother Nature Network (mnn.com) and have come up with a list that is extensive but by no means complete on common, inexpensive houseplants that we should all consider buying and keeping not just for their inherent beauty, but for the good they can do for the air we breath in our homes and offices.

The top air-purifying plant as ranked by NASA's study is the Areca palm tree. Dubbed "the most efficient air humidifier" by MetaEfficient, the Areca can be counted on to keep your home or office moist during dry times and continuously remove chemical toxins from the air. During winter, it can literally replace the use of electric humidifiers.

Tied with the Areca palm tree for NASA's top-ranked air purifying plant is the Lady palm. A versatile plant, the palm can be kept in dry or humid climates (anywhere from 20-100 degrees Fahrenheit) and is fiercely resistant to most types of plant insects.

Aloe, which is famous for being a hypoallergenic plant with a gel that can help heal cuts and burns, also boasts some remarkable air-clearing abilities, among them sucking up formaldehyde and benzene, which can be a byproduct of chemical-based cleaners, paints and more.

The Bamboo palm thrives when kept moist (but not wet) in indirect sunlight. Provided these conditions are kept stable, the Bamboo palm can be counted on to purify the indoor air of anywhere you happen to be.

Now, I know a lot of people complain that they have black thumbs—that is, they just can't seem to keep houseplants alive, but it's pretty hard, unless you're being deliberate, to kill off the hardy spider plant, which also battles benzene, formaldehyde, carbon monoxide, and xylene, which is a product used in the manufacturing of leather, rubber, and printed products.

If you or a member of your family suffers from asthma or allergies, one of the best things you can do is rush out and buy some English ivy. In fact, WebMD describes it as a "fix for allergies." In one test, about 60 percent of airborne mold in a single room vanished just six hours after an English ivy plant was brought in. And, for you cat lovers with indoor litter boxes, it's worth noting that English ivy will remove an estimated 58 percent of airborne feces.

While I've tried earlier to talk you out of buying clothes that require dry cleaning, for several reasons, one of them I haven't mentioned is that when you bring recently dry-cleaned clothes into your home you're bringing along a toxic chemical called trichloroethylene. Good news? Gerber daisies eat it up like popcorn!

An excellent plant for your bathrooms is the Snake plant, also known as mother-in-law's tongue. It's among the best for removing formaldehyde, which is common in cleaning products, toilet paper, tissues, and personal care products. Conveniently, it thrives in low light and steamy, humid conditions.

The colorful flowers of a Chrysanthemum can do a lot more than brighten a home office or living room; the blooms also help filter out benzene, which is commonly found in glue, paint, plastics and detergent. This plant loves bright light, and to encourage buds to open, you'll need to find a spot near an open window with direct sunlight.

The red edges of the Red-edged dracaena bring a pop of color, and the shrub can grow to reach your ceiling. This plant is best for removing xylene, trichloroethylene and formaldehyde, which can be introduced to indoor air through lacquers, varnishes and gasoline.

For your living room, research has determined that the weeping fig is ideal for filtering out pollutants, such as formaldehyde, benzene, and trichloroethylene that typically come in gas form out of carpeting and furniture. If there's a downside it's that the plant requires careful care but once lighting and watering conditions are found to be stable and appropriate it will flourish.

Azaleas are gorgeous flowering shrubs that do best in cooler areas such as basements or rooms that are not kept at higher temperatures most of the time. They require a decent amount of light, but are terrific for combating the formaldehyde that is one of the outgasses from plywood or foam insulation.

The list of household plants that can improve the air quality of your home and office is more extensive than I'll go into here, but let me finish by mentioning NASA's favorite plant for removing all three of the most common industrial pollutants, formaldehyde, benzene, and trichloroethylene: The peace lily. It requires a shady area and weekly watering and will return your kindness with blooms and cleaner air.

Another subject for dealing with household issues is how to get rid of unwanted or no longer used items. We know the cliché that one man's junk is another man's treasure—and that's true! A good old-fashioned yard sale can pass items that you no longer want or need to someone else that might have a use for them. But for what might be left over from that yard sale—don't just throw out the rest of your junk—take the time and make the effort to pay attention to proper disposal and recycling options. Many businesses these days will properly dispose of things like cell phones, old appliances, electronics, and the like. It may take a call or two, but it's worth the effort to properly dispose of or recycle items that can have future use.

From various sources, including the Department of Energy and the NRDC, here's a suggested twelve-month plan for improving your own personal custodianship of the planet. There's really no necessary order to how you do this, but if you tackle these suggestions you will have made a significant contribution and effort.

January: Have a home energy audit conducted, or use Internet resources cited earlier in this chapter to do your own.

February: Seal leaks and improve the insulation in your home.

March: Assess your heating—from the condition of the ducts to the efficiency of your furnace.

April: Attempt to make permanent improvements to your methods of travel, especially your daily commute.

May: Make a plan to add more houseplants to improve your indoor air quality.

June: Watch, in an overall manner what you eat and where it comes from and how it's processed; adapt a meat-free night weekly.

July: Improve how you heat and consume water, including the purchase and use of bottled water.

August: Replace inefficient light bulbs as you can afford to.

September: Do a wardrobe assessment: Make a list of what you're going to need in the coming months and plan ahead to purchase eco-friendly alternatives.

October: Replace an inefficient appliance.

November: Make your electronics more efficient—adapt habits such as power bars that can be turned off to stop "vampire" energy consumption.

December: Make an assessment of your home-cleaning practices and the chemicals you're using.

While this chapter has dealt mostly with things that you can do in your everyday life or that might make a better household, let's not forget about what you can do to help your community, your city, or your state to lower the impact of growth, save energy, lower its carbon footprint, be healthier, and in general grow in a way that is smart, strong, and sustainable. Keeping in touch with the issues in your area like zoning permits and laws, local transportation issues and options, how to renovate an old school or other public building, standards for building new structures, maintaining or adding new parks and green spaces, dealing with waste, assessing and improving air and water quality, landscaping for aesthetic and practical purposes, and the many other subjects that we've discussed are all important for the well-being and the future of our country and our planet.

Yes, it takes time and effort to get involved, to keep up with the issues, and to make changes and take action. But we can ALL make a difference if we try. There are good choices we can make—let's make them together.

Debate Versus the Undeniable:
We Can Do Better

I've ended this book with a chapter on what I can do, what my family can and is doing—and what you, as an individual and your immediate family can do to reverse the course we've been on since the dawn of the Industrial Revolution.

I can't deny the great things it's brought us, that we all enjoy and are so used to and that many of us believe we can't live without, but our Western world, the so-called "first world" way of life has come at a very high cost to our planet.

Scientists and laymen alike will argue about the cause of climate change, but in the past two or three years even the most hardened skeptics have acknowledged that we ARE experiencing a dramatic shift in our climate, in our jet streams and ocean currents.

The collapse of the cod fishery off the Newfoundland Grand Banks and the degradation of the salmon fishery off the northwest coast of the US are not debatable—they're a reality. And, as I've discovered and written (I think it's worth repeating) the cod fishery is considered in "terminal decline." It's likely never to come back, most credible scientists believe.

Scientists are also in agreement that the polar ice caps are melting. Ice fields the size of Rhode Island have cracked and fallen off the Antarctic shelf into the sea; ocean levels are rising. Most glaciers have melted down to half or less of what they were a few short decades ago. The facts are clear and undeniable—and the debate has been reduced to why it's happening. I personally believe that humans are at least a part—and perhaps a large part of the reason we're experiencing these changes—but any way you look at it, there is no denial that our planet is undergoing rapid, negative change that is affecting flora, fauna, sea life and, indeed humankind.

I've cited various sources saying we are approaching or perhaps have passed "peak oil" recovery. I acknowledge that there are some who publicly declare we've yet to reach that point and some that believe we won't reach it for another twenty-five, fifty, even a hundred years or so. Does it matter? We will run out of recoverable oil some day, and the risks of ever-more challenging recovery methods and locations were so tragically illuminated by the 2010 BP disaster off the coast of Louisiana. The ecological impact, which has yet to be determined, may have resulted in a condition that has severely damaged some of the delicate wetland ecosystems along the Gulf coast.

So we need alternatives. I am of the personal opinion that we need drastic, immediate alternatives where possible, especially in terms of how and where we build and expand our communities, villages, towns, and cities, and how we fuel our vehicles and supply electricity to our homes, businesses, schools, public buildings, and factories. No one wants to go back to the "dark ages," and that is not what I propose. Like most everyone else, I live my life grateful for the luxuries we have—the ability to travel with ease and comfort, power to keep us cool in the hot summer and warm in winter, pleasant facilities to live in and for our schools, churches, public buildings, and other structures. I don't think we have to lose these things, but we do need to think long and hard about our energy sources, the way we renovate or build, the types of appliances we use, and the way we arrange our communities. We need to be careful of how much impervious surface we put down and be mindful of how much natural land we lose. There are better ways we can do things, and I believe it's time to address these issues.

I am a committed environmentalist and conservationist, and I am personally looking for every possible alternative. As I've said from the start, I'm not a scientist. I am a family man, a piano player, and a forester.

This is not a perfect world. There is no such thing; we all know that. But we can do better, we can be innovative, we can pay closer attention to the way we live, and we can conserve and make little sacrifices that collectively make a huge difference for the better. Whether it's replacing those old light bulbs for the newer CFLs, replacing our old hot water tanks with the newer "tankless" models, buying energy star appliances when we replace the ones we wear out, using low-flow toilets, biodegradable products, motion-sensor lights, "regional" heat and cooling units, supporting solar, wind and biomass energy options, carpooling when we can, insulating our windows, walls and doors, buying hybrid cars, converting as many of our truck fleets as we can to biodiesel fuels, using organic and renewable materials like wood to build with, supporting and funding green technologies, using creative techniques like biomimicry, considering conservation easements, engaging in our town and city council meetings, making use of information resources like the Mother Nature Network (mnn.com), or generally looking for every opportunity to treat our planet better and with respect.

We hope you have learned some things from this book that will help you lower your carbon footprint and give you some food for thought concerning where we might go from here. We can't just wave a magic wand and change the world in an instant, but we can all take small steps together for a better, cleaner world for ourselves and for future generations. Remember that every journey begins with the first step, and every step we take in the right direction gets us closer to our destination—an America and a world that will grow smart, strong, and sustainable.

Resources

While I hope you will investigate many of the resources we've organized below, I would like to invite the reader to explore our website, The Mother Nature Network (mnn.com), which I'm proud to be the co-founder of along with my partner and friend, Joel Babbit. Joel and I and our fine staff have worked hard to make MNN the very best resource for the latest environmental news, education and information. We have strived to make MNN the most comprehensive and accurate environmental site in the world, and it offers many resources covering some subjects I wasn't able to fully explore in this book.

The following listed sites were all current and operating at the time of publication; however, websites are notorious for coming and going as non-profit foundations merge or lose their funding. If a particular site has gone offline, I encourage you to not be discouraged and conduct an Internet search for your topic of interest. Generally, the websites appear here in the order in which they appear in the book—though many have been repeated throughout the text as sources for different topics.

Books

Anderson, Ray. *Mid-Course Correction: Toward a Sustainable Enterprise: The Interface Model.* Atlanta: Peregrinzilla Press, 1999.

Confessions of a Radical Industrialist: Profits, People, Purpose—Doing Business While Respecting the Earth. New York: St. Martin's Press, 2009.

Dumaine, Brian. *The Plot to Save the Planet: How Visionary Entrepreneurs and Corporate Titans are Creating Real Solutions to Global Warming.* New York: Crown Business, 2009.

Hawken, Paul. *The Ecology of Commerce: A Declaration of Sustainability.* Rev. ed. New York: Harper Paperbacks, 2010.

Journals

Ehrenfeld, John and Nicholas Gertler. "Industrial Ecology in Practice." *Journal of Industrial Ecology 1,* no. 1 (January 1997): 67-79.

Websites

www.charlane.com (Remarkable sustainable plantation in middle Georgia owned and operated by Chuck and Rose Lane Leavell and their family.)

www.preservationvirginia.org/rediscovery (History of the Jamestown settlement.)

www.nrcs.usda.gov/technical/NRI (US Department of Agriculture's National Resources Inventory)

www.gfc.state.ga.us (Georgia Forestry Commission)

www.usda.gov/wps/portal/usda/farmbill2008?navid = FARMBILL2008 (2008 US Farm Bill)

www.usgs.gov (US Geological Survey)

www.fda.gov (US government's Food and Drug Administration)

www.noaa.gov (National Oceanic and Atmospheric Administration)

www.nature.org (The Nature Conservancy)

www.nrdc.org (National Resources Defense Council)

www.cleanenergy.org (Southern Alliance for Clean Energy)

www.sierraclub.org (Sierra Club)

www.coastaladvocates.com/home.php (California Coastal Protection Network)

www.americaswetland.com (America's Wetland Foundation)

www.asbpa.org (American Shore & Beach Preservation Association)

yosemite.epa.gov (American Coastal Coalition)

www.gcrmn.org (Global Reef Monitoring Network)

www.sio.ucsd.edu (Scripps Institution of Oceanography)

www.bluegoosealliance.org (part of the National Wildlife Refuge System)

www.nahbgreen.org (National Green Building Program)

www.indigodev.com/Kal.html (website detailing the remarkable spontaneous but slow evolution of the "industrial symbiosis" at Kalundborg, Denmark)

www.usbcsd.org (United States Business Council for Sustainable Development)

www.usgbc.org (LEED Green Building Rating System)

www.earthcrafthouse.com (EarthCraft Housing)

www.enertia.com (North Carolina-based home construction company Enertia)

www.epa.gov (US Environmental Protection Agency)

www.cudc.kent.edu/shrink/inst.html (Kent State University's Shrinking Cities Institute in Cleveland)

www.energy.gov (US Department of Energy)

energytaxincentives.org/

apps1.eere.energy.gov/weatherization/

www.edf.org (Environmental Defense Fund)

www.localharvest.org (A great website for information on local farmers markets and typical roadside fruit and vegetable stands can also offer foods grown in your community)

www.webecoist.com (NASA, the MetaEfficient website)

www.peachtree-city.org (Atlanta-area Peachtree City development)

www.nahbgreen.org (National Green Building Program)

SprawlCity.org (An excellent source on urban sprawl based on government census data)

www.campwinnarainbow.org (Non-profit organization playing host to numerous music festivals and charitable causes, and is home to a performing arts camp for children every summer to teach them about nature.

www.biomimicryinstitute.org (excellent site on the "new" science of biomimicry.)

www.nyrp.org (The New York Restoration Project)

www.greenhighway.net (Green Highway nonprofit group)

www.cascadeland.org (Cascade Land Conservancy)

reverb.org (Deeply rooted within the music and environmental communities, Reverb educates and engages musicians and their fans to take action toward a more sustainable future.)

Grist.org (environmental organization)

www.nature.org/initiatives/climatechange /calculator/ (Nature Conservancy's website calculator)

hes.lbl.gov/hes/ (Department of Energy's Home Energy Saver site)

greenerchoices.org (Consumer Reports)

www.simplesteps.org (Natural Resources Defense Council, which runs an excellent website for homeowners)

ase.org/content/news/detail/2609 (The Alliance to Save Energy)

www.benjerry.com/company/sear/2006/s ear06_6.1.cfm (Dairy Stewardship Alliance)

www.conservationalliance.com (The Conservation Alliance is a group of outdoor industry companies that disburses its collective annual membership dues to grassroots environmental organizations.)

www.worldwildlife.org/climate/ (World Wildlife Fund's climate change program)

www.usendowment.org/ (The US Endowment for Forestry & Communities, Inc. (Endowment) is a not-for-profit corporation established September 21, 2006, at the request of the governments of the United States and Canada in accordance with the terms of the Softwood Lumber Agreement (SLA) between the two countries.)

www.uk.brightgreenbusiness.com/ (Town in Denmark which is aiming toward zero-carbon status by the year 2029)

www.seasidefl.com/ (New-style community model in Florida)

www.mesadelsolnm.com (New-style community model in New Mexico)

www.serenbe.com (New-style community model in Georgia)

www.peachtree-city.org (New-style community model in Georgia)

www.poplargrovecharleston.com (New-style community model in Georgia) www.prairiecrossing.com (New-style community model in Illinois)

www.daybreakutah.com (New-style community model in Utah)

www.hybridcars.com (Comprehensive and up-to-date site on hybrid transportation technology, along with a useful gas mileage impact calculator.)

www.bts.gov (RITA coordinates the US Department of Transportation's research and education programs, and is working to bring advanced technologies into the transportation system.)

www.rangefuels.com (biomass-to-energy company)

www.coskata.com (biomass-to-energy company)

www.verenium.com (Verenium Corporation is a recognized pioneer in the development and commercialization of high-performance enzymes for use in industrial processes.)

www.noaa.gov (National Oceanic and Atmospheric Administration)

www.seva.org (Working in nine countries in addition to the United States, Seva Foundation provides financial resources and technical expertise to help communities build sustainable solutions to poverty and disease.)

Walmartstores.com/Sustainability/5127.aspx (partnership between Walmart and the National Fish and Wildlife Foundation to conserve critical wildlife habitats for future generations.)

www.ecomanor.com (Laura Turner Seydel and Rutherford Seydel's high-profile model for an environmentally responsible residence in Atlanta, Georgia)

www.usgbc.org (The US Green Building Council)

www.hes.lbl.gov/consumer (Department of Energy's Home Energy Saver site)

ase.org (Alliance to Save Energy)

www1.eere.energy.gov/wip/wap.html

carbonfootprint.com (A carbon-management service for businesses.)

www.musemusic.com (Musicians United to Sustain the Environment)

www.energysavers.gov (Federal government's energy saver site)

energytaxincentives.org (Federal Tax Incentives Assistance Project)

www.treesoundstudios.com (A carbon-neutral major recording studio outside of Atlanta which is an industry leader in its "mission is to educate the world on the importance of sustainable living and the impact of conscious consumerism through the power of music.)

www.grinningplanet.com (Mark Jeantheau's environmental site for encouraging environmental education through cartoons, jokes and lighthearted yet serious fare.)
purespectrumlighting.com/ (PureSpectrum is an environmentally conscientious public company headquartered in Savannah, Georgia that has positioned itself as an emerging leader in the race to introduce products and technologies that will serve as the cornerstones lighting evolution in the marketplace.)

www.coalitionforcleanair.org (California-based organization which is a model for similar clean-air initiatives across America.)

www.poet.com (The world's largest ethanol producer.)

www.goodguide.com (A website with suggestions on safer, more environmentally safe home products—they also have a cool iPhone app to go along with it.)

www.mbl.edu (Marine Biological Lab in Woods Hole, Mass., one of the world leaders in biodiversity and biological research.)

Chuck and Rose Lane Leavell proudly sponsor a scholarship at the Daniel B. Warnell School of Forestry and Natural Resources at the University of Georgia. The criterion for the scholarship is for a student to show equal interest and expertise in both forestry and wildlife studies. We have sponsored this since 1995, and are very proud of the students who have received it. If any of you are interested in contributing to this fund, we certainly encourage you do to so. Donations can be made to the following:

The Leavell Scholarship Fund
Warnell School of Forestry and Natural Resources
University of Georgia
Attention: Dean
Athens, Georgia 30602-2152
Phone: (706) 542-2686

Index